YO-CXJ-169

LLEWELLYN'S 2024

DAILY PLANETARY GUIDE

ISBN: 978-0-7387-6892-2. Astrological calculations compiled and programmed by Rique Pottenger, based on the earlier work of Neil F. Michelsen.

Astrological proofreading by Beth Koch Rosato
Cover design by Shannon McKuhen

gettyimages.com/936469074©Fug4s
gettyimages.com/489040734©Aphelleon

Llewellyn Publications
A Division of Llewellyn Worldwide Ltd.
2143 Wooddale Drive
Woodbury, MN 55125-2989
www.llewellyn.com

Printed in China

Contents

Introduction to Astrology

by Kim Rogers-Gallagher

Your horoscope is calculated using the date and time you were born from the perspective of your birth location. From this information, a clocklike diagram emerges that shows where every planet was located at the moment you made your debut. Each chart is composed of the same elements rearranged, so everyone has one of everything, but none are exactly alike. I think of planets, signs, houses, and aspects as the four astrological building blocks. Each block represents a different level of human existence.

The eight planets along with the Sun and Moon are actual physical bodies. They represent urges or needs we all have. Chiron also falls into this category. The twelve signs of the zodiac are sections of the sky, and each is 30 degrees. The signs describe the behavior a planet or house will use to express itself. The twelve houses in a chart tell us where our planets come to life. Each house represents different life concerns—values, communication, creativity, and so on—that we must live through as life and time progress.

Basically, aspects are angles. Some of the planets will be positioned an exact number of degrees apart, forming angles to one another. For example, 180 degrees is a circle divided by two and is called an opposition. A square is 90 degrees and divides the circle by four. A trine is 120 degrees and divides the circle by three, and so forth. Aspects show which planets will engage in constant dialogue with one another. The particular aspect that joins them describes the nature of their "conversation." Not all planets will aspect all other planets in the houses.

Planets: The First Building Block

Each planet acts like the director of a department in a corporation, and the corporation is, of course, you. For example, Mercury directs your Communications Department and Jupiter oversees your Abundance and Growth Department. When you have the need to communicate, you call on your Mercury; when it's time to take a risk or grow, you use your Jupiter. Let's meet each of the planets individually and take a look at which job duties fall under each planet's jurisdiction.

The Sun

Every corporation needs an executive director who makes the final decisions. The Sun is your Executive Director. The Sun in your chart is your core, your true self. Although each of the planets in your chart is important in its own right, they all "take their orders," figuratively speaking, from the Sun.

Everyone's Sun has the same inner goal: to shine. The house your Sun is in shows where you really want to do good, where you want to be appreciated and loved. Your Sun is your inner supply of pride and confidence, your identity. The Sun is you at your creative best, enjoying life to the fullest.

The Sun shows the focus of the moment, where the world's attention will be directed on that particular day. In fact, in horary and electional astrology, the two branches that pertain most to timing and prediction, the Sun represents the day, the Moon the hour, and the Midheaven the moment. In the physical body, the Sun rules the heart, upper back, and circulatory system.

The Moon

Speaking of the Moon, a good place to meet her and begin to understand her qualities is by the water on a clear night when she's full. Whether you're looking up at her or at that silvery patch she creates that shivers and dances on the water, take a deep breath and allow yourself to be still. She represents the soft interior of each of us that recalls memories, fears, and dreams.

She's a lovely lady who oversees the Department of Feelings; she's the bringer of "moods" (a great Moon word). Her house and placement in your chart reveal how your intuition works, what your emotional needs are, and how you want your needs met. She is the ultimate feminine energy, the part of you that points both to how you were nurtured and to how you will nurture others. In the body, the Moon has jurisdiction over the breasts, ovaries, and womb. She also rules our bodily fluids, the internal ocean that keeps us alive.

Mercury

♀ Back when gods and goddesses were thought to be in charge of the affairs of humanity, Mercury shuttled messages between the gods and mortals. In today's world, Mercury is the computer, the telephone, and the internet. He's the internal computer that constantly feeds you data about the world. His position and house in your chart show how you think and reason, and how you express yourself to others. You'll recognize him in your speech patterns, in your handwriting, and in the way you walk, because moving through your environment means communicating with it. He operates through your five senses and your brain, and makes you conscious of opposites—light and dark, hot and cold, up and down. He's what you use when you have a conversation, exchange a glance, gesture, or interpret a symbol. Mercury represents the side of you living totally in the present.

If you've ever tried to collect mercury after it escaped from a broken thermometer, you've learned something about Mercury. Just as your Mercury never stops collecting data, those tiny beads you tried so hard to collect brought back a bit of everything they contacted—dog hair, crumbs, and grains of dirt. In the body, Mercury also acts as a messenger. He transmits messages through his function as the central nervous system that lets your eyes and hands collaborate, your eyes blink, and breathing continue.

Venus

♀ Venus spends her energy supplying you with your favorite people, places, and things. If you want chocolate, music, flannel sheets, or the coworker you've got a mad crush on, it's your Venus that tells you how to get it. Venus enjoys beauty and comfort. She shows how to attract what you love, especially people. When you're being charming, whether by using your manners or by adorning yourself, she's in charge of all behavior that is pleasing to others—social chitchat, smiles, hugs, and kisses. Whenever you're pleased, satisfied, or content enough to purr, it's your Venus who made you feel that way. Since money is one of the ways we draw the objects we love to us, she's also in charge of finances. Venus relates to your senses—sight, smell, taste, touch, and sound—the body's receptors. After all, it's the senses that tell us what feels good and what doesn't. Venus responds to your desire for beautiful surroundings, comfortable clothing, and fine art.

Mars

♂ Mars is in charge of your Self-Defense and Action Department. He's the warrior who fights back when you're attacked—your own personal SWAT team. Your Mars energy makes you brave, courageous, and daring. His placement in your chart describes how you act on your own behalf. He's concerned only with you, and he doesn't consider the size, strength, or abilities of whomever or whatever you're up against. He's the side of you that initiates all activity. He's also in charge of how you assert yourself and how you express anger.

"Hot under the collar," "seeing red," and "all fired up" are Mars phrases. Mars is what you use to be passionate, adventurous, and bold. But he can be violent, accident-prone, and cruel, too. Wherever he is in your chart, you find constant action. Mars pursues. He shows how you "do" things. He charges through situations. This "headstrong" planet corresponds to the head, the blood, and the muscles.

Jupiter

♃ Jupiter is called "the Greater Benefic," and he heads the Department of Abundance and Growth. He's the side of you that's positive, optimistic, and generous. He's where you keep your supply of laughter, enthusiasm, and high spirits. It's Jupiter's expansive, high-spirited energy that motivates you to travel, take classes, and meet new people. Wherever he is in your chart is a place where you'll have an extensive network of friends and associates—folks you can visit, count on, and learn from. Jupiter is the side of you that will probably cause you to experience the "grass is greener" syndrome. Your Jupiter is also what you're using when you find yourself being excessive and wasteful, overdoing, or blowing something out of proportion. Words like "too" and "always" are the property of Jupiter, as are "more" and "better." In general, this planet just loves to make things bigger. In the body, Jupiter corresponds with the liver, the organ that filters what you take in and rids your body of excess. Jupiter also handles physical growth.

Saturn

♄ Saturn represents withholding and resistance to change. He heads the Boundaries and Rules Department. Locate Saturn in your chart to find out where you'll build walls to keep change out, where you may segregate yourself at times, where you'll be most likely to say no. Your Saturn is the authority inside you, the spot where you may inhibit or stall yourself throughout life—most often because you fear failure and would rather not act at all than act inappropriately. This planet teaches you to respect your elders, follow the rules, and do things right the first time. Wherever Saturn is in your chart is a place where you'll feel respectful, serious, and conservative. Your Saturn placement is where you'll know that you should never embellish the facts and never act until you're absolutely sure you're ready. Here is where you won't expect something for nothing. Saturn is also where you're at your most disciplined, where you'll teach yourself the virtues of patience, endurance, and responsibility. Because this planet is so fond of boundaries, it's also the planet in charge of organization, structures, and guidelines. In the physical body, Saturn correlates with the bones and the skin, those structures that hold your body together.

Uranus

♅ There's a spot in everyone's chart where independence is the order of the day, where rules are made specifically to be broken, and where personal freedom is the only way to go, regardless of the consequences. Here's where you'll surprise even yourself at the things you say and do. Meet Uranus, head of the Department of One Never Knows, the place in your chart where shocks, surprises, and sudden reversals are regular fare.

Your Uranus energy is what wakes you up to how confined you feel, breaks you out of the rut you're in, and sets you free. He's a computer wizard and involved in mass communications. Where he's strong in your chart, you will be strong, too. Here is where you'll have genius potential, where you'll be bold enough to ignore the old way to solve a problem and instead find a whole new way. Major scientific and technological breakthroughs like the space program and the internet were inspired by Uranus. In the body, Uranus rules the lower part of the legs, including the calves and ankles, and he co-rules with Mercury the central nervous system.

Neptune

♆ Next time you hear yourself sigh or feel yourself slip into a day-dream, think of Neptune. This is the planet in charge of romance, nostalgia, and magic. Although her official title is head of the Department of Avoidance and Fantasy, she's also one of the most creative energies you own. Wherever she is in your chart is where you're psychic. It's also where you're capable of amazing compassion and sensitivity for beings and creatures less fortunate than yourself. It's where you'll be drawn into charity or volunteer work because you realize that we're all part of a bigger plan, that there are no boundaries between you and what's out there.

This combination of sensitivity and harsh reality doesn't always mix well. This may also be a place where you'll try to escape. Sleep, meditation, and prayer are the highest uses of her energies, but alcohol and drugs are also under her jurisdiction. Neptune's place in your chart is where you're equally capable of fooling all of the people all of the time, and of being fooled yourself. In the body, Neptune and the Moon co-rule fluids. Neptune also has a connection with poisons and viruses that invisibly infiltrate our bodies and with the body's immune system, which is how we keep our barriers intact.

Pluto

♇ Pluto is head of the Department of Death, Destruction, and Decay. He's in charge of things that have to happen, and he disposes of situations that have gone past the point of no return, where the only solution is to "let go." He also oversees sex, reincarnation, recycling, regeneration, and rejuvenation. Pluto's spot in your chart is a place where intense, inevitable circumstances will arrive to teach you about agony and ecstasy. Pluto's place in your chart is where you'll be in a state of turmoil or evolution, where there will be ongoing change. This is the side of you that realizes that, like it or not, life goes on after tremendous loss. It is the side of you that will reflect on your losses down the road and try to make sense of them. Most importantly, since

Pluto rules life, death, and rebirth, here's where you'll understand the importance of process. You'll be amazingly strong where your Pluto is—he's a well of concentrated, transforming energy. In the body, Pluto is associated with the reproductive organs since here is where the invisible process of life and death begins. He is also in charge of puberty and sexual maturity. He corresponds with plutonium.

Signs: The Second Building Block

Every sign is built of three things: an element, a quality, and a polarity. Understanding each of these primary building blocks gives a head start toward understanding the signs themselves, so let's take a look at them.

The Polarities: Masculine and Feminine

The words "masculine" and "feminine" are often misunderstood or confused in the context of astrology. In astrology, masculine means that an energy is assertive, aggressive, and linear. Feminine means that an energy is receptive, magnetic, and circular. These terms should not be confused with male and female.

The Qualities: Cardinal, Fixed, and Mutable

Qualities show the way a sign's energy flows. The cardinal signs are energies that initiate change. Cardinal signs operate in sudden bursts of energy. The fixed signs are thorough and unstoppable. They're the energies that endure. They take projects to completion, tend to block change at all costs, and will keep at something regardless of whether or not it should be terminated. The mutable signs are versatile, flexible, and changeable. They can be scattered, fickle, and inconstant.

The Elements: Fire, Earth, Air, and Water

The fire signs correspond with the spirit and the spiritual aspects of life. They inspire action, attract attention, and love spontaneity. The earth signs are solid, practical, supportive, and as reliable as the earth under our feet. The earth signs are our physical envoys and are concerned with our tangible needs, such as food, shelter, work, and responsibilities. Air signs are all about the intellectual or mental sides of life. Like air itself, they are light and elusive. They love conversation, communication, and mingling. The water signs correspond to the emotional side of our natures. As changeable, subtle, and able to infiltrate as water itself, water signs gauge the mood in a room when they enter, and operate on what they sense from their environment.

Aries: Masculine, Cardinal, Fire

♈ Aries is ruled by Mars and is cardinal fire—red-hot, impulsive, and ready to go. Aries planets are not known for their patience, and they ignore obstacles, choosing instead to focus on the shortest distance between where they are and where they want to be. Planets in Aries are brave, impetuous, and direct. Aries planets are often very good at initiating projects. They are not, however, as eager to finish, so they will leave projects undone. Aries planets need physical outlets for their considerable Mars-powered energy; otherwise their need for action can turn to stress. Exercise, hard work, and competition are food for Aries energy.

Taurus: Feminine, Fixed, Earth

♉ Taurus, the fixed earth sign, has endless patience that turns your Taurus planet into a solid force to be reckoned with. Taurus folks never, ever quit. Their reputation for stubbornness is earned. They're responsible, reliable, honest as they come, practical, and endowed with a stick-to-it attitude other planets envy. They're not afraid to work hard. Since Taurus is ruled by Venus, it's not surprising to find that these people are sensual and luxury-loving, too. They love to be spoiled with the best—good food, fine wine, or even a Renoir painting. They need peace and quiet like no other, and don't like their schedules to be disrupted. However, they may need a reminder that comfortable habits can become ruts.

Gemini: Masculine, Mutable, Air

♊ This sign is famous for its duality and love of new experiences, as well as for its role as communicator. Gemini is mutable air, which translates into changing your mind, so expect your Gemini planet to be entertaining and versatile. This sign knows a little bit about everything. Gemini planets usually display at least two distinct sides to their personalities, are changeable and even fickle at times, and are wonderfully curious. This sign is ruled by Mercury, so if what you're doing involves talking, writing, gesturing, or working with hand-eye coordination, your Gemini planet will love it. Mercury also rules short trips, so any planet in Gemini is an expert at how to make its way around the neighborhood in record time.

Cancer: Feminine, Cardinal, Water

♋ Cancer is cardinal water, so it's good at beginning things. It's also the most privacy-oriented sign. Cancer types are emotionally vulnerable, sensitive, and easily hurt. They need safe "nests" to return to when the world gets to be too much. Cancer types say "I love you" by tending to your need for food, warmth, or a place to sleep. The problem is that they can become needy, dependent, or unable to function unless they feel someone or something needs them. Cancer rules the home and family. It's also in charge of emotions, so expect a Cancer to operate from his or her gut most of the time.

Leo: Masculine, Fixed, Fire

♌ Leo is fixed fire, and above all else represents pride and ego. Sun-ruled Leo wants to shine and be noticed. Natural performers, people in this sign are into drama and attract attention even when they don't necessarily want it. Occasionally your Leo friends may be touchy and high maintenance. Still, they are generous to a fault. Leo appreciates attention and praise with lavish compliments, lovely gifts, and creative outings designed to amaze and delight. Leo's specialties are having fun, entertaining, and making big entrances and exits.

Virgo: Feminine, Mutable, Earth

♍ Virgo may seem picky and critical, but that may be too simplistic. As a mutable earth sign, your Virgo planet delights in helping, and it's willing to adapt to any task. Having a keen eye for details may be another way to interpret a Virgo planet's automatic fault-finding ability. When Virgo's eye for detail combines with the ability to fix almost anything, you have a troubleshooter extraordinaire. This sign practices discrimination—analyzing, critiquing, and suggesting remedies to potential problems. This sign is also wonderful at making lists, agendas, and schedules. Keep your Virgo planet happy by keeping it busy.

Libra: Masculine, Cardinal, Air

Libra adores balance, harmony, and equal give and take—no easy task. A more charming sign would be difficult to find, though. Libra's cardinal airy nature wants to begin things, and entertaining and socializing are high priorities. These expert people-pleasing Venus-ruled planets specialize in manners, courtesy, and small talk. Alone time may be shunned, and because they're gifted with the ability to pacify, they may sell out their own needs, or the truth, to buy peace and companionship. Seeing both sides of a situation, weighing the options, and keeping their inner balance by remaining honest may be Libra's hardest tasks.

Scorpio: Feminine, Fixed, Water

Planets in this sign are detectives, excelling at the art of strategy. Your Scorpio planets sift through every situation for subtle clues, which they analyze to determine what's really going on. They're also gifted at sending subtle signals back to the environment, and at imperceptibly altering a situation by manipulating it with the right word or movement. Scorpio planets are constantly searching for intimacy. They seek intensity and may be crisis-oriented. They can be relentless, obsessive, and jealous. Remember, this is fixed water. Scorpios feel things deeply and forever. Give your Scorpio planets the opportunity to fire-walk, to experience life-and-death situations.

Sagittarius: Masculine, Mutable, Fire

The enthusiasm of this mutable fire sign, ruled by Jupiter, spreads like a brushfire. These planets tend to never feel satisfied or content, and to always wonder if there's something even more wonderful over the next mountain. Your Sagittarius planets are bored by routine; they're freedom-oriented, generous, and optimistic to a fault. They can be excessive and overindulgent. They adore outdoor activities and foreign places and foreign people. They learn by first having the big picture explained. They're only too happy to preach, advertise, and philosophize. Sagittarius planets can be quite prophetic, and they absolutely believe in the power of laughter, embarrassing themselves at times to make someone laugh.

Capricorn: Feminine, Cardinal, Earth

♑ Your Capricorn planets, ruled by Saturn, have a tendency to build things, such as erecting structures and creating a career for you. Saturn will start up an organization and turn it into the family business. These planets automatically know how to run it no matter what it is. They're authority figures. They exercise caution and discipline, set down rules, and live by them. Capricorn is the sign with the driest wit. Here's where your sense of propriety and tradition will be strong, where doing things the old-fashioned way and paying respect to elders will be the only way to go. They want a return for the time they invest, and don't mind proving how valuable they are.

Aquarius: Masculine, Fixed, Air

♒ Aquarian planets present some unexpected contradictions because they are fixed air and unpredictable. This sign's ruler, Uranus, gets the credit for Aquarius's tumultuous ways. Aquarian energy facilitates invention and humanitarian conquests, to the amazement of the masses, and planets in this sign are into personal freedom like no other. They create their own rules, fight city hall whenever possible, and deliberately break tradition. They adore change. Abrupt reversals are their specialty, so others often perceive them as erratic, unstable, or unreliable. But when Aquarius energy activates, commitment to a cause or an intellectual ideal has a steadfastness like no other sign possesses.

Pisces: Feminine, Mutable, Water

♓ Mutable Pisces can't separate itself emotionally from whatever it's exposed to. While this is the source of Pisces' well-deserved reputation for compassion, it's also the source of a desire to escape reality. Planets in this sign feel everything—for better or worse—so they need time alone to unload and reassemble themselves. Exposure to others, especially in crowds, is exhausting to your Pisces planets. Here is where you may have a tendency to take in stray people and animals and where you'll need to watch for the possibility of being victimized or taken advantage of in some way. Pisces planets see the best in people or situations, and they can be disappointed when reality sets in. These planets are the romantics of the zodiac. Let them dream in healthy ways.

Houses: The Third Building Block

Houses are represented by twelve pie-shaped wedges in a horoscope chart. (See blank chart on page 236.) They're like rooms in a house, and each reflects the circumstances we create and encounter in a specific area of life. One room, the Sixth House, relates to our daily routine and work, while the Eleventh House relates to groups we may be affiliated with, for example. The sign (Aries, Taurus, etc.) on the cusp of each house tells us something about the nature of the room behind the door. Someone with Leo on the Sixth House cusp will create different routines and work habits than a person with Capricorn on that cusp. The sign influences the type of behavior you'll exhibit when those life circumstances turn up. Since the time of day you were born determines the sign on each of the houses, an accurate birth time will result in more accurate information from your chart.

The Twelve Houses

The First House

The First House shows the sign that was ascending over the horizon at the moment you were born. Let's think again of your chart as one big house and of the houses as "rooms." The First House symbolizes your front door. The sign on this house cusp (also known as the Rising Sign or Ascendant) describes the way you dress, move, and adorn yourself, and the overall condition of your body. It relates to the first impression you make on people.

The Second House

This house shows how you handle the possessions you hold dear. That goes for money, objects, and the qualities you value in yourself and in others. This house also holds the side of you that takes care of what you have and what you buy for yourself, and the amount of money you earn. The Second House shows what you're willing to do for money, too, so it's also a description of your self-esteem.

The Third House

This house corresponds to your neighborhood, including the bank, the post office, and the gym where you work out. This is the side of you that performs routine tasks without much conscious thought. The Third House also refers to childhood and grammar school, and it shows your relationships with siblings, your communication style, and your attitude toward short trips.

The Fourth House

This house is the symbolic foundation brought from your childhood home, your family, and the parent who nurtured you. Here is where you'll find the part of you that decorates and maintains your nest. It decides what home in the adult world will be like and how much privacy you'll need. The Fourth House deals with matters of real estate. Most importantly, this house contains the emotional warehouse of memories you operate from subconsciously.

The Fifth House

Here's the side of you that's reserved for play, that only comes out when work is done and it's time to party and be entertained. This is the charming, creative, delightful side of you, where your hobbies, interests, and playmates are found. If it gives you joy, it's described here. Your Fifth House shines when you are creative, and it allows you to see a bit of yourself in those creations—anything from your child's smile to a piece of art. Traditionally this house also refers to speculation and gambling.

The Sixth House

This house is where you keep the side of you that decides how you like things to go along over the course of a day, the side of you that plans a schedule. Since it describes the duties you perform on a daily basis, it also refers to the nature of your work, your work environment, and how you take care of your health. It's how you function. Pets are also traditionally a Sixth House issue, since we tend to them daily and incorporate them into our routine.

The Seventh House

Although it's traditionally known as the house of marriage, partnerships, and open enemies, the Seventh House really holds the side of you that only comes out when you're in the company of just one other person. This is the side of you that handles relating on a one-to-one basis. Whenever you use the word "my" to describe your relationship with another, it's this side of you talking.

The Eighth House

Here's the crisis expert side of you that emerges when it's time to handle extreme circumstances. This is the side of you that deals with agony and ecstasy, with sex, death, and all manner of mergers, financial and otherwise. The Eighth House also holds information on surgeries, psychotherapy, and the way we regenerate and rejuvenate after a loss.

The Ninth House

This house holds the side of you that handles new experiences, foreign places, long-distance travel, and legal matters. Higher education, publishing, advertising, and forming opinions are handled here, as are issues involving the big picture, including politics, religion, and philosophy.

The Tenth House

This spot in your chart describes what the public knows about you. Your career, reputation, and social status are found here. This is the side of you that takes time to learn and become accomplished. It describes the behavior you'll exhibit when you're in charge, and also the way you'll act in the presence of an authority figure. Most importantly, the Tenth House describes your vocation or life's work—whatever you consider your "calling."

The Eleventh House

Here's the team player in you, the side of you that helps you find your peer groups. The Eleventh House shows the types of organizations you're drawn to join, the kind of folks you consider kindred spirits, and how you'll act in group situations. It also shows the causes and social activities you hold near and dear.

The Twelfth House

This is the side of you that only comes out when you're alone, or in the mood to retreat and regroup. Here's where the secret side of you lives, where secret affairs and dealings take place. Here, too, is where matters like hospital stays are handled. Most importantly, the Twelfth House is the room where you keep all the traits and behaviors that you were taught early on to stifle, avoid, or deny—especially in public. This side of you is very fond of fantasy, illusion, and pretend play.

Aspects and Transits: The Fourth Building Block

Planets form angles to one another as they move through the heavens. If two planets are 90 degrees apart, they form a square. If they're 180 degrees apart, they're in opposition. Planets in aspect have twenty-four-hour communication going on. The particular angle that separates any two planets describes the nature of their conversation. Astrologers use six angles most often, each of which produces a different type of relationship or "conversation" between the planets they join. Let's go over the meaning of each of the aspects.

Ptolemic Aspects

The Conjunction (0–8 degrees)

When you hear that two things are operating "in conjunction," it means they're operating together. This holds true with planets as well. Two (or more) planets conjoined are a team, but some planets pair up more easily than others. Venus and the Moon work well together because both are feminine and receptive, but the Sun and Mars are both pretty feisty by nature, and may cause conflict. Planets in conjunction are usually sharing a house in your chart.

The Sextile (60 degrees)

The sextile links planets in compatible elements. That is, planets in sextile are either in fire and air signs or earth and water signs. Since these pairs of elements get along well, the sextile encourages an active exchange between the two planets involved, so these two parts of you will be eager to work together.

The Square (90 degrees)

A square aspect puts planets at cross-purposes. Friction develops between them and one will constantly challenge the other. You can see squares operating in someone who's fidgety or constantly restless. Although they're uncomfortable and even aggravating at times, your squares point to places where tremendous growth is possible.

The Trine (120 degrees)

Trines are usually formed between planets of the same element, so they understand each other. They show an ease of communication not found in any of the other aspects, and they're traditionally thought of as "favorable." Of course, there is a downside to trines. Planets in this relationship are so comfortable that they can often get lazy and spoiled. (Sometimes they get so comfy they're boring.) Planets in trine show urges or needs that automatically support each other. The catch is that you've got to get them operating.

The Quincunx (150 degrees)

This aspect joins two signs that don't share a quality, element, or gender, which makes it difficult for them to communicate with each other. It's frustrating. For that reason, this aspect has always been considered to require an adjustment in the way the two planets are used. Planets in quincunx often feel pushed, forced, or obligated to perform. They seem to correspond to health issues.

The Opposition (180 degrees)

When two planets are opposed, they work against each other. For example, you may want to do something, and if you have two opposing planets you may struggle with two very different approaches to getting the job done. If Mars and Neptune are opposing, you may struggle between getting a job done the quick, easy way or daydreaming about all the creative possibilities open to you. It's as if the two are standing across from one another with their arms folded, involved in a debate, neither willing to concede an inch. They can break out of their standoff only by first becoming aware of one another and then compromising. This aspect is the least difficult of the traditionally known "hard" aspects because planets "at odds" with one another can come to some sort of compromise.

Transits

While your horoscope (natal chart) reflects the exact position of planets at the time of your birth, the planets, as you know, move on. They are said to be "transiting." We interpret a transit as a planet in its "today" position making an aspect to a planet in your natal chart. Transiting planets represent incoming influences and events that your natal planets will be asked to handle. The nature of the transiting planet describes the types of situations that will arise, and the nature of your natal planet tells which "piece" of you you're working on at the moment. When a planet transits through a house or aspects a planet in your chart, you will have opportunities for personal growth and change. Every transit you experience adds knowledge to your personality.

Sun Transit

A Sun transit points to the places in your chart where you'll want special attention, pats on the back, and appreciation. Here's where you want to shine. These are often times of public acclaim, when we're recognized, congratulated, or applauded for what we've done. Of course, the ultimate Sun transit is our birthday, the day when we're all secretly sure that we should be treated like royalty.

Moon Transit

When the Moon touches one of the planets in our natal chart, we react from an emotional point of view. A Moon transit often corresponds to the highs and lows we feel that last only a day or two. Our instincts are on high during a Moon transit and we're more liable to sense what's going on around us than to consciously know something.

Mercury Transit

Transiting Mercury creates activity in whatever area of life it visits. The subject is communication of all kinds, so conversation, letters, and quick errands take up our time now. Because of Mercury's love of duality, events will often occur in twos—as if Hermes the trickster were having some fun with us—and we're put in the position of having to do at least two things at once.

Venus Transit

Transiting Venus brings times when the universe gives us a small token of warmth or affection or a well-deserved break. These are often sociable, friendly periods when we do more than our usual share of mingling and are more interested in good food and cushy conditions than anything resembling work. A Venus transit also shows a time when others will give us gifts. Since Venus rules money, this transit can show when we'll receive financial rewards.

Mars Transit

Mars transiting a house can indicate high-energy times. You're stronger and restless, or perhaps cranky, angry, accident-prone, or violent. When Mars happens along, it's best to work or exercise hard to use up this considerable energy. Make yourself "too tired to be mad." These are ideal times to initiate projects that require a hard push of energy to begin.

Jupiter Transit

Under this transit you're in the mood to travel, take a class, or learn something new about the concerns of any house or planet Jupiter visits. You ponder the big questions. You grow under a Jupiter transit, sometimes even physically. Now is the time to take chances or risk a shot at the title. During a Jupiter transit you're luckier, bolder, and a lot more likely to succeed. This transit provides opportunities. Be sure to take advantage of them.

Saturn Transit

When Saturn comes along, we see things as they truly are. These are not traditionally great times, but they are often times when your greatest rewards appear. When Saturn transits a house or planet, he checks to see if the structure is steady and will hold up. You are then tested, and if you pass, you receive a symbolic certificate of some kind—and sometimes a real one, like a diploma. We will always be tested, but if we fail, life can feel very difficult. Firming up our lives is Saturn's mission. This is a great time to tap into Saturn's willpower and self-discipline to stop doing something. It is not traditionally a good time to begin new ventures, though.

Uranus Transit

The last thing in the world you'd ever expect to happen is exactly what you can expect under a Uranus transit. This is the planet of last-minute plan changes, reversals, and shock effects. So if you're feeling stuck in your present circumstances, when a Uranus transit happens along you won't be stuck for long. "Temporary people" often enter your life at these times, folks whose only purpose is to jolt you out of your present circumstances by appearing to provide exactly what you were sorely missing. That done, they disappear, leaving you with your life in a shambles. When these people arrive, enjoy them and allow them to break you out of your rut—just don't get comfortable.

Neptune Transit

A Neptune transit is a time when the universe asks only that you dream and nothing more. Your sensitivity heightens to the point that harsh sounds can actually make you wince. Compassion deepens and psychic moments are common. A Neptune transit inspires divine discontent. You sigh, wish, feel nostalgic, and don't see things clearly at all. At the end of the transit, you realize that everything about you is different, that the reality you were living at the beginning of the transit has been gradually eroded or erased right from under your feet, while you stood right there upon it.

Pluto Transit

A Pluto transit is often associated with obsession, regeneration, and inevitable change. Whatever has gone past the point of no return, whatever is broken beyond repair, will pass from your life now. As with a Saturn transit, this time is not known to be wonderful, but when circumstances peel away everything from us and we're forced to see ourselves as we truly are, we do learn just how strong we are. Power struggles often accompany Pluto's visit, but being empowered is the end result of a positive Pluto transit. The secret is to let go, accept the losses or changes, and make plans for the future.

Retrograde Planets

Retrograde literally means "backward." Although none of the planets ever really throw their engines in reverse and move backward, all of them, except the Sun and Moon, appear to do so periodically from our perspective here on Earth. What's happening is that we're moving either faster or slower than the planet that's retrograde, and since we have to look over our shoulder to see it, we refer to it as retrograde.

Mercury Retrograde: A Communication Breakdown

The way retrograde planets seem to affect our affairs varies from planet to planet. In Mercury's case, it means often looking back at Mercury-ruled things—communications, contracts, and so on. Keep in mind that Mercury correlates with Hermes, the original trickster, and you'll understand how cleverly disguised some of these errors can be. Communications become confused or are delayed. Letters are lost or sent to Auckland instead of Oakland, or they end up under the car seat for three weeks. We sign a contract or agreement and find out later that we didn't have all the correct information and what we signed was misleading in some way. We try repeatedly to reach someone on the telephone but can never catch them, or our communications devices themselves break down or garble information in some way. We feel as if our timing is off, so short trips often become more difficult. We leave the directions at home or write them down incorrectly. We're late for appointments due to circumstances beyond our control, or we completely forget about them.

Is there a constructive use for this time period? Yes. Astrologer Erin Sullivan has noted that the ratio of time Mercury spends moving retrograde (backward) and direct (forward) corresponds beautifully with the amount of time we humans spend awake and asleep—about a third of our lives. So this period seems to be a time to take stock of what's happened over the past three months and assimilate our experiences.

A good rule of thumb with Mercury retrograde is to try to confine activities to those that have "re" attached to the beginning of a word, such as reschedule, repair, return, rewrite, redecorate, restore, replace, renovate, or renew.

Retrogrades of the Other Planets

With Venus retrograde every eighteen months for six weeks, relationships and money matters are delayed or muddled.

With Mars retrograde for eleven weeks and then direct for twenty-two months, actions initiated are often rooted in confusion or end up at cross-purposes to our original intentions. Typically under a Mars retrograde, the aggressor or initiator of a battle is defeated.

Jupiter retrogrades for four months and is direct for nine months. Saturn retrogrades for about the same amount of time. Each of the outer planets—Uranus, Neptune, and Pluto—stays retrograde for about six or seven months of every year. In general, remember that actions ruled by a particular planet quite often need to be repeated or done over when that planet is retrograde. Just make sure that whatever you're planning is something you don't mind doing twice.

Moon Void-of-Course

The Moon orbits Earth in about twenty-eight days, moving through each of the signs in about two days. As she passes through the thirty degrees of each sign, she visits with the planets in order by forming angles, or aspects, with them. Because she moves one degree in just two to two and a half hours, her influence on each planet lasts only a few hours. As she approaches the late degrees of the sign she's passing through, she eventually forms what will be her final aspect to another planet before leaving the sign. From this point until she actually enters the new sign, she is referred to as being "void-of-course" (v/c).

The Moon symbolizes the emotional tone of the day, carrying feelings of the sign she's "wearing" at the moment. She rules instincts. After she has contacted each of the planets, she symbolically "rests" before changing her costume, so her instincts are temporarily on hold. It's during this time that many people feel fuzzy, vague, or scattered. Plans or decisions do not pan out. Without the instinctual knowing the Moon provides as she touches each planet, we tend to be unrealistic or exercise poor judgment. The traditional definition of the void-of-course Moon is that "nothing will come of this," and it seems to be true. Actions initiated under a void-of-course Moon are often wasted, irrelevant, or incorrect—usually because information needed to make a sound decision is hidden or missing or has been overlooked.

Now, although it's not a good time to initiate plans when the Moon is void, routine tasks seem to go along just fine. However, this period is really ideal for what the Moon does best: reflection. It's at this time that we can assimilate what has occurred over the past few days. Use this time to meditate, ponder, and imagine. Let your conscious mind rest and allow yourself to feel.

On the lighter side, remember that there are other good uses for the void-of-course Moon. This is the time period when the universe seems to be most open to loopholes. It's a great time to make plans you don't want to fulfill or schedule things you don't want to do. In other words, like the saying goes, "To everything, there is a season." Even void-of-course Moons.

The Moon's Influence

As the Moon goes along her way, she magically appears and disappears, waxing to full from the barest sliver of a crescent just after she's new, then waning back to her invisible new phase again. The four quarters—the New Moon, the second quarter, the Full Moon, and the fourth quarter—correspond to the growth cycle of every living thing.

The Quarters

First Quarter

This phase begins when the Moon and the Sun are conjunct one another in the sky. At the beginning of the phase, the Moon is invisible, hidden by the brightness of the Sun as they travel together. The Moon is often said to be in her "dark phase" when she is just new. The New Moon can't actually be seen until 5½ to 12 hours after its birth. Toward the end of the first-quarter phase, as the Moon pulls farther away from the Sun and begins to wax toward the second quarter stage, a delicate silver crescent appears. This time corresponds to all new beginnings; this is the best time to begin a project.

Second Quarter

The second quarter begins when the Moon has moved 90 degrees away from the Sun. At this point the waxing Moon rises at about noon and sets at about midnight. It's at this time that she can be seen in the western sky during the early evening hours, growing in size from a crescent to her full beauty. This period corresponds to the development and growth of life, and with projects that are coming close to fruition.

Third Quarter

This phase begins with the Full Moon, when the Sun and Moon are opposite each other in the sky. It's now that the Moon can be seen rising in the east at sunset, a bit later each night as this phase progresses. This time corresponds to the culmination of plans and to maturity.

Fourth Quarter

This phase occurs when the Moon has moved 90 degrees past the full phase. She is decreasing in light, rises at midnight, and can be seen now in the eastern sky during the late evening hours. She doesn't reach the highest point in the sky until very early in the morning. This period corresponds to "disintegration"—a symbolic "drawing back" to reflect on what's been accomplished. It's now time to reorganize, clear the boards, and plan for the next New Moon stage.

The Moon Through the Signs

The signs indicate how we'll do things. Since the Moon rules the emotional tone of the day, it's good to know what type of mood she's in at any given moment. Here's a thumbnail sketch to help you navigate every day by cooperating with the Moon no matter what sign she's in.

Aries

The Moon in Aries is bold, impulsive, and energetic. It's a period when we feel feisty and maybe a little argumentative. This is when even the meekest aren't afraid to take a stand to protect personal feelings. Since Aries is the first sign of the zodiac, it's a natural starting point for all kinds of projects, and a wonderful time to channel all that "me first" energy to initiate change and new beginnings. Just watch out for a tendency to be too impulsive and stress-oriented.

Taurus

☽ ♉ The Moon in Taurus is the Lady at her most solid and sensual, feeling secure and well rooted. There's no need to stress or hurry—and definitely no need to change anything. We tend to resist change when the Moon is in this sign, especially change that's not of our own making. We'd rather sit still, have a wonderful dinner, and listen to good music. Appreciating the beauty of the earth, watching a sunset, viewing some lovely art, or taking care of money and other resources are Taurus Moon activities.

Gemini

☽ ♊ This mutable air sign moves around so quickly that when the Moon is here we're a bit more restless than usual, and may find that we're suddenly in the mood for conversation, puzzles, riddles, and word games. We want two—at least two—of everything. Now is a great time for letter writing, phone calls, or short trips. It's when you'll find the best shortcuts, and when you'll need to take them, too. Watch for a tendency to become a bit scattered under this fun, fickle Moon.

Cancer

☽ ♋ The Moon in this cardinal water sign is at her most nurturing. Here the Moon's concerns turn to home, family, children, and mothers, and we respond by becoming more likely to express our emotions and to be sympathetic and understanding toward others. We often find ourselves in the mood to take care of someone, to cook for or cuddle our dear ones. During this time, feelings run high, so it's important to watch out for becoming overly sensitive, dependent, or needy. Now is a great time to putter around the house, have family over, and tend to domestic concerns.

Leo

♌ The Leo Moon loves drama with a capital *D*. This theatrical sign has long been known for its big entrances, love of display, and need for attention. When the Moon is in this sign, we're all feeling a need to be recognized, applauded, and appreciated. Now, all that excitement, pride, and emotion can turn into melodrama in the blink of an eye, so it's best to be careful of overreacting or being excessively vain during this period. It's a great time to take in a show (or star in one), be romantic, or express your feelings for someone in regal style.

Virgo

♍ The Moon is at her most discriminating and detail-oriented in Virgo, the sign most concerned with fixing and fussing. This Moon sign puts us in the mood to clean, scour, sort, troubleshoot, and help. Virgo, the most helpful of all the signs, is also more health conscious, work-oriented, and duty bound. Use this period to pay attention to your diet, hygiene, and daily schedules.

Libra

♎ The Libra Moon is most oriented toward relationships and partnerships. Since Libra's job is to restore balance, however, you may find yourself in situations of emotional imbalance that require a delicate tap of the scales to set them right. In general, this is a social, polite, and friendly time, when others will be cooperative and agree more easily to compromise. A Libra Moon prompts us to make our surroundings beautiful, or to put ourselves in situations where beauty is all around us. This is a great time to decorate, shop for the home, or visit places of elegant beauty.

Scorpio

♏ Scorpio is the most intense sign, and when the Moon is here, she feels everything to the *n*th degree—and needless to say, we do, too. Passion, joy, jealousy, betrayal, love, and desire can take center stage in our lives now, as our emotions deepen to the point of possible obsession. Be careful of a tendency to become secretive or suspicious, or to brood over an offense that was not intended.

Now is a great time to investigate a mystery, do research, "dig"—both figuratively and literally—and allow ourselves to become intimate with someone.

Sagittarius

☽ ♐ The Moon is at her most optimistic and willing to let go of things in Sagittarius. Jupiter, the planet of long-distance travel and education of the higher mind, makes this a great time to take off for adventure or attend a seminar on a topic you've always been interested in—say, philosophy or religion. This is the sign with the gift of prophecy and wisdom. When the Moon is in this sign, spend time outdoors, be spontaneous, and laugh much too loudly; just watch for a tendency toward excess, waste, and overdoing.

Capricorn

☽ ♑ The Moon is at her most organized, practical, and business-like in Capricorn. She brings out the dutiful, cautious, and pessimistic side of us. Our goals for the future become all-important. Now is the time to tend to the family business, act responsibly, take charge of something, organize any part of our lives that has become scattered or disrupted, set down rules and guidelines, or patiently listen and learn. Watch for the possibility of acting too businesslike at the expense of others' emotions.

Aquarius

☽ ♒ The Aquarius Moon brings out the rebel in us. This is a great time to break out of a rut, try something different, and make sure everyone sees us for the unique individuals we are. This sign is ruled by Uranus, so personal freedom and individuality are more important than anything now. Our schedules become topsy-turvy, and our causes become urgent. Watch for a tendency to become fanatical, act deliberately rebellious without a reason, or break tradition just for the sake of breaking it.

Pisces

☽ ♓ When the Moon slips into this sign, sleep, meditation, prayer, drugs, or alcohol is often what we crave to induce a trancelike state that will allow us to escape from the harshness of reality. Now is when we're most susceptible to emotional assaults of any kind, when we're feeling dreamy, nostalgic, wistful, or impressionable. It's also when we're at our most spiritual, when our boundaries are at their lowest, when we're compassionate, intuitive, and sensitive to those less fortunate. This is the time to attend a spiritual group or religious gathering.

2024 Eclipse Dates

March 25

Lunar Eclipse at 5° ♎ 07'

(3:00 a.m. EDT/12:00 a.m. PDT)

April 8

Solar Eclipse at 19° ♈ 24'

(2:21 p.m. EDT/11:21 a.m. PDT)

September 17

Lunar Eclipse at 25° ♓ 41'

(10:34 p.m. EDT/7:34 p.m. PDT)

October 2

Solar Eclipse at 10° ♎ 04'

(2:49 p.m. EDT/11:49 a.m. PDT)

2024 New and Full Moons

- ● New Moon, 20 ♑ 44, January 11, 6:57 a.m. EST
- ○ Full Moon, 5 ♌ 15, January 25, 12:54 p.m. EST
- ● New Moon, 20 ♒ 41, February 9, 5:59 p.m. EST
- ○ Full Moon, 5 ♍ 23, February 24, 7:30 a.m. EST
- ● New Moon, 20 ♓ 17, March 10, 5:00 a.m. EDT
- ○ Full Moon/Lunar Eclipse, 5 ♎ 07, March 25, 3:00 a.m. EDT
- ● New Moon/Solar Eclipse, 19 ♈ 24, April 8, 2:21 p.m. EDT
- ○ Full Moon, 4 ♏ 18, April 23, 7:49 p.m. EDT
- ● New Moon, 18 ♉ 02, May 7, 11:22 p.m. EDT
- ○ Full Moon, 2 ♐ 55, May 23, 9:53 a.m. EDT
- ● New Moon, 16 ♊ 18, June 6, 8:38 a.m. EDT
- ○ Full Moon, 1 ♑ 07, June 21, 9:08 p.m. EDT
- ● New Moon, 14 ♋ 23, July 5, 6:57 p.m. EDT
- ○ Full Moon, 29 ♑ 09, July 21, 6:17 a.m. EDT
- ● New Moon, 12 ♌ 34, August 4, 7:13 a.m. EDT
- ○ Full Moon, 27 ♒ 15, August 19, 2:26 p.m. EDT
- ● New Moon, 11 ♍ 04, September 2, 9:56 p.m. EDT
- ○ Full Moon/Lunar Eclipse, 25 ♓ 41, Sept. 17, 10:34 p.m. EDT
- ● New Moon/Solar Eclipse, 10 ♎ 04, October 2, 2:49 p.m. EDT
- ○ Full Moon, 24 ♈ 35, October 17, 7:26 a.m. EDT
- ● New Moon, 9 ♏ 35, November 1, 8:47 a.m. EDT
- ○ Full Moon, 24 ♉ 01, November 15, 4:28 p.m. EST
- ● New Moon, 9 ♐ 33, December 1, 1:21 a.m. EST
- ○ Full Moon, 23 ♊ 53, December 15, 4:02 a.m. EST
- ● New Moon, 9 ♑ 44, December 30, 5:27 p.m. EST

2024 Planetary Motions

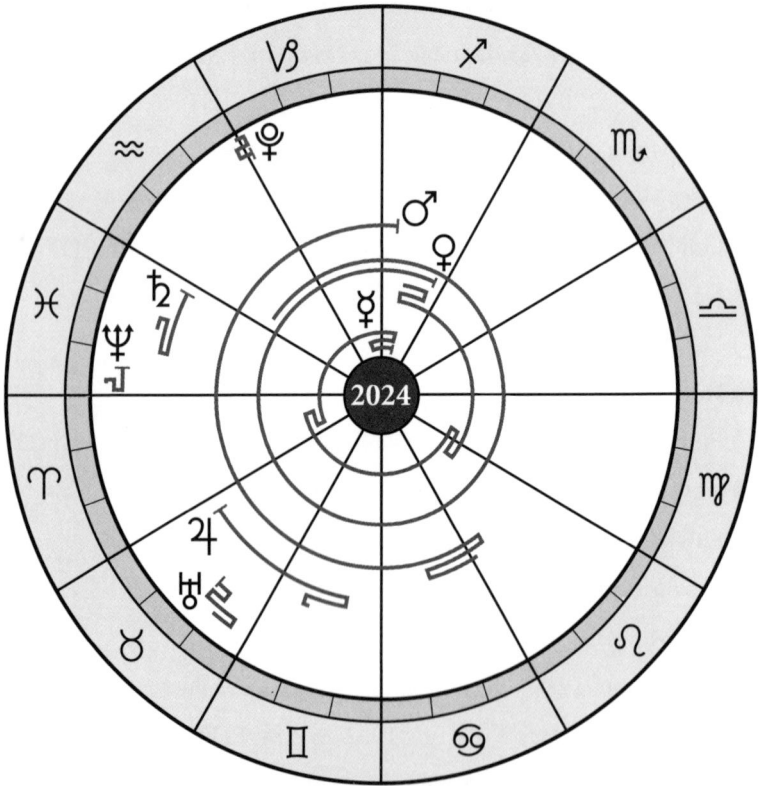

2024 Travel			*Stationary Points*				
Planet	Begins	Ends	Station	Date	Position	Eastern	Pacific
Mercury	22 ♐ 15	20 ♐ 08	SR	12/13/23	8 ♑ 29	2:09 am	
			SD	1/1	22 ♐ 11	10:08 pm	**7:08 pm**
			SR	4/1	27 ♈ 13	6:14 pm	**3:14 pm**
			SD	4/25	15 ♈ 59	8:54 am	**5:54 am**
			SR	8/4	4 ♍ 06		**9:56 pm**
			SR	8/5	4 ♍ 06	12:56 am	
			SD	8/28	21 ♌ 25	5:14 pm	**2:14 pm**
			SR	11/25	22 ♐ 40	9:42 pm	**6:42 pm**
			SD	12/15	6 ♐ 24	3:56 pm	**12:56 pm**

2024 Travel			Stationary Points				
Planet	Begins	Ends	Station	Date	Position	Eastern	Pacific
Venus	2♐52	27♒56	No change in direction in 2024				
Mars	27♐28	1♌51	SR	12/6	6♌10	6:33 pm	**3:33 pm**
			SD	2/23/25	17♋01	9:00 pm	**6:00 pm**
Jupiter	5♉35	13♊12	SR	10/9	21♊20	3:05 am	**12:05 am**
			SD	2/4/25	11♊17	4:40 am	**1:40 am**
Saturn	3♓16	14♓32	SR	6/29	19♓26	3:07 pm	**12:07 pm**
			SD	11/15	12♓42	9:20 am	**6:20 am**
Uranus	19♉23	23♉38	SR	8/28/23	23♉05	10:39 pm	**7:39 pm**
			SD	1/26	19♉05		**11:35 pm**
			SD	1/27	19♉05	2:35 am	
			SR	9/1	27♉15	11:18 am	**8:18 am**
			SD	1/30/25	23♉16	11:22 am	**8:22 am**
Neptune	25♓05	27♓18	SR	7/2	29♓56	6:40 am	**3:40 am**
			SD	12/7	27♓08	6:43 pm	**3:43 pm**
Pluto	29♑22	1♒04	SR	5/2	2♒06	1:46 pm	**10:46 am**
			SD	10/11	29♑39	8:34 pm	**5:34 pm**

SR = stationary, moving retrograde

SD = stationary, moving direct

Times corrected for Daylight Saving Time from March 10 to November 3

2024 Retrograde Planets

Planet	Begin	Eastern	Pacific	End	Eastern	Pacific
Uranus	8/28/23	10:39 pm	**7:39 pm**	1/26		**11:35 pm**
				1/27	2:35 am	
Mercury	12/12/23		**11:09 pm**	1/1	10:08 pm	**7:08 pm**
	12/13/23	2:09 am				
Mercury	4/1	6:14 pm	**3:14 pm**	4/25	8:54 am	**5:54 am**
Pluto	5/2	1:46 pm	**10:46 am**	10/11	8:34 pm	**5:34 pm**
Saturn	6/29	3:07 pm	**12:07 pm**	11/15	9:20 am	**6:20 am**
Neptune	7/2	6:40 am	**3:40 am**	12/7	6:43 pm	**3:43 pm**
Mercury	8/4		**9:56 pm**	8/28	5:14 pm	**2:14 pm**
	8/5	12:56 am				
Uranus	9/1	11:18 am	**8:18 am**	1/30/25	11:22 am	**8:22 am**
Jupiter	10/9	3:05 am	**12:05 am**	2/4/25	4:40 am	**1:40 am**
Mercury	11/25	9:42 pm	**6:42 pm**	12/15	3:56 pm	**12:56 pm**
Mars	12/6	6:33 pm	**3:33 pm**	2/23/25	9:00 pm	**6:00 pm**

Times corrected for Daylight Saving Time from March 10 to November 3

2024 Planetary Ingresses

January

Ingress	day	ET	PT
♂ ♑	4	9:58 am	**6:58 am**
☿ ♑	13	9:49 pm	**6:49 pm**
☉ ♒	20	9:07 am	**6:07 am**
♇ ♒	20	7:50 pm	**4:50 pm**
♀ ♑	23	3:50 am	**12:50 am**

February

Ingress	day	ET	PT
☿ ♒	4		**9:10 pm**
☿ ♒	5	12:10 am	
♂ ♒	12		**10:05 pm**
♂ ♒	13	1:05 am	
♀ ♒	16	11:05 am	**8:05 am**
☉ ♓	18	11:13 pm	**8:13 pm**
☿ ♓	22		**11:29 pm**
☿ ♓	23	2:29 am	

March

Ingress	day	ET	PT
☿ ♈	9	11:03 pm	**8:03 pm**
♀ ♓	11	5:50 pm	**2:50 pm**
☉ ♈	19	11:06 pm	**8:06 pm**
♂ ♓	22	7:47 pm	**4:47 pm**

April

Ingress	day	ET	PT
♀ ♈	4		**9:00 pm**
♀ ♈	5	12:00 am	
☉ ♉	19	10:00 am	**7:00 am**
♀ ♉	29	7:31 am	**4:31 am**
♂ ♈	30	11:33 am	**8:33 am**

May

Ingress	day	ET	PT
☿ ♉	15	1:05 pm	**10:05 am**
☉ ♊	20	8:59 am	**5:59 am**
♀ ♊	23	4:30 pm	**1:30 pm**
♃ ♊	25	7:15 pm	**4:15 pm**

June

Ingress	day	ET	PT
☿ ♊	3	3:37 am	**12:37 am**
♂ ♉	8		**9:35 pm**
♂ ♉	9	12:35 am	
♀ ♋	16		**11:20 pm**
♀ ♋	17	2:20 am	
☿ ♋	17	5:07 am	**2:07 am**
☉ ♋	20	4:51 pm	**1:51 pm**

July

Ingress	day	ET	PT
☿ ♌	2	8:50 am	**5:50 am**
♀ ♌	11	12:19 pm	**9:19 am**
♂ ♊	20	4:43 pm	**1:43 pm**
☉ ♌	22	3:44 am	**12:44 am**
☿ ♍	25	6:42 pm	**3:42 pm**

August

Ingress	day	ET	PT
♀ ♍	4	10:23 pm	**7:23 pm**
☿ ♌	14	8:16 pm	**5:16 pm**
☉ ♍	22	10:55 am	**7:55 am**
♀ ♎	29	9:23 am	**6:23 am**

September

Ingress	day	ET	PT
♇ ♑	1	8:10 pm	**5:10 pm**
♂ ♋	4	3:46 pm	**12:46 pm**
☿ ♍	8		**11:50 pm**
☿ ♍	9	2:50 am	
☉ ♎	22	8:44 am	**5:44 am**
♀ ♏	22	10:36 pm	**7:36 pm**
☿ ♎	26	4:09 am	**1:09 am**

October

Ingress	day	ET	PT
☿ ♏	13	3:23 pm	**12:23 pm**
♀ ♐	17	3:28 pm	**12:28 pm**
☉ ♏	22	6:15 pm	**3:15 pm**

November

Ingress	day	ET	PT
☿ ♐	2	3:18 pm	**12:18 pm**
♂ ♌	3	11:10 pm	**8:10 pm**
♀ ♑	11	1:26 pm	**10:26 am**
♇ ♒	19	3:29 pm	**12:29 pm**
☉ ♐	21	2:56 pm	**11:56 am**

December

Ingress	day	ET	PT
♀ ♒	6		**10:13 pm**
♀ ♒	7	1:13 am	
☉ ♑	21	4:21 am	**1:21 am**

Times corrected for Daylight Saving Time from March 10 to November 3

2024 Moon Void-of-Course Data

JANUARY

Last aspect Date	Time	Moon enters Date	Sign	Time
2	6:36 pm	2	♎	7:47 pm
5	6:41 am	5	♏	7:39 am
7	3:22 pm	7	♐	4:08 pm
9	1:24 pm	9	♑	8:33 pm
11	9:33 pm	11	♒	10:01 pm
13	4:59 am	13	♓	10:29 pm
15	11:33 pm	15	♈	11:49 pm
18	3:03 am	18	♉	3:12 am
20	8:57 am	20	♊	8:58 am
22	3:40 pm	22	♋	4:51 pm
24	5:58 am	25	♌	2:37 am
26	4:19 pm	27	♍	2:11 pm
29	6:20 pm	30	♎	3:04 am

FEBRUARY

Last aspect Date	Time	Moon enters Date	Sign	Time
1	4:03 am	1	♏	3:37 pm
3	10:24 pm	4	♐	1:28 am
6	12:06 am	6	♑	7:08 am
8	2:52 am	8	♒	8:59 am
9	5:59 pm	10	♓	8:42 am
12	7:32 am	12	♈	8:26 am
14	5:21 am	14	♉	10:02 am
16	10:01 am	16	♊	2:39 pm
18	10:21 pm	18	♋	10:25 pm
21	1:38 am	21	♌	8:40 am
22	11:18 pm	23	♍	8:38 pm
26	2:35 am	26	♎	9:29 am
27	1:22 pm	28	♏	10:09 pm

MARCH

Last aspect Date	Time	Moon enters Date	Sign	Time
2	2:47 am	2	♐	8:56 am
4	10:41 am	4	♑	4:15 pm
6	2:35 pm	6	♒	7:38 pm
8	1:56 pm	8	♓	8:03 pm
10	3:45 pm	10	♈	8:19 pm
12	7:08 am	12	♉	8:28 pm
14	6:29 pm	14	♊	11:16 pm
17	12:43 am	17	♋	5:40 am
19	2:52 pm	19	♌	3:33 pm
22	2:34 am	22	♍	3:42 am
24	11:49 am	24	♎	4:37 pm
26	7:09 pm	27	♏	5:03 am
29	11:40 am	29	♐	3:52 pm
31	8:16 pm	4/1	♑	12:05 am

APRIL

Last aspect Date	Time	Moon enters Date	Sign	Time
3/31	8:16 pm	1	♑	12:05 am
3	1:40 am	3	♒	5:08 am
5	1:40 am	5	♓	7:13 am
7	4:27 am	7	♈	7:25 am
8	10:39 pm	9	♉	7:23 am
11	6:04 am	11	♊	8:59 am
13	10:46 pm	13	♋	1:45 pm
15	7:22 pm	15	♌	10:24 pm
18	8:02 am	18	♍	10:10 am
20	8:20 pm	20	♎	11:08 pm
22	7:24 pm	23	♏	11:20 am
25	7:17 pm	25	♐	9:37 pm
28	3:31 am	28	♑	5:37 am
30	11:19 am	30	♒	11:20 am

MAY

Last aspect Date	Time	Moon enters Date	Sign	Time
2	5:28 am	2	♓	2:52 pm
4	3:06 pm	4	♈	4:41 pm
6	1:57 am	6	♉	5:42 pm
8	5:55 pm	8	♊	7:20 pm
10	9:49 pm	10	♋	11:13 pm
13	5:13 am	13	♌	6:36 am
15	12:41 pm	15	♍	5:33 pm
18	5:09 am	18	♎	6:23 am
19	11:48 am	20	♏	6:34 pm
23	3:28 am	23	♐	4:24 am
25	10:47 am	25	♑	11:36 am
27	4:02 pm	27	♒	4:45 pm
29	10:20 am	29	♓	8:33 pm
31	10:55 pm	31	♈	11:28 pm

JUNE

Last aspect Date	Time	Moon enters Date	Sign	Time
2	6:04 pm	3	♉	1:55 am
5	4:09 am	5	♊	4:36 am
7	8:16 am	7	♋	8:41 am
9	3:05 pm	9	♌	3:29 pm
11	3:16 pm	12	♍	1:39 am
14	1:54 pm	14	♎	2:12 pm
17	2:05 am	17	♏	2:38 am
19	12:19 pm	19	♐	12:32 pm
21	6:58 pm	21	♑	7:08 pm
23	11:05 pm	23	♒	11:14 pm
25	6:30 pm	26	♓	2:08 am
28	4:45 am	28	♈	4:52 am
30	12:56 am	30	♉	8:00 am

JULY

Last aspect Date	Time	Moon enters Date	Sign	Time
2	11:43 am	2	♊	11:50 am
4	4:44 pm	4	♋	4:51 pm
6	11:47 pm	6	♌	11:56 pm
9	2:04 am	9	♍	9:48 am
11	9:55 pm	11	♎	10:06 pm
13	6:49 pm	14	♏	10:53 am
16	9:10 pm	16	♐	9:25 pm
19	3:58 am	19	♑	4:14 am
21	7:26 am	21	♒	7:43 am
23	5:38 am	23	♓	9:23 am
25	10:31 am	25	♈	10:52 am
26	6:14 pm	27	♉	1:23 pm
29	4:59 pm	29	♊	5:28 pm
31	10:46 pm	31	♋	11:19 pm

AUGUST

Last aspect Date	Time	Moon enters Date	Sign	Time
3	6:31 am	3	♌	7:10 am
5	11:16 am	5	♍	5:17 pm
8	4:40 am	8	♎	5:31 am
9	5:45 pm	10	♏	6:34 pm
13	5:01 am	13	♐	6:01 am
15	12:52 pm	15	♑	1:51 pm
17	4:43 pm	17	♒	5:45 pm
19	2:26 pm	19	♓	6:52 pm
21	5:54 pm	21	♈	7:02 pm
23	8:44 am	23	♉	8:00 pm
25	9:40 pm	25	♊	11:04 pm
28	3:14 am	28	♋	4:47 am
30	11:24 am	30	♌	1:09 pm

SEPTEMBER

Last aspect Date	Time	Moon enters Date	Sign	Time
1	8:25 pm	1	♍	11:48 pm
4	12:06 pm	4	♎	12:12 pm
7	1:08 am	7	♏	1:18 am
9	1:11 pm	9	♐	1:26 pm
11	8:21 pm	11	♑	10:38 pm
14	3:35 am	14	♒	3:53 am
16	1:04 am	16	♓	5:39 am
18	5:02 am	18	♈	5:24 am
20	4:39 am	20	♉	5:03 am
22	6:14 am	22	♊	6:24 am
24	7:59 am	24	♋	10:50 am
26	6:12 pm	26	♌	6:47 pm
28	11:36 pm	29	♍	5:42 am

OCTOBER

Last aspect Date	Time	Moon enters Date	Sign	Time
1	5:39 pm	1	♎	6:20 pm
4	6:40 am	4	♏	7:22 am
6	6:52 pm	6	♐	7:34 pm
9	1:54 am	9	♑	5:38 am
11	11:53 am	11	♒	12:31 pm
13	10:11 am	13	♓	3:55 pm
15	4:00 pm	15	♈	4:34 pm
17	3:26 pm	17	♉	4:00 pm
19	3:33 pm	19	♊	4:07 pm
21	5:00 pm	21	♋	6:50 pm
24	12:47 am	24	♌	1:24 am
26	4:04 am	26	♍	11:47 am
28	11:54 pm	29	♎	12:30 am
31	12:57 pm	31	♏	1:29 pm

NOVEMBER

Last aspect Date	Time	Moon enters Date	Sign	Time
3	12:51 am	3	♐	1:19 am
5	5:23 am	5	♑	10:17 am
7	5:38 pm	7	♒	5:58 pm
9	7:23 pm	9	♓	11:00 pm
12	1:13 am	12	♈	1:26 am
14	1:50 am	14	♉	1:59 am
16	2:03 am	16	♊	2:09 am
17	11:09 pm	18	♋	3:50 am
20	6:20 am	20	♌	8:51 am
22	8:15 am	22	♍	6:01 pm
25	12:35 am	25	♎	6:20 am
27	4:14 am	27	♏	7:21 pm
30	1:19 am	30	♐	6:53 am

DECEMBER

Last aspect Date	Time	Moon enters Date	Sign	Time
2	10:47 am	2	♑	4:09 pm
4	6:34 pm	4	♒	11:21 pm
6	7:01 pm	7	♓	4:49 am
9	3:45 am	9	♈	8:38 am
10	5:13 pm	11	♉	10:55 am
13	7:39 am	13	♊	12:22 pm
15	9:32 am	15	♋	2:21 pm
17	1:33 pm	17	♌	6:39 pm
20	12:19 am	20	♍	2:37 am
22	8:27 am	22	♎	2:08 pm
24	5:44 am	25	♏	3:06 am
27	9:24 am	27	♐	2:46 pm
29	6:34 pm	29	♑	11:37 pm

Times in EST/EDT

2024 Planetary Phenomena

Information on Uranus and Neptune assumes the use of a telescope. Resource: *Astronomical Phenomena for the Year 2024,* prepared jointly with His Majesty's Nautical Almanac Office of the United Kingdom Hydrographic Office and the United States Naval Observatory's Nautical Almanac Office. The dates are expressed in Universal Time and must be converted to your Local Mean Time. (See the World Map of Time Zones on page 221.)

Planets Visible in Morning and Evening

Planet	Morning	Evening
Mercury	Jan. 1 – Feb. 16 April 20 – June 7 Aug. 27 – Sept. 20 Dec. 12 – Dec. 31	March 9 – April 4 June 22– Aug. 12 Oct. 15 – Nov. 30
Venus	Jan. 1 – April 28	July 11 – Dec. 31
Mars	Jan. 10 – Dec. 31	
Jupiter	June 2 – Dec. 7	Jan. 1 – May 5 Dec. 7 – Dec. 31
Saturn	March 17 – Sept. 8	Jan. 1 – Feb. 12 Sept. 8 – Dec. 31

Mercury

Mercury can only be seen low in the east before sunrise or low in the west after sunset.

Venus

Venus is a brilliant object in the morning sky from the beginning of the year until late April, when it becomes too close to the Sun for observation. In the second week of July it reappears in the evening sky, where it stays until the end of the year.

Mars

Mars can be seen in the morning sky from the second week of January. It can be seen for more than half the night from the beginning of October until the end of the year.

Jupiter

Jupiter can be seen only in the evening sky from late January until early May, when it becomes too close to the Sun for observation. It reappears in the morning sky in early June. Its westward elongation gradually increases until December 7, when it is visible throughout the night.

Saturn

Saturn can be seen in the evening sky until mid-February, when it becomes too close to the Sun for observation. It reappears in the morning sky in mid-March. Its westward elongation gradually increases until September 8, when it is visible throughout the night. Its eastern elongation then gradually decreases until early December, when it can be seen only in the evening sky.

Uranus

Uranus is visible in the sky at the beginning of the year. From early February until the end of the third week of April, it can be seen only in the evening sky. It then becomes too close to the Sun for observation, reappearing in early June in the morning sky.

Neptune

Neptune is visible at the beginning of the year in the evening sky. In late February it becomes too close to the Sun for observation and reappears in early April in the morning sky. Its eastern elongation gradually decreases, and in late December it can be seen only in the evening sky.

DO NOT CONFUSE Mercury with Mars from mid-January to early February, when Mercury is the brighter object.

2024 Weekly Forecasts

by Michelle Perrin, aka Astrology Detective

Overview of 2024

After popping in for a trial run for a few months during 2023, Pluto finally moves into Aquarius for good in 2024. This is a major astrological event—so much so that this entire introduction is devoted to it. It takes Pluto 248 years to orbit the Sun, meaning its transit of a single sign can take over a decade or two. Therefore, in astrology, Pluto is used to define eras.

The previous era we just experienced was Pluto in Capricorn. Pluto is the planet of complete, often radical transformation, while Capricorn is the sign of institutional power. Pluto entered Capricorn in 2008 at the very beginning of the financial crisis and is ending its transit of this sign with the Covid pandemic. Over the last fifteen years, the main organizations in our lives—Big Government, Big Media, Big Pharma, Big Tech, Big Business, etc.—all underwent radical, profound changes. Local, national powers seemed to be losing ground as we moved to a "one world" model of governance, with global institutions often setting policy for the entire planet. The iPhone was invented in 2007, which completely revolutionized online communication. It's hard to remember a time when we weren't addicted to our screens and social media, but it wasn't that long ago.

With Pluto moving into democratically minded Aquarius, a lot of the overreach of power that was accumulated during the Pluto in Capricorn era could start to see pushback from ordinary people, and we can expect this trend to accelerate over the upcoming years. Pluto in Aquarius is Davey fighting Goliath—and winning. The last Pluto in Aquarius era was from 1777 to 1798. While the US was founded in 1776, most of the Revolutionary War (1775–83) took place during Pluto in Aquarius. This entire era was known as the Age of Revolution, as citizens around the globe were inspired by what was going on in the US and staged their own democratic rebellions against ossified, unfair regimes. Most famously, the French Revolution overthrew the country's monarchy.

The Pluto in Aquarius era prior to this one was from 1532 to 1553—the height of the Reformation in Europe, a time when the newly formed Protestant movement stood up against the hierarchical Roman Catholic Church. This era was ushered in by Henry VIII's secret marriage to Anne Boleyn and saw the Church of England break away from Rome.

Pluto in Aquarius represents progress against tyranny, but it can also usher in its own cultlike, zealous authoritarianism—think of the Reign of Terror that followed the French Revolution. However, many countries transitioned more peacefully, so this is not a given, but more a cautionary tale to be aware of.

Aquarius also rules technology, so we can expect the digital realm to be used in ever more tyrannical ways to control us. From social credit scores to digital currencies that could be used to track and limit what we spend our money on, technology may become an increasingly authoritarian force in our lives. As the world becomes more and more globalized, individuals may try to reorganize their local environments so they can be around people who share their same ideals, instead of living in geographical configurations with others who have polar-opposite views on life and living.

Overall, Pluto in Aquarius will represent a chance for average people to stand up and take back control over encroachments by government and technology. This Pluto transit will last until 2044; amazing progress can be achieved over the next two decades as people rise up against oppression to usher in a more egalitarian, democratic, idealistic society that is of the people and for the people.

January 1–7

The new year starts off with vibes that are both lazy and inspired, so feel free to enjoy the holiday by sleeping in, relaxing, and letting your imagination roam free. Tuesday is a different story, however. It's time to get back to work after the festive season, and your brain may have a hard time firing up and focusing after all the mirth and merry. While the day starts out low-energy, a sense of drive and purpose returns by early evening. Wednesday and Thursday are perfect for brainstorming and teamwork, although egos may clash in after-hour relationships. You could plow through huge amounts of chores and duties on Friday thanks to a mega-burst of industrious energy. If you feel worn-out at the end of the day, you may want to just turn in early instead of hitting the town. **Weekend outlook:** Saturday afternoon is great for socializing, while Sunday promotes art, romance, and bonding. Try not to get too emotional if plans go awry on Saturday night. Just go with the flow. Sunday evening is a perfect time for lounging about, reading, and binge-watching.

Tips for a five-star week: Don't push yourself to produce on Monday and Tuesday; it's okay to proceed at a slow pace. You'll want to preserve your energy for the rest of the workweek, when the speed picks up and you'll be running on all cylinders. You might want to avoid dating on Wednesday and Saturday evenings and instead schedule a rendezvous for Sunday afternoon.

Top astrological event of the week: *Monday:* Mercury direct: The new year starts off on a promising note as Mercury turns direct on January 1, putting an end to indecision, confusion, and miscommunications. You can easily turn your attention now to planning and making resolutions for 2024.

January 8–14

Monday and Tuesday are great moments for team building and brainstorming new plans, but it may be difficult to get any actual work done, as things could quickly devolve into social chitchat and time-wasting. A strong work ethic comes bouncing back on Tuesday evening, however, making for a highly productive rest of the week. If you are a freelancer, you may even want to enjoy your daytime hours and tackle your work duties in the evening, when you will be revved up on overdrive. Thursday's New Moon in Capricorn is the perfect time to implement New Year's resolutions, maximizing the chance they will come to fruition over the course of the upcoming twelve months. This is also a great date night, as it will be easy to emotionally bond with the object of your affection. The workweek ends with another burst of gung-ho energy, making Friday the perfect day to seek a job, go on an interview, pitch a sale, or finally start your own business. **Weekend outlook:** Saturday is a great night to catch up with friends. It also favors connections forged through communication, so make sure to plan on going someplace where you can have long, meandering conversations. Sunday is a great day to catch up on chores or partake in physical activities.

Tips for a five-star week: Don't push yourself to be productive during the first two days of the week. Your fire will come raging back midweek, making you an unstoppable inferno on the job.

Top astrological event of the week: *Friday:* Mars in Capricorn trine Jupiter in Taurus: This aspect bestows the Midas touch on all business activities, so get out there and make your dreams come true. Luck will open like a lotus flower.

January 15–21

Monday is Martin Luther King Jr. Day in the US, and the heavens are tapping into this leader's inextinguishable spirit. This is the perfect day to set about making the world a better place by getting involved with grassroots organizations, where you can truly make an impact in your community. Your energy could be easily depleted on Tuesday and Wednesday, so instead of ruminating on your problems, surround yourself with the company of those you love, as they will instantly lift your mood. Productivity returns on Thursday, which is an excellent day for both the planning and the execution of projects. Contacts made in the afternoon could prove fruitful in the future, while the evening will be a great time to hit the gym and get in shape. People could be quite emotionally touchy on Friday morning, so give a wide berth to overly sensitive types. Luckily, the energy bounces back for an afternoon filled with spontaneity and excitement. **Weekend outlook:** The Sun gives a kiss goodbye to Pluto as it prepares for its exit from Capricorn on Saturday, making the daytime hours incredibly auspicious for career ambitions. Even though it's a Saturday, you may want to work on an entrepreneurial endeavor, look for your dream job, or put in extra hours at your existing one. The evening is a bit low-energy, so you may prefer something chill. There isn't a major astrological cloud in the sky on Sunday, so life is truly what you make it on this day.

Tips for a five-star week: Stop thinking about how you can help yourself and instead focus on how you can help those around you. In the end, it will make you feel more capable and confident.

Top astrological event of the week: *Saturday:* Pluto enters Aquarius: This is such a momentous event that the entire introduction is dedicated to it—go read it now!

January 22–28

A lazy T-square could have everyone irritable on Monday, so try to avoid working in a team, as people may not take criticism well. The grumpy energy continues on Tuesday, when people could be quick to anger or even resurrect arguments from the past. Wednesday represents the calm eye of the week's storm, so enjoy the peace while it lasts. Schedule all meetings and social outings on this day to take advantage of the positive vibes. Thursday's Full Moon is part of a T-square that drags in Pluto and Jupiter, creating an explosive mix that could detonate without warning. The Moon is urging us to move on from disordered people who squash our spirit and individuality. If you bear this in mind, this seemingly harsh energy could have massive benefits in the long run. **Weekend outlook:** While the workweek is filled with moments of drama, the weekend is the exact opposite. Saturday is a great time to spend with friends and family or go on a daytime date. It is equally auspicious for getting physically fit or plowing through piled-up chores. Sunday's incredibly harmonious vibes make this an excellent time for romance, art, and socializing. This is one of the best date nights of the month, so start swiping!

Tips for a five-star week: If you feel there are people in your life who have you walking on eggshells, it may be time to march on to better pastures. Keep your sights on the weekend, when romance is in store for couples and singles alike.

Top astrological event of the week: *Sunday:* Venus in Capricorn trine Jupiter in Taurus: If you're looking for a reliable partner who will have your back through thick and thin, this energy will make your search a whole lot easier.

January 29–February 4

After starting off with an energetic bang, the week's energy quickly dissipates into more laid-back vibes, so get all your important chores and duties done on Monday and Tuesday. If you put yourself out there and get out of your comfort zone, you could break down doors and spontaneously make things happen. If you're single, the rest of the week is not the best for dating, as petty squabbles and power games could erupt. Instead, set your sights on a fairy-tale Saturday soiree. Friday is a great day for artistic endeavors, but work of a more practical nature could mushroom out of control. **Weekend outlook:** Love is in the air on Saturday, making it a perfect time for the trifecta of romance: physical passion, sweet courtly love, and intellectual connection. Choose your strong point and go for it! Sunday's lackadaisical energy makes it a good day to relax and recuperate, so put off errands for another day.

Tips for a five-star week: Monday and Saturday are the two superstar days of a rather uneventful week, so schedule your time wisely to make the most of these energies.

Top astrological event of the week: *Monday:* Mars in Capricorn trine Uranus in Taurus: Baby, I'm going to make you a star! This energy will take the ingénue chorus girl and turn her into an overnight sensation, so get out (or go online) and network professionally. You never know who you might meet.

February 5–11

This week is all about the need for change. No matter how scary it seems, sometimes radical adjustments are needed for new, better things to take root. The highly visionary vibes found early in the week will help you plot a redesigned route to success. If you want something different in your love life, you couldn't find a more auspicious day than Wednesday to seek a new suitor or alter an existing situation. Look to revamp and revise all other aspects of your life at Friday's New Moon. **Weekend outlook:** While disagreements could pop up early Saturday morning, by the evening everything is sorted and good times are in store for all. Another lazy Sunday is in store, so sit back and take it easy.

Tips for a five-star week: Opportunities for finding true love abound on Wednesday, so if you're single, don't allow this occasion to go to waste. You may meet a fairy-tale soulmate in a spontaneous situation, so keep your eyes open.

Top astrological event of the week: *Wednesday:* Mars in Capricorn sextile Neptune in Pisces: Idealism and romance are in abundance on this day. Leave the rose-colored glasses on, so reality and dreams can blend into one beautiful plane of existence.

February 12–18

You may be best off scheduling your yearly Valentine's rendezvous a day early, as competitive, domineering energies will hold court midweek. In a quest for power, some folks will want to show off and run roughshod over other people's feelings. On Monday, Tuesday, and Friday, however, the vibes are totally different. These sweetly amorous days are worthy of any romance novel, where tender feelings of affection combine with passion and intellectual connection to create lasting bonds. **Weekend outlook:** When out on the town on Friday evening, be careful not to overindulge in intoxicating substances or you could end up getting into petty fights by telling friends exactly how you feel about them. Saturday and Sunday are rather lackadaisical days when it is better to pursue the arts and reading than to tackle heavy chores.

Tips for a five-star week: Stay away from control freaks and those with volatile emotions on Wednesday and Thursday. Their mood swings have no logic, so don't waste your time trying to come to an understanding.

Top astrological event of the week: *Tuesday:* Mars enters Aquarius: Mars joins Pluto in Aquarius on February 13, helping us all adjust to this new cosmic era with fortitude and aplomb.

February 19–25

Monday and Tuesday are highly productive days when work ethic and inspiration go seamlessly hand in hand. Energies shift on Wednesday, when idealists could butt heads with the more Machiavellian players; beware of manipulators who come off as smooth operators, especially in the romance department. **Weekend outlook:** The weekend may start off with feelings of mental, physical, and emotional exhaustion, so take it easy on Friday evening and Saturday. Plan spontaneous outings on Sunday, when an up-for-anything electricity fills the air. Adventures off the beaten path will help recharge your batteries.

Tips for a five-star week: Suitors who rush in to sweep you off your feet may not be as charming and wonderful as they seem. While it may be hard to resist love bombers, try to remain emotionally detached until you can better evaluate the situation.

Top astrological event of the week: *Saturday:* Full Moon in Virgo opposite the Sun, Mercury, and Saturn in Pisces and trine Jupiter in Taurus: This Full Moon will help reveal any false friends and lovers who are feeding off your kindness, thereby allowing you to return to a place of emotional stability.

February 26–March 3

Happy leap year! As a special gift from the universe, 2024 holds an extra day on Thursday, bursting with opportunities for long-term romance, compromise, and understanding. There is one catch, however. We must break free from entrenched, stagnant ways and open ourselves up to new opportunities to take full advantage of this energy. Luckily, a square between Mars and Jupiter on Tuesday will give us the push needed to get out of any long-standing ruts. Wednesday, meanwhile, is an excellent day for intellectual work that requires a high degree of focus and concentration. **Weekend outlook:** It might be best to avoid dating on Friday night, when jealousy and emotional volatility will likely abound. Instead, plan a daytime get-together on Saturday, when strong feelings of cosmic connection infuse the air. It may be hard to get out of bed in the morning on Sunday, so enjoy a good rest instead. Spend the day on energetic outings that don't require a lot of intellectual input. The evening is perfect for a romantic, cozy date night.

Tips for a five-star week: Learn to let go and allow things to come to you instead of trying to plan and micromanage every small detail of your life.

Top astrological event of the week: *Tuesday:* Mars in Aquarius square Jupiter in Taurus: The winds of progress and social change are blasting away worn-out social conventions and traditions. It is time to embrace the new on both the personal and the societal level.

March 4–10

While it may seem hard to get into the swing of things on Monday morning, by the afternoon a burst of reinvigorating intellectual energy puts winds in your sails. These buoyant vibes continue through Wednesday. Whether you are doing visionary, creative work or are in the stages of executing a project, you will have plenty of drive, enthusiasm, and determination to get it all done without suffering from feelings of exertion. You may need to slow down to refill your batteries on Thursday before putting in a final push to round out a highly productive week. **Weekend outlook:** Everyone is up for a fight on Saturday afternoon, so put off dates or socializing until Sunday. Saturday could be an accident-prone time, so avoid high-risk adventure sports and pay extra attention when driving. A highly romantic, creative New Moon on Sunday, however, could bring a soulmate into the lives of singles or restore the bonds of couples.

Tips for a five-star week: If there are any work projects you need to get done, tackle them this week and the universe will infuse you with all the ideas and energy you need to bring them to completion. If love is what you're after, there is no better day than Sunday to plant new seeds of amour.

Top astrological event of the week: *Saturday:* Mars in Aquarius square Uranus in Taurus: In the fight for progress, there is often a rush to tear it all down. Whether personally or in terms of societal structures, it is best not to completely destroy our rich heritage, as building a future from scratch is not as easy as it may seem.

March 11–17

Overall, this is a pretty chill week, devoid of any major transits. Romantic Venus enters starry-eyed Pisces on Monday, setting the tone for a relatively relaxed, harmonious seven-day period. Tuesday and Thursday are excellent for art and love, while Wednesday's industrious vibes are perfect for tackling work projects. **Weekend outlook:** Saturday's extroverted energy is brimming with passion, so spend time with friends or searching for love. Enjoy St. Patrick's Day on Sunday, a five-star day for socializing or going on a date.

Tips for a five-star week: The week's mellow vibes require no heavy lifting, so sit back and enjoy this period of relative calm.

Top astrological event of the week: *Monday:* Venus enters Pisces: This affectionate, tender transit is auspicious for all types of relationships—friends, love, and family. Spend the upcoming weeks nurturing everyone you care about.

March 18–24

The Sun enters Aries on Tuesday, ushering in the spring and kicking off the astrological new year. This is a time of new beginnings, and if there are any 2024 resolutions you have let lapse, this is the perfect time to renew them. Monday is an excellent day to tackle work, as long as it is not of a deeply intellectual nature, which would be better to deal with on Thursday. **Weekend outlook:** With Mars entering Pisces on Friday, this weekend is less about chores and duties and more about socializing and having fun. Saturday promises a cornucopia of joy, as long as you remain spontaneous and don't overplan. Schedule dates for Sunday brunch or afternoon, as it will be easier to form a pure romantic connection in the daytime than amid the temptations of the night.

Tips for a five-star week: Consider this week a second chance at a brand-new start. If you have been on autopilot since the beginning of 2024, now is the time to awake from your slumber and start building the future you truly desire.

Top astrological event of the week: *Tuesday:* Sun enters Aries: The Sun enters fiery Aries on March 19, putting an end to the cold winter and allowing new seeds of possibility and growth to bloom.

March 25–31

The week starts out with a massive onslaught of intense cosmic energy, which just as suddenly deflates into a whimper for the rest of the week. Monday's Lunar Eclipse in Libra pushes us to give up our competitive, individualistic, ego-driven outlook and seek out the power of the collective. Being an active participant in a greater community can bring feelings of peace and acceptance in the long term. The rest of the week is pretty laid-back. Schedule spontaneous dates or look for love on Thursday; you may be able to find someone who is slightly rebellious but also responsible and dependable. **Weekend outlook:** If you feel depleted on Saturday, don't push yourself to catch up on chores. Instead, have a cheerful brunch with friends or family. Suspicions of deception could become evident on Sunday, so use your sleuthing skills to get to the truth.

Tips for a five-star week: Hang on tight on Monday. Once you put that day's intense energies behind you, the rest of week will be a cakewalk.

Top astrological event of the week: *Monday:* Lunar Eclipse in Libra: This is the perfect time to free yourself from suffocating, isolating, codependent relationships and instead spread your energies throughout a greater group. The more people you can count on to have your back, the better.

April 1–7

The universe is playing its own April Fools' joke when Mercury goes retrograde on Monday, bringing potential mishaps and miscommunications in its wake. This is not an auspicious period for negotiations or peace agreements, as parties may not hold up their own end of the deal. You may want to wait until after the 25th to extend an olive branch. Tuesday and Friday are excellent days for brainstorming, seeking inspiration, and getting things done, while Wednesday promotes teamwork and romance. **Weekend outlook:** Whether you want to tackle chores, catch up on work, paint the town red, or seek a soulmate, Saturday's abundance of positive energy provides everything you need and more. Sunday's delicate vibes promote gentle, courtly love, so much so that an ultra-romantic suitor could magically appear if you dare look for them.

Tips for a five-star week: Except for some energy-draining confusion on Monday and Thursday, the week is brimming with possibilities for work and romance—but you'll need to take action. These energies won't manifest without some input on your part.

Top astrological event of the week: *Monday:* Mercury retrograde in Aries: The best-laid plans could go haywire at this time, so be extra careful with travel plans and communications. If possible, avoid signing contracts until the 25th. If not, make sure to read all the fine print.

April 8–14

Monday's Solar Eclipse in Aries is shaking things up, leading to breakthroughs in terms of personal healing. There is no better day to reach out to an estranged loved one. If you seek counseling at this time, you could reach an epiphany regarding the root cause of your pain. Wednesday is one of the most productive days of the year, so focus on bringing a dream project to life. Thursday favors big ideas, teamwork, and compromise, so bring people together and see what pans out. Finish up projects before Friday, when energies are more dissipated and lackadaisical. **Weekend outlook:** Trust may be an issue on Saturday, so put off dating or seeking a new suitor to a more auspicious time. Sunday is an excellent day for tackling chores, duties, and projects, or spending time doing solitary adventure sports.

Tips for a five-star week: If you dare to dig deep into your past and inner psyche, you can finally slay the inner demons that have been plaguing you for a lifetime.

Top astrological event of the week: *Wednesday:* Mars conjunct Saturn in Pisces: Feelings of extraordinary strength, bravery, and fearlessness will infuse the core of your being. Just like Superman, you'll be faster than a speeding bullet, more powerful than a loco-motive, and able to leap tall buildings in a single bound. Get out and start saving the world.

April 15–21

This week is a mixed bag, with a majority of days serving up a com-bination of positive and challenging energies. On Monday, things will go smoothly, as long as you put your own individualistic, ego-driven desires on the back burner to focus on upholding tradition and famil-ial duties. Wednesday, however, requires an opposite approach: use this day to unleash your inner rebel, dream up new ideas, and shake up the status quo. The pendulum swings yet again on Friday, when energies are best funneled into renovating and sprucing up old things. Practice sustainability by reinterpreting old clothes and furnishings to give them a new, modern flair. **Weekend outlook:** Saturday is one of the most adventurous days of the year. Even if you're feeling tired or drained, if you dare to go off the beaten path, out-of-the-ordinary experiences could create lifelong memories. People may be in a grumpy mood on Sunday and want to take it out on the world, so try to avoid the control freaks in your life.

Tips for a five-star week: Go with the flow this week. Just because things are traditional or outdated doesn't mean they can't serve as in-spiration for future innovations. Instead of embracing the totally new, try to figure out how you can transform what you already have to take you into the next chapter.

Top astrological event of the week: *Saturday:* Jupiter conjunct Uranus in Taurus: This rare aspect happens about once every twelve years, acting like a nuclear bomb of excitement, adventure, and radi-cal change. If you open yourself to new experiences, anything could happen.

April 22–28

On Monday, try not to ruminate too much on emotional pain caused by loved ones. Instead, use the energy conjured up by Tuesday's Full Moon to take back your personal power and extricate yourself from any manipulative forces in your life that are holding you down. If you are being bullied by a group or a person in authority, summon up the courage to speak out and seek help, or simply move on. Once Mercury turns direct on Thursday, the confusion of the past few weeks will dissipate, leading to a dynamic, straightforward day where honesty and trust prevail. **Weekend outlook:** Saturday is a better day for engaging in intellectual pursuits than for tackling chores or duties, while Sunday promotes romance and socializing—just be careful of wolves in sheep's clothing who may be selling you a false set of goods.

Tips for a five-star week: Stop seeking affirmation from those around you, and instead focus on building your own confidence.

Top astrological event of the week: *Tuesday:* Full Moon in Scorpio square Pluto in Aquarius: Don't allow your image to be crafted and controlled by nefarious forces who wish to keep you down. It may be better to leave a group than to be surrounded by those who don't properly value you and see you for who you are.

April 29–May 5

This week is ushered in with vibes that are highly romantic and poetic. Whether you want to concentrate on an art project, seek out new love, or bask in the warm glow of an existing relationship, forget about getting back into the daily grind on Monday and instead focus on the softer side of life. On Tuesday, Mars roars into Aries, which it rules, bringing an aura of gung-ho enthusiasm, ambition, and confidence. Both Tuesday and Friday are excellent days to impress higher-ups at work, ask for a raise or promotion, start an entrepreneurial endeavor, seek new employment, or schedule a job interview. People may be emotionally touchy on Wednesday, so it is better to lie low midweek. **Weekend outlook:** Saturday is auspicious for a wide range of activities, from spending time with family and carrying out home renovations to art, love, and adventure sports. No matter what you end up doing, you will enjoy it to the max. Sunday is nearly free of any major astrological transits, so there is nothing standing in your way of doing whatever you'd like.

Tips for a five-star week: Focus on romance and art on Monday, but then quickly shift to pursuing career goals on Tuesday in order to take advantage of this week's cornucopia of opportunities.

Top astrological event of the week: *Monday:* Mars conjunct Neptune in Pisces: Even shrinking violets will bloom confidently on this day. The entire world is vibrating with the limitless possibilities of romance and glamour, so go out and gather ye rosebuds while ye may.

May 6–12

If you are looking for a stable, reliable partner, Tuesday's New Moon could bring the suitor of your dreams into your life. If you are already in a relationship, you may want to discuss taking things to the next level by considering marriage, having children, or moving in together. Seeds planted at this time will bloom into a beautiful garden over the course of the upcoming year. Wednesday is another powerful day, perfect for romance, creativity, and getting out of a rut by implementing swift, radical change. Take a chance and dare to be different!

Weekend outlook: If you're going on a date on Friday night, be careful of Casanovas who are all about the thrill of the chase but have zero desire for an actual relationship. Arguments could flare on Saturday, but harmony returns in time for Mother's Day, when feelings of love and respect for familial roots abound.

Tips for a five-star week: Let down your barriers and take a chance on trusting those around you. The week's beneficent vibes promote sharing, nurturing, and pooling resources for the betterment of all.

Top astrological event of the week: *Tuesday:* New Moon in Taurus: This generous New Moon is sandwiched between Venus, Uranus, and Jupiter in grounded, good-hearted Taurus. This is a good day to create domestic plans for the future. Look for a house, take out a mortgage, or move in with your significant other; it's time to create a stable base for your own personal happily ever after.

May 13–19

A rather bumpy midweek hump on Wednesday could throw a wrench into a largely positive week. Small disagreements could suddenly explode into massive standoffs, but hold on tight—you may be jostled, but the challenging energies will pass by Friday afternoon, when a rather stubborn Cold War thaws into détente and peace. Monday is an excellent date night if you're looking for someone dependable and trustworthy. **Weekend outlook:** Electrifying romance could suddenly sweep you off your feet, sucking you into a vortex of true, destined love. Friday and Saturday are overflowing with passion and random good luck. A chance meeting could morph into something significant, so don't be afraid to bump into a passing stranger; the stars will give you the confidence to strike up a conversation. Sunday's laid-back energy favors a more subtle, sweet approach to courtship.

Tips for a five-star week: This has the potential to be an erratic week, when nothing goes according to plan. Be Zen and go with the flow. If you dig in your heels, you will only kick up more stress.

Top astrological event of the week: *Saturday:* Venus conjunct Uranus in Taurus: You could fall in love at first sight on this day, so take off your blinders and look for love outside of your regular, routine haunts.

May 20–26

A vibrant Sun moves into effervescent Gemini on Monday, setting the tone for a lively, vivacious few weeks. The more superficial aspects of life will be emphasized now, so put a stop to moping about the world's problems and get out there and enjoy. Venus and Jupiter also enter this sparkling sign on Thursday and Saturday, respectively, bringing an added boost of glamorous romance and beneficent socializing. Wednesday is an auspicious day to forge new alliances in order to reach your overall objectives. Thursday's Full Moon is jam-packed with astrological influences to help shake off tired, stagnant routines or emotional obligations, so you can feel free of baggage from the past and realign yourself with forces and people who really have your best interests in mind. If you've been surrounded by vultures who take rather than give, this is the day to turn that dynamic around. Kindness and loyalty are out there if you look. **Weekend outlook:** Saturday is a powerful day for those seeking "the one." The possibility to meet a soulmate is strong, so grab every opportunity. Sunday is a great day to tackle chores, but you may feel exhausted by late evening, so plan on turning in early.

Tips for a five-star week: Free yourself from the chains of one-way obligations. There is nothing wrong with seeking out fun and good cheer. Not all of life needs to be serious to be worthwhile.

Top astrological event of the week: *Saturday:* Jupiter enters Gemini: The upcoming twelve months are all about increasing your sphere of influence through communication, social media, and all other forms of reaching out. With an open-minded, upbeat mindset, you will be able to attract a wide range of people who put a spring in your step instead of dragging you down.

May 27–June 2

Monday is a five-star day for socializing. If you are in the US, use the Memorial Day holiday as an excuse to throw a shindig. Instead of the usual circle of friends and family, expand your horizons by inviting an array of artistic, bohemian, and eccentric types to brighten your world. Tuesday is an excellent date night, but the week's uplifting vibes take a downbeat turn midweek. After the excitement of the past few days, Wednesday's energy is productive, but clashes could arise over how to get things done, leading to hurt feelings and resentment on Thursday. The workweek ends on a positive note, however, when it is possible to iron out disagreements and collaborate on a common goal. **Weekend outlook:** Friday is a highly dreamy date night. Schedule a trip to the cinema or an art exhibit to escape into the realm of romance. Saturday is another ideal day for socializing and love, while Sunday is incredibly beneficial for joining groups or forming alliances that will put you in a powerful position for the future.

Tips for a five-star week: This week is best spent widening your circle of acquaintances, whether through friendship, networking for work, joining volunteer organizations, or looking for love.

Top astrological event of the week: *Sunday:* Jupiter in Gemini trine Pluto in Aquarius: If ever there was a day for humanity to come together to save the world, it is this one. Each individual can do their part by seeking out like-minded, idealistic global citizens to form groups that bring massive change for the betterment of all.

June 3–9

You can get further this week by pooling your mental and physical resources with others than by going it alone. Tuesday is an optimal day for group brainstorming and teamwork, as it will generate out-of-the-box solutions that bring long-term benefits. On Wednesday, sharing, generosity, and understanding pave the way to true power. Even the most resolute lone wolf may want to rethink their relationship status at Thursday's New Moon, as the romantic seeds planted at this time have the potential to blossom into a loving, emotional, compassionate support system over the upcoming year. **Weekend outlook:** After a lazy morning, Saturday's vibes become more productive as the day goes on, so schedule chores and duties for the late afternoon and early evening. Sunday is a different story, when few will be in the mood for work. However, if you dedicate yourself to art, romance, or film, you can enjoy a day of heightened, poetic emotions.

Tips for a five-star week: Whether it be in work or love, it's time to lower your barriers and let others into your life. Worthwhile people make life's experience easier and more abundant; it depends on who you let in. Choose wisely.

Top astrological event of the week: *Thursday:* New Moon conjunct Venus in Gemini: The New Moon meets the planet of true love. Could there be a more promising time to search for new romantic possibilities or strengthen the bonds of an existing alliance?

June 10–16

There is no denying that this is one of the grumpier weeks of the year. People will likely be feeling super competitive and using every dirty, manipulative tactic to be the head honcho in the room. Whether in work, friendship, or love, you may want to remove yourself from the pettiness and banality of it all. Tuesday could be an especially cutthroat day, and Wednesday and Thursday may be no better, when suspicions, paranoia, and resentments run high. There is no sense brooding over those around you who have gotten ahead on unearned merit; it will only eat you up inside without resolving anything. After an emotionally volatile morning, good vibes and a positive outlook return by Friday afternoon. The evening is an especially good time to bask in the warmth of close, jovial friends. **Weekend outlook:** Saturday is one of those rare days that is completely devoid of all major astrological transits, so life is literally what you make it. On Sunday, there could be temptations to escape the problems of the world through drugs or alcohol, so if these are issues for you, be extremely diligent. Otherwise, Father's Day promises moments of warmth and laid-back joy.

Tips for a five-star week: Stay away from difficult people this week, especially bossy control freaks who have to be the center of attention. Put your energies into yourself and your own goals instead of trying to one-up others over things that don't even really matter to you.

Top astrological event of the week: *Tuesday:* Mars in Taurus square Pluto in Aquarius: This warlike energy pits forces of tradition and control against rebellious spirits who want to tear it all down and start anew. Perhaps the wisest strategy would be to watch from the sidelines.

June 17–23

This week is defined by a number of dissonant planetary aspects to Neptune. All these vibes could seductively lure us into deception—or self-deception—by enticing us into seemingly utopian dreamscapes that end up not being what they were cracked up to be. It is important to keep your wits about you to avoid getting suckered by a sideshow huckster selling a phony cure-all. This is especially true in love on Monday. Luckily, rational Mercury is on your side to help you weed out wanton Casanovas and Loreleis whose charms will only lead you to destruction. **Weekend outlook:** Saturday is an excellent time for sports, adventure, and getting things done, but mental projections based on past hurts could throw a monkey wrench into romantic plans. It is better to put off amorous rendezvous until Sunday, when you may even meet someone new out of the blue who decides to stick around.

Tips for a five-star week: Avoid decision-making this week, unless you want to build up your Florida swampland portfolio.

Top astrological event of the week: *Friday:* Moon in Sagittarius square Neptune in Pisces right before the New Moon in Capricorn: It's time to put an end to pipe dreams. Either work to make them happen or move on.

June 24–30

After a couple slightly challenging weeks, good vibes return once more. This is a pretty laid-back period that is especially auspicious for planning out the long-term future. Monday morning is filled with revved-up energy and good cheer, although feelings of fatigue could arise by late afternoon, so it may be better to put off social events to another evening. Wednesday and Thursday are excellent for brainstorming, finding lasting solutions to problems, and mapping out goals. Feelings of industriousness, focus, and innovation abound; if you have entrepreneurial dreams, this is a great time to plot out a business plan. Wednesday is the week's best date night, but Friday is also overflowing with romantic generosity and creativity, especially for social outings. **Weekend outlook:** Saturday is defined by passion, courtly love, and electric inspiration. You could get knocked off your feet by someone who is sweetly considerate and spicily seductive—a rare combination. If someone catches your eye or randomly approaches you, it may be worth it to take a chance on romance. Avoid overexerting yourself or overbooking your schedule on Sunday, as the day's exhaustive energies are not that conducive to getting things done.

Tips for a five-star week: Design your future path and embark on it immediately. It's time to make your dreams spring to life!

Top astrological event of the week: *Wednesday:* Mercury in Cancer trine Saturn in Pisces: Your intuition will be spot-on when it comes to solving problems and building foundations for new endeavors. Logic will lead the way.

July 1–7

Canadian and American readers are celebrating holidays this week, and their respective dates are filled with good cheer and upbeat vibes. Monday, Canada Day, is an excellent time for socializing and strengthening the caring bonds of friendship and family. If you dare to go off the beaten path and break stagnant routines, you will be awarded with exhilarating, memorable experiences. Tuesday is auspicious for making fairy-tale dreams come true. Schedule weddings, proposals, moving in together, or taking things to the next level on this day. If you're single, you couldn't ask for a better day to look for love-term love or go on a date. Seek kind, responsible partners and you can't go wrong. Wednesday's stubborn energy could lead to resentment against authority figures, while Thursday is infused with slightly lazy vibes. Luckily for Americans, this is July 4th, so many people will have the day off. Gung-ho, get-it-done energies burst back on the scene on Friday—a day when you can get massive amounts of work done and make major headway on business goals. **Weekend outlook:** Saturday is filled with a wide array of positive energies that you can apply to any aspect of life, from work to family, adventure, friends, and love. If you're single, afternoon and evening dates are equally romantic. Sunday starts off with slightly manipulative energies, but the subterfuge soon ends, allowing mental clarity and a spirit of generosity and sharing to return by late afternoon.

Tips for a five-star week: Enjoy the holiday spirit by spending time with friends and relatives. Romance is in the air, making this an upbeat, positive week for dating and spending time with existing partners.

Top astrological event of the week: *Friday:* Mars in Taurus sextile Saturn in Pisces: If you want to look for a new job, pitch a work project, or start your own business, this is one of the best days of the year to put plans into action.

July 8–14

The workweek kicks off with an explosion of inspired, innovative problem-solving energy. Monday is a great day for brainstorming as a team—after all, two heads are better than one. After this frenzy of activity, a sense of mild exhaustion could set in by evening and last until midweek. You may want to burn the midnight oil on Wednesday, however, as its late-night energy is happily productive. The focus shifts to the softer side of life on Thursday. Instead of work, place your focus firmly on romance, adventure, and expanding your horizons. This is by far one of the best date nights of the year, overflowing with an abundance of passion and poetry. Friday is a day that functions best if one abides by the existing hierarchy. Sometimes bosses and authority figures do know best, due to their abundance of lived experience. If you go against the powers that be, you will probably be shot down, so put off suggestions to another day. **Weekend outlook:** While you may wake up with a perfect schedule for Saturday's activities, by evening you could be too worn-out to accomplish everything. Go with the flow. On Sunday, petty arguments could flare up, leading to hurt feelings. Put off dating and avoid controlling friends and family members.

Tips for a five-star week: Take care of business on Monday and dedicate Thursday to love and romance.

Top astrological event of the week: *Thursday:* Venus in Cancer trine Neptune in Pisces: Fairy godmothers may appear to turn your pumpkin into a chariot on the road to true love. This is a day when fairy tales could become reality and anything could happen. Family members could assist you in your quest for romance, so see if someone can set you up on a blind date.

July 15–21

This week will bring an abundance of courage and bravery, allowing us all to shake off stagnant or constricting situations and worn-out routines. It is time to explore new horizons and encounter all the awe-inspiring abundance the world has to offer. Starting on Monday, focus on career ambitions and seeking the job you truly desire. Random encounters could lead to new opportunities, so go to networking events and have your business card ready. Thursday is another auspicious day for throwing off the chains of tradition for a more individualized outlook. It's better to take it easy or work as a team on Tuesday and Wednesday; otherwise there is the tendency to bite off more than you can chew. **Weekend outlook:** If you're an artist, Saturday is an excellent time to practice your craft. It's also perfect for a romantic weekend getaway or day trip. Have nothing planned? Be spontaneous! Sunday's Full Moon is all about putting an end to conformity and instead embracing the offbeat, eccentric, and adventurous. It's time to put some joy and fun into life, especially after several years of serious societal influences. Sunday also offers up passion in spades. If you're looking for your soulmate, they may appear on the horizon during the evening hours. If you've already found yours, lock the doors, turn off the lights, and enjoy the heat of summer!

Tips for a five-star week: This is no time for routine and duties. Break free, be daring, and take the road less traveled.

Top astrological event of the week: *Monday:* Mars conjunct Uranus in Taurus: *Carpe diem*—or, in other words, seize the day. Open yourself to completely new experiences by letting go of any inhibitions that are holding you back.

July 22–28

Whether single or in a couple, you will want to schedule dates and romantic rendezvous on Thursday or Friday, as the rest of the week could be a bit tense. Group dynamics have the potential to crush the individual spirit on Tuesday. Beware of sharing details of your life with a colleague or friend who will only use it as ammunition to gossip about you behind your back. While you may feel overwhelmed with duties on Wednesday, the will and energy to tackle all chores returns by late afternoon. Thursday is by far the best day of the week, filled with love, compassion, and good times. Spend the day with those you care about to recharge your batteries. **Weekend outlook:** Clashing egos dominate Saturday's vibes, but if you keep your cool and rely on your wits, things will work out to your advantage. Sunday is an excellent time to catch up on chores.

Tips for a five-star week: Lie low on Monday and Tuesday so you are fully rested to take advantage of Thursday's positive vibes. Joyous good times are abundant on Thursday evening, so schedule time with friends or suitors.

Top astrological event of the week: *Thursday:* Sun in Leo sextile Mars in Gemini: This is a five-star day for socializing and dating. There will be no such thing as a wallflower at this time, as even the shyest, most introverted people will be up for mingling and busting loose.

July 29–August 4

If you can let go of your mental and emotional blocks, you could implement positive, life-altering changes on Monday and Tuesday. While the heart is willing, you may be too overburdened by work on Wednesday to truly enjoy the day's lightly romantic vibes. Thursday is auspicious for out-of-the-box thinking and innovative problem-solving, while Friday could see some hurt feelings—better to focus on your work rather than your relationships. **Weekend outlook:** Although power struggles might abound on Saturday, artistic activities are favored. Seek understanding of the human condition through fine art, literature and great works of cinema. The week ends with Sunday's vibrant New Moon in Leo—an incredibly auspicious time for widening your social circle. On this day it will be easy to meet new, interesting people who could grow into worthwhile friends over the course of the next year.

Tips for a five-star week: Throw off the shackles of shyness to expand your worldview and your circle of friends.

Top astrological event of the week: *Sunday:* New Moon in Leo: This glamorous New Moon is in auspicious aspect with extroverted Mars and beneficent Jupiter in sparkling Gemini. This is a day for fun, glitz, and charm.

August 5–11

Mercury goes retrograde on Monday, ushering in a period of potential confusion and setbacks. However, if you long to reach out to the one who got away, Monday or Wednesday would be an excellent time to do so. Tuesday is auspicious for work of an intellectual nature, but you could become easily exhausted when undertaking physical labor. If you bite off more than you can chew on Wednesday, you could soon find yourself overwhelmed and destabilized; but energy comes roaring back on Friday, when mountains can be moved and piled-up chores can be over and done with once and for all. **Weekend outlook:** If any misunderstandings pop up on Saturday, they can be talked through calmly and worked out later that evening. Sunday is an excellent time for romance and family.

Tips for a five-star week: With Mercury moving retrograde on Monday, this week is all about the past—making amends with estranged friends and family, reconnecting with lost loves, and clearing out old duties before taking on new ones.

Top astrological event of the week: *Monday:* Mercury retrograde in Virgo: When Mercury is retrograde, even the best-laid plans can go awry. If traveling for summer holidays, you may experience delays, cancellations, strikes, or mix-ups with reservations. Try to stay flexible and give yourself plenty of time for flights and trains.

August 12–18

You'll be able to get a lot done at work on Monday as long as you go it alone, as team projects could devolve into battling egos. Tuesday and Wednesday are dominated by a quick succession of squares and oppositions by the Moon, which are exacerbated by an explosive conjunction between Mars and Jupiter. Small skirmishes could quickly expand into metaphorical nuclear wars. There is a gleeful zestfulness to this energy, as if there is a thrill in wanton destruction and watching it all burn. It is imperative to focus on achieving justice as opposed to judgment and payback. While Thursday seems to bring a bit of peace and harmony, it would also be easy to be deluded into a false sense of well-being. The week ends with a challenging square between Mars and Saturn in the mutable signs of Gemini and Pisces, respectively. Be sure you are fighting the good fight before picking up your torch and pitchfork. **Weekend outlook:** After a stressful week, good times return for the weekend. Visit a museum or spend meaningful time with those you care about to strengthen your bonds on Saturday, and use Sunday for catching up with old friends and family you haven't heard from in a while.

Tips for a five-star week: Resist the temptation to join the masses; instead, take the time to learn about the nuances of the past before cancelling it in ignorance.

Top astrological event of the week: *Wednesday:* Mars conjunct Jupiter in Gemini: Jupiter's expansive energy is pouring gasoline on the bellicose aggression of Mars. Arguments and altercations could erupt like a long-dormant volcano. If you can, burn off excess physical energy at the gym instead of taking it out on others and the world around you.

August 19–25

An entire chapter could be written on Monday's transits alone. This Full Moon is a cosmic megaphone loudly broadcasting what we need to change in our lives—starting with love. A Venusian T-square pulls in Jupiter and Saturn. If a long-term love situation is not defined by joy, closeness, and a sense of sharing, what is it bringing to your life? Could it be time to move on? Nearby Mars conjures up the courage to break away from a toxic, controlling, or stagnant partner. The Full Moon is also in a T-square with Uranus, the Sun, and Mercury retrograde. There may be the impetus to make rash decisions. On one hand, it may be better to reflect with logic and reason, but on the other, if all you're doing is stewing in thoughts of the past without ever moving into a state of action, that situation needs to change now. While Wednesday morning is a bit of an emotional tinderbox, harmonious vibes return by evening, making it an excellent date night for singles or couples. The same can't be said for Thursday, however, when romance could morph into nothing but drama. Friday is an excellent day for getting things done at work and then socializing with friends in the evening. **Weekend outlook:** Saturday is a day to get out there and start ticking things off your bucket list, while Sunday is oozing with romance and amorous possibilities. Dare to strike up a conversation with any charming potential suitors who cross your path.

Tips for a five-star week: Allow your impulses to drag you out of long-standing detrimental situations, especially if logic isn't leading you to make the right choices.

Top astrological event of the week: *Monday:* Saturn in Pisces square Jupiter in Gemini and opposite Venus in Virgo: Controlling romantic situations could become almost unbearable. There is also a Full Moon on this day, and Full Moons are times for endings and letting go. Maybe it's time to add more verve, spontaneity, and equality to your relationship or simply move on.

August 26–September 1

A heady air of heightened romance infuses the entire week, so if you still haven't had your fill of summer lovin', get out there and reap your rosebuds before it's too late. Sometimes the right decision in love is not to choose a dutiful, reliable partner, but to opt for someone who is exciting, spontaneous, passionate, and mentally inspiring. If you dare to go outside your "sure thing" comfort zone on Tuesday, you may actually find someone who thrills you to your core. If you've been under any delusions concerning a suitor, Mercury turns direct on Wednesday, bringing clarity back into your love life. You may need to face the harsh realities of a betrayal or deception, but that is better than living a lie. Thursday is a powerful day for finding a long-term soulmate, popping the question, or getting married. Finally, Friday ends with a happily ever after. If a white knight or brave princess randomly crosses your path, ride off with them into the sunset to check out new realms of romance. You may need to loosen your sense of control in order to open yourself up to love, but it will be well worth it. **Weekend outlook:** Saturday is nearly devoid of any major transits, leading to calm skies, while Sunday ends the week with a bang when Pluto retrogrades back into Capricorn, bringing up issues related to Big Business, Big Government, Big Pharma, Big Tech, or Big Anything that rules our everyday lives.

Tips for a five-star week: The summer is drawing to a close, but new opportunities for romance are just beginning. Go out and find someone whose company you enjoy without being overly critical of their tiniest traits. Let love unfold slowly and organically.

Top astrological event of the week: *Sunday:* Pluto retrogrades back into Capricorn: Pluto first entered Capricorn in 2008, and it may feel like this transit will never end. After having moved into Aquarius in January, ushering in a new era, Pluto is returning to Capricorn for a last hurrah until November 19, when it leaves this sign once and for all—or at least until 2254. Issues regarding governmental and corporate control may rear their ugly heads again during this period, tearing us apart instead of bringing us together.

September 2–8

Both the US and Canada are celebrating Labor (or Labour) Day on Monday. The New Moon in Virgo that day rules nutrition, and holiday barbecues and festivities are an excellent excuse to usher in healthier eating strategies. The summer is over and we may not be ready to get back to the grind on Tuesday. Resentment and laziness are like lead balloons hanging over the entire day, making exertion exhausting—a feeling that lasts into Wednesday. Thursday is the week's best date night, while Friday evening is an excellent time to chitchat with friends. Make sure to go to a place where the music isn't too loud, so you can enjoy each other's conversations. **Weekend outlook:** On Saturday, it may be easy to jump to the wrong conclusion, leading to power struggles and paranoia. If you are experiencing a confusing situation, take time out to investigate before confronting someone, especially if they are a friend, family member, or romantic partner. Sunday starts off lazy, but a sense of industriousness and joviality is ushered in by midmorning.

Tips for a five-star week: If you don't feel like working this week, don't push yourself to get things done. If you don't have any urgent deadlines to meet, it's better to take it slow.

Top astrological event of the week: *Tuesday:* Mars in Gemini square Neptune in Pisces: It would be easy to get distracted into daydreams today and lose any desire or determination to tackle reality.

September 9–15

With Mercury's move on Monday into diligent Virgo, one of the signs it rules, the mind is ready to get back to work; but where the mind goes, the body and spirit don't necessarily follow. It may be difficult to stay focused on the task at hand for almost the entire week. On Tuesday, thoughts wander off to intoxicating reveries of love, while on Wednesday, it will be easy to become distracted and get caught up in the weeds of utopian ideals so that nothing ever gets done—although the late-night hours do offer up a sizzling dose of passion. Thursday is another day that is good for brainstorming and communication, although it may be difficult to actually implement things. The pace finally picks up on Friday, when it is easy to get happily lost in one's work. **Weekend outlook:** Saturday is a great day for art, museum visits, and strengthening alliances with friends and family, while Sunday is one of the best days of the entire year for dating, with daytime dates being particularly fruitful.

Tips for a five-star week: Try to do planning and visionary work from Monday to Thursday, as it will be easy to come up with great ideas but harder to implement them. Love is here, there, and everywhere on Sunday, so if you are single, start looking online or in real life.

Top astrological event of the week: *Sunday:* Venus in Libra trine Jupiter in Gemini: Venus, the planet of true love, is in Libra, one of the signs it rules, sending positive vibes to generous, bighearted Jupiter. The universe is bursting with romance for singles and couple alike.

September 16–22

Tuesday's Lunar Eclipse may rip off the rose-colored glasses, forcing us to face the harsh reality of a situation that was being brushed under the rug for far too long. Festering problems can no longer be ignored, and it's time to deal with them once and for all. While these challenges may be difficult to unravel intellectually, a solution will be found in time as long as you start thinking about it now. Lovers' squabbles could flare up on Thursday, so avoid scheduling romantic outings that evening. If you feel like someone is trying to manipulate or deceive you on Friday, act swiftly to put them in their place. **Weekend outlook:** If you think only with your head on Saturday, you may grow paranoid and suspicious; but if you tap into your heart and inner sense of compassion, you will be able to arrive at the truth. Sunday is an excellent day to devote to activities you love.

Tips for a five-star week: The Lunar Eclipse on Tuesday may stir up some disturbing information, but it is better to live in truth than waste your life chasing pipe dreams.

Top astrological event of the week: *Tuesday:* Lunar Eclipse in Pisces: The Lunar Eclipse is very close to Neptune and opposite Mercury in Virgo. The investigative powers of the logical mind are on overdrive, blowing apart false narratives and forcing a shift back to reality.

September 23–29

This week, a trickle of work duties could quickly turn into a tsunami, so don't agree to take on loads you can't bear. Confusion and doubt may reign on Tuesday morning, so put off meetings, decisions, or signing contracts until later in the afternoon, when mental clarity returns. Wednesday is a great day for focus, concentration, and getting things done, while Thursday is incredibly inspirational and innovative—a perfect time for creative visualization, so you can achieve your personal dream goals. **Weekend outlook:** Although you may want to avoid dating on Saturday, when emotions could be all over the place, romance is in the cards for everyone on Sunday, whether single or in a couple.

Tips for a five-star week: Try to schedule your most important work meetings on Thursday, as an abundance of positive energy will put wind in your sails.

Top astrological event of the week: *Thursday:* Mercury in Virgo trine Pluto in Capricorn: Innovative ideas will impress the powers that be today, so make pitches and send out résumés.

September 30–October 6

Monday is for the ambitious and those looking to broaden their professional path. If you put your mind and energy on your career, you can move toward long-lasting success today. While there may be a lot of confusion on Tuesday, you don't need to solve all problems alone. Seek the wisdom and experience of mentors and bosses to help you make the right decisions. An electrifying Solar Eclipse in Libra on Wednesday will provide the answers to many of life's questions if you just reflect on them. Friday afternoon is perfect for team-building activities, or you may even want to take a few swipes on a dating app, as you may meet a promising long-term partner. **Weekend outlook:** The weekend is all about romance and adventure. If you need to take care of chores, get them done on Saturday morning, because after that, attention turns to love and passion. If you're looking for a sweet, poetic suitor, plan a daytime rendezvous, but if you're up for passion and excitement, schedule your date for the early evening. Who knows, it may even last into the night. Forget work on Sunday. Instead, plan a romantic outing to an art museum or avant-garde cinema.

Tips for a five-star week: Focus on your career early in the week, because starting on Thursday, the vibes shift to love.

Top astrological event of the week: *Friday:* Venus in Scorpio trine Saturn in Pisces: Scorpio is one of the most loyal, reliable signs, while Saturn is all about building sturdy foundations for the future. Throw in Venus, the planet of love, into the mix, and you have an incredibly auspicious day for dating or taking things to the next level.

October 7–13

This week's energy is like a pendulum that shifts from one extreme to the other, but it all will be quite easy to manage if you schedule well. Tuesday's uplifting vibes are filled with romance, excitement, and inspiration. Work will be a breeze and love may sweep you off your feet. Schedule dates, meetings, and interviews on this day. Thursday's loose Grand Cross in the cardinal signs, however, is a bit more challenging. Old wounds could be opened up, causing emotional hurt while bruising one's ego. Everyone is up for a fight and will be willing to run roughshod over anyone standing in the way of their ambitions, so lie low, stay away from competitive colleagues, and don't get caught up in squabbles. Inner strength and power suddenly return on Friday morning, obliterating any pain that may have been dredged up the previous day. Meaning can be found in art and human connection, so spend the day surrounded by those you care about. **Weekend outlook:** Saturday's energy is cheerful and up for anything, while Sunday is a mixed bag. You will want to be on the lookout for mental power games and malicious gossip carried out by manipulative people. Luckily, an abundance of goodwill also exists on this day, along with the intuitive insight to quickly detect snakes in the grass.

Tips for a five-star week: Don't waste your time with toxic people, but instead bask in the warm glow of trusted, tried-and-true friends and coworkers who bring meaning and positivity into your life.

Top astrological event of the week: *Tuesday:* Venus in Scorpio trine Mars in Cancer: This is an excellent day to spend with family and children. If you're trying to conceive, squeeze in some early-morning loving.

October 14–20

Monday is Thanksgiving in Canada, with the potential for a heaping side dish of familial dysfunction. Fights could flare up and authoritarians could try to exert their power, flinging everyone back into dynamics that were best left behind in childhood. Instead of taking these vibes to heart, embrace them as kindred tradition. Luckily, Tuesday is an ebullient day overflowing with heady hopes and opportunities for romance. Schedule a date night, dedicate yourself to art, or seek out your dream job. Thursday's Full Moon forms a loose Grand Cross that may seem challenging at first, but if you focus on healing old wounds caused by bullies and those in power, you may be able to move on once and for all. Friday favors busywork over that of a visionary nature. **Weekend outlook:** Saturday is an extremely productive, high-octane day that is perfect for hobbies or getting things done. You may want to avoid dating, however, as the risk of being seduced by a love-them-and-leave-them lothario runs high. Sunday's mood is lazy and sluggish; there is nothing wrong with recharging your batteries lounging at home.

Tips for a five-star week: A lot of emotions from the past could bubble up this week. Instead of dwelling on them, seek out new love, spend time with a current supportive partner, or immerse yourself in art.

Top astrological event of the week: *Thursday:* Full Moon in Aries in a loose Grand Cross conjunct Chiron, opposite the Sun in Libra, and square Pluto in Capricorn and Mars in Cancer: Even though you may have had no control over people hurting you in the past, you do control whether they continue to harm you emotionally in the future. This is the time to shut and lock the door on past abuse. If you can, schedule a session with a therapist.

October 21–27

This week is bursting with active, ambitious energy, allowing you to go after all your personal and professional goals. Just one word of advice: you'll get the most done if you go off in a corner and work without oversight, as bosses and management could ax your most innovative, successful ideas. Try to stay off the radar instead of seeking outward affirmation. **Weekend outlook:** This weekend is a bit of a repetition of the last one. Saturday is filled with cheerful, upbeat vibes, making the evening a perfect time for socializing with friends, while Sunday's lethargic mood promotes relaxing and lounging at home.

Tips for a five-star week: If you have a business idea, now is the time to get it off the ground. This week is especially auspicious for innovative entrepreneurs who go their own way.

Top astrological event of the week: *Thursday:* Mars in Cancer sextile Uranus in Taurus: An abundance of energy combined with eureka-like inspiration could lead to breakthroughs at work. This is also a passionate date night that could end in a sudden pregnancy for couples looking to conceive; singles should make sure they are protected.

October 28–November 3

Happy Halloween! This week lives up to its spooky reputation, serving up an abundance of challenging tricks that could scare you into making the wrong decision, so ponder all decisions before taking action, especially on Monday and Wednesday. If you've had problems with addiction in the past, Monday's stressors could lead you to temptation, so have a sober friend on call if your defenses are feeling low. Halloween's lunar T-square could bring out the monsters around us who try to impose their will on everyone else, no matter the cost. Luckily, by Thursday evening the energy shifts, leading to a highly creative, social, and festive night—go all out on your costume! Friday's New Moon is highly productive, making it the best day of the week to get things done and plan for the future. **Weekend outlook:** Saturday is a great time to tackle chores, while that evening and the wee hours of Sunday are geared toward romance and passion; don't hesitate to schedule a date night. Sunday morning, however, is a different story, when egos could clash.

Tips for a five-star week: It will be easy to be led down the garden path early in the week, so avoid implementing change at this time.

Top astrological event of the week: *Sunday:* Mars in Cancer opposite Pluto in Capricorn: This passive-aggressive, rebellious energy will refuse to take any kind of orders, even from wise, benevolent leaders, potentially leading to insubordination and an inability to compromise.

November 4–10

Although the you may feel overwhelmed with chores and duties on the first day of the week, the universe will give you all the stamina and focus you need on Monday and Wednesday. Stick-in-the-muds could come down hard on the artistic and eccentric on Thursday; instead of fighting back, disengage from the drama and go your own way. It may be best to avoid socializing and dating on Thursday, as many people will be too exhausted and cranky to relax and enjoy themselves. **Weekend outlook:** It may be hard to drag yourself out of bed on Saturday morning, so stay in the sack and catch up on REM sleep. The evening will be a sparkling time for romance and socializing. Put off chores until Sunday evening, when they can be tackled with aplomb.

Tips for a five-star week: Try to check out of the office early and get home before tempers start to flare early Friday evening.

Top astrological event of the week: *Monday:* Sun in Scorpio trine Saturn in Pisces: You may receive an adrenaline rush from the universe, enabling you to move mountains without exerting any major effort. Charm and cheerfulness promote teamwork and networking to form solid alliances for the future.

November 11–17

Monday is Veterans Day in the US and Remembrance Day in Canada. If you are one of the lucky workers who get the day off, spend your time being spontaneous with those you care about. Everyone can take advantage of the evening's romantic vibes to schedule a date night. While there is energy to spare on Tuesday, it may be difficult deciding how to get things done. After a grumpy start, Thursday's charming, harmonious vibes make it an excellent time for team projects, while Friday's New Moon is pushing us to take a chance on something new—especially when it comes to love. **Weekend outlook:** The best-laid plans could go haywire on Saturday evening, leading to hurt feelings from last-minute cancellations by flaky friends. Have a plan B in store. You may want to turn in early on Sunday, as fatigue could set in easily.

Tips for a five-star week: Concentrate on love and romance during the workweek, as the weekend energies are a bit more erratic, emotionally sensitive, and lethargic.

Top astrological event of the week: *Saturday:* Sun in Scorpio opposite Uranus in Taurus: You will need to be flexible and patient when faced with Saturday's wild-card energy. Absolutely anything could happen—likely in a challenging way—so it would be better to schedule important events for another evening.

November 18–24

The start of the workweek will require a great deal of mental exertion, but even if you feel worn-out and tired at the start of Monday evening, don't go home early or you may miss out on a chance on love. This is an excellent date night for singles and couples, when artsy outings bring magic and romance. If someone tries to push you around and tell you what to do on Wednesday morning, you will have sufficient courage to stick up for yourself and carve your own path. The Sun's entry into Sagittarius on Thursday brings an abundance of adventurous, generous vibes, while Friday's fast-moving, anxiety-ridden energies could take the wind out of your sails, as it might be hard to keep pace with all the change. **Weekend outlook:** Even if you're feeling bored and moody early Saturday evening, make an effort to go out. Friendship and romance will help make your spirits soar and lift you out of any momentary funk. Sunday will offer only tediousness if you insist on planning everything to a T. Instead, be spontaneous and expand your worldview to previously unknown horizons.

Tips for a five-star week: It's better to roll with things this week than to try to control everything around you.

Top astrological event of the week: *Monday:* Mercury in Sagittarius opposite Jupiter in Gemini: Your brain will be firing on all cylinders, while the phone rings off the hook and your inbox overflows with messages. It may be difficult to keep up with communications, so take a deep breath and do one task at a time.

November 25–December 1

Thursday is Thanksgiving in the US. This could cause delays and frustrations while traveling, so be prepared and take a book to read in the airport waiting area. Mercury retrograde could also trigger memories from the past, as so often happens during the holidays. While some nostalgia and reflection can be spiritually beneficial, try not to brood too much over days gone by—and especially avoid trying to hook up with an ex on Tuesday. Monday and Wednesday are energetic, powerful days bursting with action and activities. While minor squabbles could flare up on Thanksgiving morning, by the evening feelings of tradition and heritage will bring everyone together. **Weekend outlook:** Schedule outings and dates for Saturday, when feelings of enthusiasm and passion abound. Sunday's New Moon in adventurous Sagittarius is a time to move on from worn-out routines as well as shut out all emotional vampires and time-wasters, so you can put the focus back on what you want from life.

Tips for a five-star week: On Thursday, be thankful for your roots. Even if they are gnarled in places, they nourish who you are in the current day.

Top astrological event of the week: *Monday:* Mercury goes retrograde in Sagittarius: Sagittarius is a high-octane sign that is all about keeping busy, while Mercury retrograde favors reflection and pause. The more you try to advance over the coming weeks, the more you could fall behind. This is a better period to do research and lay the groundwork than to launch new projects.

December 2–8

This is a week when artistic, innovative, eccentric ideas will clash with conformist, conventional, paint-by-numbers outlooks. This may not be the best time to make new pitches or proposals at work due to the challenging, stodgy energy. This is especially true on Wednesday. However, if you shift your focus to your love life and dating, soulmate-level romance is in store. Social outings on Friday could be dragged down by intellectually ponderous conversations, leading to arguments over ideology. Mars also turns retrograde this evening, slowing down action and activity, as well as making it difficult to get projects off the ground. Expect delays and setbacks. **Weekend outlook:** The weekend swings between too hot and too cold. Egos could run out of control on Saturday, so try to rein in boastfulness and feelings of invincibility. Sunday, however, is a time when cold logic could lead to bad decision-making, as human intuitiveness is cut off.

Tips for a five-star week: There is tremendous pressure this week to conform. If you insist on sticking out like a nail, be prepared to be hammered down.

Top astrological event of the week: *Friday:* Mars goes retrograde in Leo: Mars will be retrograde until February 23, 2025, and will remain in Leo through the end of the year. Mars retrograde slows things down to super slo-mo speed, which does not suit the dynamic sign of Leo very well. You may feel frustrated that things are not going as quickly as you'd like, so try to be patient. This is not a good period to have any unnecessary, purely cosmetic procedures done, as things could take a long time to heal or not turn out as expected. Instead, try nonpermanent changes to your look if you feel like a change.

December 9–15

The workweek is bookended by wonderfully harmonious transits, while the hump will be quite bumpy indeed. After a dreamy, ethereal Monday and a witty, joyful Tuesday, stubborn energies kick in on Wednesday. People are not in the mood to compromise, so put off negotiations to another day. Thursday showcases a battle of the bullies, where emotional manipulators and aggressive ruffians face off. Who will win? If you don't want to find out, stay out of the drama by concentrating on your work. Friday brings a sudden burst of kumbaya vibes, when people can work together toward a common goal without feelings of competition or envy. **Weekend outlook:** On Saturday, forget about catching up on errands and instead dedicate the day to love and socializing. Mercury goes direct on Sunday following the Gemini Full Moon, putting an end to several weeks of problems regarding electronics and communications.

Tips for a five-star week: Schedule all important meetings for Monday, Tuesday, and Friday. Midweek is best for focusing on solitary pursuits.

Top astrological event of the week: *Sunday:* Mercury direct in Sagittarius: Mercury goes direct just in time for the holidays, ensuring that online shopping problems will be ironed out and gifts will arrive in time for Christmas. The potential for travel headaches will also be minimized.

December 16–22

The last full workweek before the Christmas holidays is overflowing with an abundance of bustling activity and merry good cheer. Monday is an excellent day to get caught up at work or finish buying presents for friends and family. Wednesday, however, could be a bit lazy, when it is easy to slip into daydreams. It is an excellent night for socializing, but maybe hold off on romance until Thursday, which is one of the most amorous nights of the entire year. It will be almost impossible not to fall madly in love. **Weekend outlook:** The weekend is a bit more challenging, starting with Saturday's lunar T-square in the mutable signs. You may have a long list of things to get done in preparation for the holidays, but try not to feel too overwhelmed. This time of year should be more about people than material surroundings. Even if you start out feeling sluggish on Sunday morning, by the afternoon you will be on fire.

Tips for a five-star week: Whether you are single or in a couple, do not let Thursday's five-star romantic vibes pass you by.

Top astrological event of the week: *Thursday:* Venus in Aquarius trine Jupiter in Gemini: An H-bomb of true love will explode across the universe on Thursday, promising dazzling new encounters for singles, while couples could reignite the excitement of when they first met. This is also an excellent day for volunteering to help others who may be in need during the holiday season.

December 23–31

Christmas is a time when extended families come from far and wide to meet together under one roof, bringing their own disparate personalities and ways of doing things. It should come as no surprise that this could cause discomfort and clashes, as various factions want to do things their own way. That doesn't mean there is a lack of love, however. On Christmas Eve, the more laid-back, easygoing, free-wheeling members of the family could be at odds with the overplanning control freaks who want to uphold every tradition and plan everything to a T.

Luckily, all this energy calms down by midday Christmas, ensuring the holiday is emotionally warm and cozy. When we look back at the holiday, however, resentments could linger on Thursday and Friday. It is best not to dwell too much on things. **Weekend outlook through New Year's Eve:** Friday evening is a festive night to spend with friends, while Saturday dredges up the feelings and dynamics from Christmas Eve. Use the New Moon on Monday, December 30, to set your resolutions for 2025. New Year's Eve itself promises exciting times that will bring you closer to the ones you love, especially if you are spontaneous or do something new.

Tips for a five-star week: Realize that your family members mean well, even if they are completely, totally different from you. You only need to roll with it for a few days.

Top astrological event of the week: *Tuesday:* Jupiter in Gemini square Saturn in Pisces: Jupiter, the planet of expansion, enters into a challenging aspect with Saturn, the orb of constriction. These two opposing forces do not form a happy union, creating the tension of extremes. Try to compromise.

About the Astrologer

Michelle Perrin, aka Astrology Detective, has built a reputation as one of the world's most trusted and sought-after astrologers for more than ten years. Her work has appeared in some of the most influential titles online and in print, making her one of the few astrologers who has garnered respect from both a mass audience and the astrological community. Her horoscopes have appeared on the websites for Canada's W Dish and Slice TV Networks, Tarot.com's Daily Horoscope site, and *Dell Horoscope* magazine, among others. Her writings have also been featured in *The Mountain Astrologer*, the leading trade journal for the astrological community, and astrology.com. She is also a long-term contributor to Llewellyn's annual *Moon Sign Book* and *Moon Sign Datebook*. Her website is www.astrologydetective.com or follow her at https://www.instagram.com/hashtaghoroscopes/.

Finding Opportunity Periods

by Jim Shawvan

There are times when the most useful things you can do are ordinary tasks such as laundry, cooking, listening to music, reading, learning, or meditating. There are other times when the universe opens the gates of opportunity. Meetings, decisions, or commitments during these "Opportunity Periods" can lead to new and positive developments in your life. Most people are unaware of these subtle changes in the energies, so they wind up doing laundry when they could be signing an important contract, or they go out to try to meet a new sweetheart when the energies for such a thing are totally blocked.

I developed the Opportunity Periods system over more than thirty years, as I tested first one hypothesis and then another in real life. In about 1998, when I studied classical astrology with Lee Lehman, the system got some added zing, including William Lilly's idea that the Moon when void-of-course in the signs of the Moon and Jupiter "performeth somewhat." The signs of the Moon and Jupiter are Taurus, Cancer, Sagittarius, and Pisces. For those who want to understand the details of the system, they are explained here. If you simply want to use the system, all the information you need is on the calendar pages (you don't need to learn the technicalities).

An Opportunity Period (OP) is a period in which the aspects of the transiting Moon to other transiting planets show no interference with the free flow of decision and action.

Opportunity Periods apply to everyone in the world all at once; although, if the astrological influences on your own chart are putting blocks in your path, you may not be able to use every OP to the fullest. Nevertheless, you are always better off taking important actions and making crucial decisions during an Opportunity Period.

Signs of the Moon and Jupiter

Taurus: the Moon's exaltation
Cancer: the Moon's domicile and Jupiter's exaltation
Sagittarius: Jupiter's fiery domicile
Pisces: Jupiter's watery domicile

Steps to Find Your Opportunity Periods

Under Sun's Beams

Step 1: Determine whether the Moon is "under Sun's beams"; that is, less than 17 degrees from the Sun. If it is, go to step 7. If not, continue to step 2.

Moon Void-of-Course

Step 2: Determine when the Moon goes void-of-course (v/c). The Moon is said to be void-of-course from the time it makes the last Ptolemaic aspect (conjunction, sextile, square, trine, or opposition) in a sign until it enters the next sign.

In eight of the twelve signs of the zodiac, Moon-void periods are NOT Opportunity Periods. In the other four signs, however, they are! According to seventeenth-century astrologer William Lilly, the Moon in the signs of the Moon and Jupiter "performeth somewhat." Lee Lehman says that she has taken this to the bank many times—and so have I.

Stressful or Easy Aspect

Step 3: Determine whether the aspect on which the Moon goes void is a stressful or an easy aspect. Every square is stressful, and every trine and every sextile is easy. Conjunctions and oppositions require judgment according to the nature of the planet the Moon is aspecting, and according to your individual ability to cope with the energies of that planet. For example, the Moon applying to a conjunction of Jupiter, Venus, or Mercury is easy, whereas, for most purposes, the Moon applying to a conjunction of Saturn, Mars, Neptune, Pluto, or Uranus is stressful. However, if you are a person for whom Uranus or Pluto is a familiar and more or less comfortable energy, you may find that the period before the Moon's conjunction to that planet is an Opportunity Period for you. (Since this is true for relatively few people, such periods are not marked as OPs in this book.)

Oppositions can work if the Moon is applying to an opposition of Jupiter, Venus, Mercury, or the Sun (just before the Full Moon). The Moon applying to a conjunction with the Sun (New Moon) presents a whole set of issues on its own. See step 7.

Easy Equals Opportunity

Step 4: If the aspect on which the Moon goes void is an easy aspect, there is an Opportunity Period before the void period. If the aspect on which the Moon goes void is a stressful aspect, there is no Opportunity Period preceding the void period in that sign. To determine the beginning of the Opportunity Period, find the last stressful aspect the Moon makes in the sign. The Opportunity Period runs from the last stressful aspect to the last aspect (assuming that the last aspect is an easy one). If the Moon makes no stressful aspects at all while in the sign, then the Opportunity Period begins as soon as the Moon enters the sign, and ends at the last aspect.

When Is an Aspect Over?

Step 5: When is an aspect over? There are three different answers to this question, and I recommend observation to decide. I also recommend caution.

- An aspect is over (in electional astrology) as soon as it is no longer exact. For example, if the Moon's last stressful aspect in a sign is a square to Saturn at 1:51 p.m., the Opportunity Period (if there is one) would be considered to begin immediately. This is the way the Opportunity Periods are shown in this book.

- Lee Lehman says an aspect is effective (for electional purposes) until it is no longer partile. An aspect is said to be partile if the two planets are in the same degree numerically. For example, a planet at 0° Aries 00' 00" is in partile trine to a planet at 0° Leo 59' 59", but it is not in partile conjunction to a planet at 29° Pisces 59' 59", even though the orb of the conjunction is only one second of arc ($\frac{1}{3,600}$) of a degree.

- An aspect is effective until the Moon has separated from the exact aspect by a full degree, which takes about two hours. This is the most cautious viewpoint. If you have doubts about the wisdom of signing a major contract while the Moon is still within one degree of a nasty aspect, then for your own peace of mind you should give it two hours, to get the one-degree separating orb.

Translating Light and Translating Darkness

Step 6: One should avoid starting important matters when the Moon is translating light from a stressful aspect with a malefic planet to an ostensibly easy aspect with another malefic planet—or even a series of such aspects uninterrupted by any aspects to benefic planets. I refer to this as "translating darkness." Translation of light is a concept used primarily in horary astrology, and it is discussed in great detail in books and on websites on that subject. For example, the Moon's last difficult aspect is a square to Saturn, and there is an apparent Opportunity Period because the Moon's next aspect is a trine to Mars, on which the Moon goes void-of-course. The problem is this: the Moon is translating light from one malefic to another, and this vitiates what would otherwise be an Opportunity Period. The same would be true if the sequence were, for example, Moon square Saturn, then Moon trine Mars, then Moon sextile Neptune—an unbroken series of malefics.

For the purpose of this system, we may regard all of the following planets as malefics: Mars, Saturn, Uranus, Neptune, and Pluto. I can almost hear the howls of protest from the folks who believe there is no such thing as a malefic planet or a bad aspect. On the level of spiritual growth, that is doubtless true, but this book is meant to be used to make your everyday life easier. Anyone who urges others to suffer more than absolutely necessary in the name of spirituality is indulging in great spiritual arrogance themselves.

New Moon, Balsamic Phase, and Cazimi Notes

Step 7: Here are some notes on the period around the New Moon: waxing, waning, Balsamic, under beams, combust, and Cazimi.

As it separates from conjunction with the Sun (New Moon) and moves toward opposition (Full Moon), the Moon is said to be waxing, or increasing in light. Traditionally the period of the waxing Moon is considered favorable for electional purposes.

Then after the Full Moon, as the Moon applies to a conjunction with the Sun, the Moon is said to be waning, or decreasing in light. Traditionally this period is regarded as a poor choice for electional purposes, and the closer the Moon gets to the Sun, the worse it is said to be. In practice, I find that problems seem to occur only as the Moon gets very close to the Sun.

When the Moon is applying to a conjunction with the Sun (New Moon) and is less than 45 degrees away from the Sun, the Moon is said to be in its Balsamic phase. This phase is associated with giving things up and is considered especially unfavorable for starting things you wish to increase.

Any planet within 17 degrees of the Sun is said to be under Sun's beams. Traditionally this weakens the planet, particularly for electional and horary purposes.

Any planet within 8 degrees of the Sun is said to be combust. Traditionally this weakens the planet even more, particularly in electional and horary work.

Any planet whose center is within 17 minutes of arc of the center of the Sun in celestial longitude is said to be Cazimi. Oddly, this is considered the highest form of accidental dignity. In other words, a planet is thought to be weak when under Sun's beams, weaker still when combust, but—surprisingly—very powerful and benefic when Cazimi!

The average speed of the Moon is such that it remains Cazimi for about an hour; that is, half an hour before and half an hour after the exact conjunction with the Sun (New Moon). Other things being equal, you can use the Cazimi Moon to start something if you really want it to succeed.

However, please do not attempt to use the Cazimi Moon at the time of a Solar Eclipse, nor if the Moon is moving from the Cazimi into a stressful aspect. Cazimi is powerful, but it cannot override the difficulties shown by a Solar Eclipse, nor those shown by, say, the Moon's application to a square of Saturn.

If you really need to start something around the time of the New Moon, and you cannot use the Cazimi, it is a good idea to wait until the first Opportunity Period after the Moon has begun waxing. Even if the Moon is still under Sun's beams at that time, it is better than starting the new project while the Moon is still waning. However, if you can reasonably do so, it is best to wait for the first Opportunity Period after the Moon is no longer under Sun's beams; that is, after the Moon has separated from the Sun by at least 17 degrees. For the principles to use at that time, see step 2.

About the Astrologers

Paula Belluomini, CAP ISAR, began studying astrology as a teenager while living in Brazil. Growing up, she became fascinated with the movement of the stars and was passionate about learning how their positions affected life on Earth. She immersed herself in all the literature she could find on the subject, and moved to Southern California in the 1990s to continue her studies through independent coursework.

Paula completed the steps required to become a Certified Astrological Professional (CAP) by the International Society for Astrological Research (ISAR) in 2015, and participated in several astrological conferences promoted by ISAR and UAC. She was introduced to Jim Shawvan's Opportunity Periods system in Anaheim (ISAR 2003), and has followed his work ever since.

Paula's main areas of expertise and interest include modern astrology with predictive techniques, relationship analysis, and relocational astrology, as well as electional, mundane, and traditional astrology. More recently, horary astrology has piqued her interest because of its practicality and ability to answer questions in a more objective way.

In addition to providing astrology consulting services, Paula writes articles and posts about current astrological events, gives lectures about specific topics, participates in research and study groups, and continues educating herself on the stars.

Aside from astrology, Paula has a degree in marketing and is an experienced graphic and web designer who often creates artwork with astrological themes. For more information, please visit her website at astropaula.com.

Jim Shawvan developed the system of Opportunity Periods over a period of three decades, out of his interest in electional astrology—the art of picking times for important actions such as getting married, opening a business, or incorporating a company (or even matters of only medium importance). Jim began the study of astrology in 1969. He taught classes in predictive astrology and lectured numerous times to the San Diego Astrological Society and other astrological groups and conferences.

Jim's articles appeared in *The Mountain Astrologer* and other publications. He predicted the delay in the results of the US presidential election of 2000, and in early 2001 he predicted that, in response to anti-American terrorism, the US would be at war in Afghanistan in the first two years of George W. Bush's presidency.

Jim studied cultural anthropology and structural linguistics at Cornell University, and later became a computer programmer and systems analyst. From 1989 to 1997 he was the technical astrologer at Neil Michelsen's Astro Communications Services, handling the most difficult questions and orders. He held the Certified Astrological Professional certificate issued by the International Society for Astrological Research.

Business Guide

Collections

Try to make collections on days when your Sun is well aspected. Avoid days when Mars or Saturn are aspected. If possible, the Moon should be in a cardinal sign: Aries, Cancer, Libra, or Capricorn. It is more difficult to collect when the Moon is in Taurus or Scorpio.

Employment, Promotion

Choose a day when your Sun is favorably aspected or the Moon is in your tenth house. Good aspects of Venus or Jupiter are beneficial.

Loans

Moon in the first and second quarters favors the lender; in the third and fourth it favors the borrower. Good aspects of Jupiter or Venus to the Moon are favorable to both, as is Moon in Leo, Sagittarius, Aquarius, or Pisces.

New Ventures

Things usually get off to a better start during the increase of the Moon. If there is impatience, anxiety, or deadlock, it can often be broken at the Full Moon. Agreements can be reached then.

Partnerships

Agreements and partnerships should be made on a day that is favorable to both parties. Mars, Neptune, Pluto, and Saturn should not be square or opposite the Moon. It is best to make an agreement or partnership when the Moon is in a mutable sign, especially Gemini or Virgo. The other signs are not favorable, with the possible exception of Leo or Capricorn. Begin partnerships when the Moon is increasing in light, as this is a favorable time for starting new ventures.

Public Relations

The Moon rules the public, so this must be well aspected, particularly by the Sun, Mercury, Uranus, or Neptune.

Selling

Selling is favored by good aspects of Venus, Jupiter, or Mercury to the Moon. Avoid aspects to Saturn. Try to get the planetary ruler of your product well aspected by Venus, Jupiter, or the Moon.

Signing Important Papers

Sign contracts or agreements when the Moon is increasing in a fruitful sign. Avoid days when Mars, Saturn, Neptune, or Pluto are afflicting the Moon. Don't sign anything if your Sun is badly afflicted.

Calendar Pages
How to Use Your *Daily Planetary Guide*

Both Eastern and Pacific times are given in the datebook. The Eastern times are listed in the left-hand column. The Pacific times are in the right-hand column in bold typeface. Note that adjustments have been made for Daylight Saving Time. The void-of-course Moon is listed to the right of the daily aspect at the exact time it occurs. It is indicated by "☽ v/c." On days when it occurs for only one time zone and not the other, it is indicated next to the appropriate column and then repeated on the next day for the other time zone. Note that the monthly ephemerides in the back of the book are shown for midnight Greenwich Mean Time (GMT). Opportunity Periods are designated by the letters "OP." See page 79 for a detailed discussion on how to use Opportunity Periods.

Symbol Key

Planets/	☉	Sun	♃	Jupiter
Asteroids	☽	Moon	♄	Saturn
	☿	Mercury	♅	Uranus
	♀	Venus	♆	Neptune
	♂	Mars	♇	Pluto
	⚷	Chiron		

Signs	♈	Aries	♎	Libra
	♉	Taurus	♏	Scorpio
	♊	Gemini	♐	Sagittarius
	♋	Cancer	♑	Capricorn
	♌	Leo	♒	Aquarius
	♍	Virgo	♓	Pisces

Aspects	☌	Conjunction (0°)	△	Trine (120°)
	✶	Sextile (60°)	⚻	Quincunx (150°)
	□	Square (90°)	☍	Opposition (180°)

Motion	℞	Retrograde	D	Direct

Moon Phases	●	New Moon	◑	2nd Quarter
	○	Full Moon	◐	4th Quarter

25 Mon
2nd ♊
CHRISTMAS DAY

☽♊ ✶ ♅♈	7:21 am	**4:21 am**	
♀♏ △ ♆♓	12:15 pm	**9:15 am**	
☽♊ ☍ ♂♐	9:08 pm	**6:08 pm**	
☽♊ □ ♆♓		**9:57 pm**	
☽♊ ⚻ ♀♏		**11:15 pm**	
☽♊ ☍ ☿♐		**11:55 pm**	☽ v/c

26 Tue
2nd ♊
○ Full Moon 4 ♋ 58
KWANZAA BEGINS
BOXING DAY (CANADA & UK)
CHIRON DIRECT

☽♊ □ ♆♓	12:57 am		
☽♊ ⚻ ♀♏	2:15 am		
☽♊ ☍ ☿♐	2:55 am		☽ v/c
☽♊ ⚻ ♇♑	8:45 am	**5:45 am**	
☽ enters ♋	10:15 am	**7:15 am**	
☽♋ △ ♄♓	3:30 pm	**12:30 pm**	
☽♋ ☍ ☉♑	7:33 pm	**4:33 pm**	
☽♋ ✶ ♃♉	8:45 pm	**5:45 pm**	
♅ D	10:10 pm	**7:10 pm**	
☿♐ □ ♆♓		**11:43 pm**	

27 Wed
3rd ♋

☿♐ □ ♆♓	2:43 am		
☉♑ △ ♃♉	10:28 am	**7:28 am**	
☽♋ □ ♅♈	3:23 pm	**12:23 pm**	
☿♐ ☌ ♂♐	7:31 pm	**4:31 pm**	
☽♋ ✶ ♅♉	11:04 pm	**8:04 pm**	

28 Thu
3rd ♋

☽♋ ⚻ ☿♐	7:40 am	**4:40 am**	
☽♋ ⚻ ♂♐	9:17 am	**6:17 am**	
☽♋ △ ♆♓	9:45 am	**6:45 am**	
☽♋ △ ♀♏	5:12 pm	**2:12 pm**	
♂♐ □ ♆♓	5:16 pm	**2:16 pm**	
☽♋ ☍ ♀♑	5:57 pm	**2:57 pm**	☽ v/c
☽ enters ♌	7:23 pm	**4:23 pm**	
♀♏ ✶ ♀♑		**10:01 pm**	
☽♌ ⚻ ♄♓		**10:15 pm**	

♀♏ ⚹ ♀♈ 1:01 am
☽♌ ⚻ ♄♓ 1:15 am
☽♌ □ ♃♉ 6:18 am **3:18 am**
☽♌ ⚻ ☉♈ 10:19 am **7:19 am**
♀ enters ♐ 3:24 pm **12:24 pm**
☽♌ △ ♅♈ **10:46 pm**

Fri 29
3rd ♌

☽♌ △ ♅♈ 1:46 am
☽♌ □ ♅♉ 9:39 am **6:39 am**
☽♌ △ ☿♐ 4:00 pm **1:00 pm**
☽♌ ⚻ ♆♓ 8:57 pm **5:57 pm**
♃ D 9:40 pm **6:40 pm**
☽♌ △ ♂♐ **9:18 pm** ☽ v/c

Sat 30
3rd ♌
JUPITER DIRECT

OP: After Moon squares Uranus today until v/c Moon today or on Sunday. Despite Mercury being retrograde, this OP is excellent for creativity and celebrating a happy new year.

☽♌ △ ♂♐ 12:18 am ☽ v/c
☽♌ ⚻ ♀♈ 5:34 am **2:34 am**
☽ enters ♍ 6:53 am **3:53 am**
☽♍ □ ♀♐ 11:23 am **8:23 am**
☽♍ ☍ ♄♓ 1:24 pm **10:24 am**
☽♍ △ ♃♉ 6:10 pm **3:10 pm**

Sun 31
3rd ♌
New Year's Eve

Eastern Standard Time (EST) plain / **Pacific Standard Time (PST) bold**

NOVEMBER 2023
S	M	T	W	T	F	S
			1	2	3	4
5	6	7	8	9	10	11
12	13	14	15	16	17	18
19	20	21	22	23	24	25
26	27	28	29	30		

DECEMBER 2023
S	M	T	W	T	F	S
					1	2
3	4	5	6	7	8	9
10	11	12	13	14	15	16
17	18	19	20	21	22	23
24	25	26	27	28	29	30
31						

JANUARY
S	M	T	W	T	F	S
	1	2	3	4	5	6
7	8	9	10	11	12	13
14	15	16	17	18	19	20
21	22	23	24	25	26	27
28	29	30	31			

JANUARY

Mercury Note: Mercury goes direct on Monday, January 1, but remains in its Storm, moving slowly, until January 7.

1 MON
3rd ♍
NEW YEAR'S DAY
KWANZAA ENDS
MERCURY DIRECT

☽♍ △ ☉♑	3:59 am	**12:59 am**
♀♐ □ ♄♓	8:26 am	**5:26 am**
☽♍ ⊼ ⚷♈	2:14 pm	**11:14 am**
☿ D	10:08 pm	**7:08 pm**
☽♍ △ ♅♉	10:09 pm	**7:09 pm**

2 TUE
3rd ♍

☽♍ □ ☿♐	3:54 am	**12:54 am**
☽♍ ☍ ♆♓	9:50 am	**6:50 am**
☽♍ □ ♂♐	5:13 pm	**2:13 pm**
☽♍ △ ♀♑	6:36 pm	**3:36 pm** ☽ v/c
☽ enters ♎	7:47 pm	**4:47 pm**
☽♎ ⊼ ♄♓		**11:47 pm**

3 WED
3rd ♎
◑ 4th Quarter 13 ♎ 15

☽♎ ⊼ ♄♓	2:47 am	
♀♐ ⊼ ♃♉	5:55 am	**2:55 am**
☽♎ ⊼ ♃♉	7:07 am	**4:07 am**
☽♎ ⚹ ♀♐	7:15 am	**4:15 am**
☽♎ □ ☉♑	10:30 pm	**7:30 pm**
☽♎ ☍ ⚷♈		**11:59 pm**

4 THU
4th ♎

☽♎ ☍ ⚷♈	2:59 am	
♂ enters ♑	9:58 am	**6:58 am**
☽♎ ⊼ ♅♉	10:37 am	**7:37 am**
☽♎ ⚹ ☿♐	5:25 pm	**2:25 pm**
☽♎ ⊼ ♆♓	10:08 pm	**7:08 pm**

☽♎□♇♑	6:41 am	**3:41 am**	☽ v/c
☽ enters ♏	7:39 am	**4:39 am**	
☽♏⚹♂♑	9:03 am	**6:03 am**	
☽♏△♄♓	2:49 pm	**11:49 am**	
☽♏☍♃♉	6:35 pm	**3:35 pm**	

Fri 5
4th ♎

☉♑□⚷♈	3:35 am	**12:35 am**	
☽♏⚻⚷♈	1:22 pm	**10:22 am**	
☽♏⚹☉♑	2:12 pm	**11:12 am**	
☽♏☍♅♉	8:24 pm	**5:24 pm**	

Sat 6
4th ♏

OP: After Moon opposes Uranus today until v/c Moon on Sunday. Take advantage of this intense energy during the Last Quarter Moon to clear away clutter and recycling.

☽♏△♆♓	7:21 am	**4:21 am**	
☽♏⚹♇♑	3:22 pm	**12:22 pm**	☽ v/c
☽ enters ♐	4:08 pm	**1:08 pm**	
☽♐□♄♓	11:11 pm	**8:11 pm**	
☽♐⚻♃♉		**11:23 pm**	

Sun 7
4th ♏

Eastern Standard Time (EST) plain / **Pacific Standard Time (PST) bold**

DECEMBER 2023

S	M	T	W	T	F	S
					1	2
3	4	5	6	7	8	9
10	11	12	13	14	15	16
17	18	19	20	21	22	23
24	25	26	27	28	29	30
31						

JANUARY

S	M	T	W	T	F	S
	1	2	3	4	5	6
7	8	9	10	11	12	13
14	15	16	17	18	19	20
21	22	23	24	25	26	27
28	29	30	31			

FEBRUARY

S	M	T	W	T	F	S
				1	2	3
4	5	6	7	8	9	10
11	12	13	14	15	16	17
18	19	20	21	22	23	24
25	26	27	28	29		

January

Mercury Note: Mercury finally leaves its Storm on Monday. Look over your notes on any ideas that occurred to you while Mercury was retrograde or slow. How do they look now?

8 Mon
4th ♐

☽♐ ⚻ ♃♉	2:23 am	
☽♐ ☌ ♀♐	1:44 pm	**10:44 am**
☽♐ △ ♅♈	7:44 pm	**4:44 pm**
☿♐ □ ♆♓	8:24 pm	**5:24 pm**
☽♐ ⚻ ♅♉		**11:10 pm**

9 Tue
4th ♐

☽♐ ⚻ ♅♉	2:10 am	
☽♐ □ ♆♓	12:27 pm	**9:27 am**
☽♐ ☌ ☿♐	1:24 pm	**10:24 am** ☽ v/c
☉♑ △ ♅♉	7:07 pm	**4:07 pm**
☽ enters ♑	8:33 pm	**5:33 pm**
♂♑ ✳ ♄♓	9:40 pm	**6:40 pm**

10 Wed
4th ♑

☽♑ ✳ ♄♓	3:29 am	**12:29 am**
☽♑ ☌ ♂♑	3:45 am	**12:45 am**
☽♑ △ ♃♉	6:14 am	**3:14 am**
☽♑ □ ♅♈	10:27 pm	**7:27 pm**

11 Thu
4th ♑
● New Moon 20 ♑ 44

☽♑ △ ♅♉	4:26 am	**1:26 am**
☽♑ ☌ ☉♑	6:57 am	**3:57 am**
♀♐ △ ♅♈	9:36 am	**6:36 am**
☽♑ ✳ ♆♓	2:20 pm	**11:20 am**
☽♑ ☌ ♀♑	9:33 pm	**6:33 pm** ☽ v/c
☽ enters ♒	10:01 pm	**7:01 pm**

♂♑△♃♉	5:42 am	**2:42 am**
☽≈□♃♉	7:29 am	**4:29 am**
☽≈⚹♅♈	11:12 pm	**8:12 pm**
☽≈⚹♀♐		**11:32 pm**

Fri 12
1st ≈

☽≈⚹♀♐	2:32 am	
☽≈□♅♉	4:59 am	**1:59 am** ☽ v/c
☿ enters ♑	9:49 pm	**6:49 pm**
☽ enters ♓	10:29 pm	**7:29 pm**
☽♓⚹☿♑	10:32 pm	**7:32 pm**

Sat 13
1st ≈

☽♓♂♄♓	5:50 am	**2:50 am**
♀♐⊼♅♉	8:03 am	**5:03 am**
☽♓⚹♃♉	8:08 am	**5:08 am**
☽♓⚹♂♑	10:40 am	**7:40 am**

Sun 14
1st ♓

Eastern Standard Time (EST) plain / **Pacific Standard Time (PST) bold**

DECEMBER 2023								JANUARY								FEBRUARY					
S	M	T	W	T	F	S		S	M	T	W	T	F	S		S	M	T	W	T	F	S
					1	2			1	2	3	4	5	6						1	2	3
3	4	5	6	7	8	9		7	8	9	10	11	12	13		4	5	6	7	8	9	10
10	11	12	13	14	15	16		14	15	16	17	18	19	20		11	12	13	14	15	16	17
17	18	19	20	21	22	23		21	22	23	24	25	26	27		18	19	20	21	22	23	24
24	25	26	27	28	29	30		28	29	30	31					25	26	27	28	29		
31																					

15 Mon
1st ♓

Martin Luther King Jr. Day

OP: After Moon conjoins Neptune until Moon enters Aries. This is a great time to develop and implement ambitious and far-reaching projects.

☽♓ ✶ ♅♉	5:47 am	**2:47 am**	
☽♓ □ ♀♐	7:48 am	**4:48 am**	
☽♓ ✶ ☉♑	3:47 pm	**12:47 pm**	
☽♓ ♂ ♆♓	4:03 pm	**1:03 pm**	
☉♑ ✶ ♆♓	7:38 pm	**4:38 pm**	
☽♓ ✶ ♀♑	11:33 pm	**8:33 pm**	☽ v/c
☽ enters ♈	11:49 pm	**8:49 pm**	

16 Tue
1st ♈

☽♈ □ ☿♑	4:05 am	**1:05 am**
☽♈ □ ♂♑	3:14 pm	**12:14 pm**
☽♈ ♂ ☊♈		**11:20 pm**

17 Wed
1st ♈
◐ 2nd Quarter 27 ♈ 32

☽♈ ♂ ☊♈	2:20 am	
☽♈ △ ♀♐	3:22 pm	**12:22 pm**
☽♈ □ ☉♑	10:53 pm	**7:53 pm**

18 Thu
2nd ♈

☽♈ □ ♀♑	3:03 am	**12:03 am**	☽ v/c
☽ enters ♉	3:12 am	**12:12 am**	
☿♑ ✶ ♄♓	3:49 am	**12:49 am**	
☽♉ ✶ ♄♓	11:57 am	**8:57 am**	
☽♉ △ ☿♑	12:42 pm	**9:42 am**	
☽♉ ♂ ♃♉	2:05 pm	**11:05 am**	
☽♉ △ ♂♑	10:26 pm	**7:26 pm**	

Fri 19
2nd ♉

☿♑ △ ♃♉	4:31 am	**1:31 am**
♀♐ □ ♆♓	10:49 am	**7:49 am**
☽♉ ☌ ♅♉	1:11 pm	**10:11 am**
☽♉ ⚹ ♆♓		**9:40 pm**
☽♉ ⚻ ♀♐		**11:04 pm**

OP: After Moon conjoins Uranus today until Moon enters Gemini on Saturday. Highly productive time, excellent to invest in what you want to see grow.

Sat 20
2nd ♉

Sun enters Aquarius

☽♉ ⚹ ♆♓	12:40 am		
☽♉ ⚻ ♀♐	2:04 am		
☉♑ ☌ ♇♑	8:46 am	**5:46 am**	
☽♉ △ ♇♑	8:56 am	**5:56 am**	
☽♉ △ ☉♑	8:57 am	**5:57 am**	☽ v/c
☽ enters ♊	8:58 am	**5:58 am**	
☉ enters ♒	9:07 am	**6:07 am**	
☽♊ □ ♄♓	6:32 pm	**3:32 pm**	
♇ enters ♒	7:50 pm	**4:50 pm**	
☽♊ ⚻ ☿♑		**9:45 pm**	

Sun 21
2nd ♊

☽♊ ⚻ ☿♑	12:45 am	
☽♊ ⚻ ♂♑	8:23 am	**5:23 am**
☽♊ ⚹ ⚷♈	2:04 pm	**11:04 am**

Eastern Standard Time (EST) plain / **Pacific Standard Time (PST) bold**

DECEMBER 2023

S	M	T	W	T	F	S
					1	2
3	4	5	6	7	8	9
10	11	12	13	14	15	16
17	18	19	20	21	22	23
24	25	26	27	28	29	30
31						

JANUARY

S	M	T	W	T	F	S
	1	2	3	4	5	6
7	8	9	10	11	12	13
14	15	16	17	18	19	20
21	22	23	24	25	26	27
28	29	30	31			

FEBRUARY

S	M	T	W	T	F	S
				1	2	3
4	5	6	7	8	9	10
11	12	13	14	15	16	17
18	19	20	21	22	23	24
25	26	27	28	29		

22 Mon
2nd ♊

☽♊ □ ♅♓	8:22 am	**5:22 am**	
☽♊ ☍ ♀♐	3:40 pm	**12:40 pm**	☽ v/c
☽ enters ♋	4:51 pm	**1:51 pm**	
☽♋ ⊼ ♇♒	4:58 pm	**1:58 pm**	
☽♋ ⊼ ☉♒	9:43 pm	**6:43 pm**	

23 Tue
2nd ♋

OP: After Moon opposes Mars today until Moon enters Leo on Wednesday or Thursday. This OP starts full of energy and ends with mellow Neptunian vibes. Use it for taking the initiative or engaging in anything that interests you.

☽♋ △ ♄♓	3:15 am	**12:15 am**
♀ enters ♓	3:50 am	**12:50 am**
☽♋ ✶ ♃♉	5:13 am	**2:13 am**
☽♋ ☍ ☿♓	3:53 am	**12:53 am**
☽♋ ☍ ♂♓	8:44 pm	**5:44 pm**
☽♋ □ ♇♈	11:04 pm	**8:04 pm**

24 Wed
2nd ♋

☽♋ ✶ ♅♉	5:24 am	**2:24 am**	
☽♋ △ ♆♓	5:58 pm	**2:58 pm**	☽ v/c
☽ enters ♌		**11:37 pm**	
☽♌ ☍ ♇♒		**11:53 pm**	

25 Thu
2nd ♋
○ Full Moon 5 ♌ 15

☽ enters ♌	2:37 am	
☽♌ ☍ ♇♒	2:53 am	
☽♌ ⊼ ♀♓	7:50 am	**4:50 am**
♂♓ □ ♇♈	12:15 pm	**9:15 am**
☽♌ ☍ ☉♒	12:54 pm	**9:54 am**
☽♌ ⊼ ♄♓	1:52 pm	**10:52 am**
☽♌ □ ♃♉	3:46 pm	**12:46 pm**

☿♑ □ ♅♈	9:49 am	**6:49 am**
☽♌ △ ♅♈	9:55 am	**6:55 am**
☽♌ ⚻ ☿♑	9:56 am	**6:56 am**
☽♌ ⚻ ♂♑	11:19 am	**8:19 am**
☽♌ □ ♅♉	4:19 pm	**1:19 pm** ☽ v/c
☉≈ □ ♃♉		**11:18 pm**
♅ D		**11:35 pm**

Fri 26
3rd ♌
Uranus direct (Pacific)

☉≈ □ ♃♉	2:18 am	
♅ D	2:35 am	
☽♌ ⚻ ♆♓	5:25 am	**2:25 am**
☿♑ ☌ ♂♑	9:59 am	**6:59 am**
☽ enters ♍	2:11 pm	**11:11 am**
☽♍ ⚻ ♇≈	2:38 pm	**11:38 am**
♀♑ ✳ ♄♓		**10:03 pm**
☽♍ ☍ ♄♓		**11:20 pm**
☽♍ △ ♀♑		**11:28 pm**

Sat 27
3rd ♌
Uranus direct (Eastern)

♀♑ ✳ ♄♓	1:03 am	
☽♍ ☍ ♄♓	2:20 am	
☽♍ △ ♀♑	2:28 am	
☽♍ △ ♃♉	4:10 am	**1:10 am**
☽♍ ⚻ ☉≈	6:23 am	**3:23 am**
☿♑ △ ♅♉	4:07 pm	**1:07 pm**
♀♑ △ ♃♉	8:02 pm	**5:02 pm**
☽♍ ⚻ ♅♈	10:28 pm	**7:28 pm**

Sun 28
3rd ♍

Eastern Standard Time (EST) plain / **Pacific Standard Time (PST) bold**

DECEMBER 2023						
S	M	T	W	T	F	S
					1	2
3	4	5	6	7	8	9
10	11	12	13	14	15	16
17	18	19	20	21	22	23
24	25	26	27	28	29	30
31						

JANUARY						
S	M	T	W	T	F	S
	1	2	3	4	5	6
7	8	9	10	11	12	13
14	15	16	17	18	19	20
21	22	23	24	25	26	27
28	29	30	31			

FEBRUARY						
S	M	T	W	T	F	S
				1	2	3
4	5	6	7	8	9	10
11	12	13	14	15	16	17
18	19	20	21	22	23	24
25	26	27	28	29		

29 Mon
3rd ♍

☽♍ △ ♂♑	3:54 am	**12:54 am**
☽♍ △ ♅♉	4:51 am	**1:51 am**
☽♍ △ ☿♑	6:38 am	**3:38 am**
☽♍ ☍ ♆♓	6:20 pm	**3:20 pm** ☽ v/c
♂♑ △ ♅♉	6:41 pm	**3:41 pm**

30 Tue
3rd ♍

☽ enters ♎	3:04 am	**12:04 am**
☽♎ △ ♀♒	3:41 am	**12:41 am**
☽♎ ⊼ ♄♓	3:55 pm	**12:55 pm**
☽♎ ⊼ ♃♉	5:40 pm	**2:40 pm**
☽♎ □ ♀♑	10:34 pm	**7:34 pm**
☽♎ △ ☉♒		**10:07 pm**

31 Wed
3rd ♎

☽♎ △ ☉♒	1:07 am	
☽♎ ☍ ⚷♈	11:36 am	**8:36 am**
☽♎ ⊼ ♅♉	5:48 pm	**2:48 pm**
☽♎ □ ♂♑	9:00 pm	**6:00 pm**

1 Thu
3rd ♎

☽♎ □ ☿♑	4:03 am	**1:03 am** ☽ v/c
☽♎ ⊼ ♆♓	7:13 am	**4:13 am**
☽ enters ♏	3:37 pm	**12:37 pm**
☽♏ □ ♀♒	4:23 pm	**1:23 pm**

☽♏︎ △ ♄ ⯑	4:39 am	**1:39 am**
☿♑︎ ⚹ ♆ ⯑	5:55 am	**2:55 am**
☽♏︎ ☍ ♃ ♉︎	6:17 am	**3:17 am**
☽♏︎ ⚹ ♀ ♑︎	5:09 pm	**2:09 pm**
☽♏︎ □ ☉ ♒︎	6:18 pm	**3:18 pm**
☽♏︎ ⚻ ⚷ ♈︎	11:08 pm	**8:08 pm**

FRI 2

3rd ♏︎
◑ 4th Quarter 13 ♏︎ 36
GROUNDHOG DAY
IMBOLC

☽♏︎ ☍ ♅ ♉︎	4:55 am	**1:55 am**
☽♏︎ ⚹ ♂ ♑︎	11:42 am	**8:42 am**
☽♏︎ △ ♆ ⯑	5:42 pm	**2:42 pm**
☽♏︎ ⚹ ☿ ♑︎	10:24 pm	**7:24 pm** ☽ v/c
☽ enters ♐︎		**10:28 pm**
☽♐︎ ⚹ ♀ ♒︎		**11:19 pm**

SAT 3

4th ♏︎

OP: After Moon opposes Uranus until v/c Moon. This is a great time to bring focus, intensity, and commitment to your projects at hand.

☽ enters ♐︎	1:28 am	
☽♐︎ ⚹ ♀ ♒︎	2:19 am	
☽♐︎ □ ♄ ⯑	2:10 pm	**11:10 am**
☽♐︎ ⚻ ♃ ♉︎	3:39 pm	**12:39 pm**
☿ enters ♒︎		**9:10 pm**

SUN 4

4th ♏︎

JANUARY						
S	M	T	W	T	F	S
	1	2	3	4	5	6
7	8	9	10	11	12	13
14	15	16	17	18	19	20
21	22	23	24	25	26	27
28	29	30	31			

FEBRUARY						
S	M	T	W	T	F	S
				1	2	3
4	5	6	7	8	9	10
11	12	13	14	15	16	17
18	19	20	21	22	23	24
25	26	27	28	29		

MARCH						
S	M	T	W	T	F	S
					1	2
3	4	5	6	7	8	9
10	11	12	13	14	15	16
17	18	19	20	21	22	23
24	25	26	27	28	29	30
31						

5 Mon
4th ♐

☿ enters ≈	12:10 am	
♀♑ □ ♃♈	6:49 am	**3:49 am**
☽♐ ✶ ☉≈	6:55 am	**3:55 am**
☽♐ △ ♃♈	6:57 am	**3:57 am**
☉≈ ✶ ♃♈	7:27 am	**4:27 am**
☿≈ ☌ ♀≈	7:58 am	**4:58 am**
☽♐ ⊼ ♅♉	12:11 pm	**9:11 am**
☽♐ □ ♆♓		**9:06 pm** ☽ v/c

6 Tue
4th ♐

OP: After Moon enters Capricorn today until v/c Moon on Wednesday or Thursday. This OP is ideal for practical matters, like organizing, during the Balsamic phase of the Moon. A time to be industrious aided by Mars in Capricorn.

☽♐ □ ♆♓	12:06 am	☽ v/c
☽ enters ♑	7:08 am	**4:08 am**
☽♑ ✶ ♄♓	7:18 pm	**4:18 pm**
☽♑ △ ♃♉	8:41 pm	**5:41 pm**

7 Wed
4th ♑

☽♑ □ ♃♈	10:33 am	**7:33 am**
☽♑ ☌ ♀♑	3:12 pm	**12:12 pm**
☽♑ △ ♅♉	3:19 pm	**12:19 pm**
♀♑ △ ♅♉	4:25 pm	**1:25 pm**
♂♑ ✶ ♆♓	7:20 pm	**4:20 pm**
☽♑ ✶ ♆♓		**11:30 pm**
☽♑ ☌ ♂♑		**11:52 pm** ☽ v/c

8 Thu
4th ♑

☽♑ ✶ ♆♓	2:30 am	
☽♑ ☌ ♂♑	2:52 am	☽ v/c
☉≈ □ ♅♉	5:46 am	**2:46 am**
☽ enters ≈	8:59 am	**5:59 am**
☽≈ ☌ ♀≈	9:57 am	**6:57 am**
☽≈ ☌ ☿≈	6:25 pm	**3:25 pm**
☽≈ □ ♃♉	10:10 pm	**7:10 pm**

☽≈ ✶ ♂♈ 11:06 am **8:06 am**
☽≈ □ ♅♉ 3:35 pm **12:35 pm**
☽≈ ☌ ☉≈ 5:59 pm **2:59 pm** ☽ v/c

FRI 9
4th ≈
● New Moon 20 ≈ 41

☿≈ □ ♃♉ 8:25 am **5:25 am**
☽ enters ♓ 8:42 am **5:42 am**
☽♓ ☌ ♄♓ 8:45 pm **5:45 pm**
☽♓ ✶ ♃♉ 10:05 pm **7:05 pm**

SAT 10
1st ≈
LUNAR NEW YEAR (DRAGON)

☽♓ ✶ ♅♉ 3:07 pm **12:07 pm**
☽♓ ✶ ♀♑ 11:31 pm **8:31 pm**
☽♓ ☌ ♆♓ **11:11 pm**

SUN 11
1st ♓

Eastern Standard Time (EST) plain / **Pacific Standard Time (PST) bold**

		JANUARY				
S	M	T	W	T	F	S
	1	2	3	4	5	6
7	8	9	10	11	12	13
14	15	16	17	18	19	20
21	22	23	24	25	26	27
28	29	30	31			

		FEBRUARY				
S	M	T	W	T	F	S
				1	2	3
4	5	6	7	8	9	10
11	12	13	14	15	16	17
18	19	20	21	22	23	24
25	26	27	28	29		

		MARCH				
S	M	T	W	T	F	S
					1	2
3	4	5	6	7	8	9
10	11	12	13	14	15	16
17	18	19	20	21	22	23
24	25	26	27	28	29	30
31						

February

12 Mon
1st ♓

OP: After Moon conjoins Neptune on Sunday or today until **Moon enters Aries today.** (Pisces is one of the four signs in which the v/c Moon is a good thing. See page 79.) Use your intuition and imagination during this waxing Moon OP to start new, purposeful projects.

☽♓ ♂ ♆♓	2:11 am	
☽♓ ⚹ ♂♑	7:32 am	**4:32 am** ☽ v/c
☽ enters ♈	8:26 am	**5:26 am**
☽♈ ⚹ ♀♒	9:36 am	**6:36 am**
♂ enters ♒		**10:05 pm**

13 Tue
1st ♈

Mardi Gras (Fat Tuesday)

♂ enters ♒	1:05 am	
☽♈ ⚹ ☿♒	5:44 am	**2:44 am**
♀♑ ⚹ ♆♓	8:36 am	**5:36 am**
☽♈ ♂ ⚷♈	11:22 am	**8:22 am**
♂♒ ♂ ♀♒		**10:06 pm**
☽♈ ⚹ ☉♒		**10:40 pm**

14 Wed
1st ♈

Valentine's Day
Ash Wednesday

♂♒ ♂ ♀♒	1:06 am	
☽♈ ⚹ ☉♒	1:40 am	
☽♈ □ ♀♑	5:21 am	**2:21 am** ☽ v/c
☽ enters ♉	10:02 am	**7:02 am**
☽♉ □ ♀♒	11:22 am	**8:22 am**
☽♉ □ ♂♒	11:56 am	**8:56 am**
☽♉ ⚹ ♄♓	11:57 pm	**8:57 pm**
☽♉ ♂ ♃♉		**10:31 pm**

15 Thu
1st ♉

☽♉ ♂ ♃♉	1:31 am	
☿♒ ⚹ ⚷♈	8:16 am	**5:16 am**
☽♉ □ ☿♒	3:36 pm	**12:36 pm**
☽♉ ♂ ♅♉	7:27 pm	**4:27 pm**

Fri 16
1st ♉
◐ 2nd Quarter 27 ♉ 26

☽♉ ⚹ ♆♓	7:55 am	**4:55 am**
☽♉ □ ☉♒	10:01 am	**7:01 am** ☽ v/c
♀ enters ♒	11:05 am	**8:05 am**
☽ enters ♊	2:39 pm	**11:39 am**
☽♊ △ ♀♒	3:02 pm	**12:02 pm**
☽♊ △ ♇♒	4:11 pm	**1:11 pm**
☽♊ △ ♂♒	7:56 pm	**4:56 pm**
☿♒ □ ♅♉	10:53 pm	**7:53 pm**

Sat 17
2nd ♊

♀♒ ☌ ♇♒	3:48 am	**12:48 am**
☽♊ □ ♄♓	5:57 am	**2:57 am**
☽♊ ⚹ ⚷♈	9:18 pm	**6:18 pm**

Sun 18
2nd ♊
Sun enters Pisces

☽♊ △ ☿♒	6:22 am	**3:22 am**
☽♊ □ ♆♓	3:28 pm	**12:28 pm**
☽♊ △ ☉♒	10:21 pm	**7:21 pm** ☽ v/c
☽ enters ♋	10:25 pm	**7:25 pm**
☉ enters ♓	11:13 pm	**8:13 pm**
☽♋ ⚻ ♇♒		**9:10 pm**

OP: After Moon squares Neptune until v/c Moon. Wait two hours after the square for clarity and use this time for reasoning, creativity, and communication.

Eastern Standard Time (EST) plain / **Pacific Standard Time (PST) bold**

JANUARY

S	M	T	W	T	F	S
	1	2	3	4	5	6
7	8	9	10	11	12	13
14	15	16	17	18	19	20
21	22	23	24	25	26	27
28	29	30	31			

FEBRUARY

S	M	T	W	T	F	S
				1	2	3
4	5	6	7	8	9	10
11	12	13	14	15	16	17
18	19	20	21	22	23	24
25	26	27	28	29		

MARCH

S	M	T	W	T	F	S
					1	2
3	4	5	6	7	8	9
10	11	12	13	14	15	16
17	18	19	20	21	22	23
24	25	26	27	28	29	30
31						

19 Mon
2nd ♋

Presidents' Day

OP: After Moon enters Cancer on Sunday until Moon enters Leo on Wednesday. This long and dynamic OP is perfect to get your projects off the ground. Suitable for anything you want to see grow.

☽♋ ⚻ ♀♒	12:10 am		
☽♋ ⚻ ♀♒	4:53 am	**1:53 am**	
☽♋ ⚻ ♂♒	7:38 am	**4:38 am**	
☽♋ △ ♄♓	3:02 pm	**12:02 pm**	
☽♋ ⚹ ♃♉	5:00 pm	**2:00 pm**	

20 Tue
2nd ♋

☽♋ □ ♅♈	6:45 am	**3:45 am**	
☽♋ ⚹ ♅♉	11:45 am	**8:45 am**	
☽♋ ⚻ ☿♒		**10:32 pm**	
☽♋ △ ♆♓		**10:38 pm**	☽ v/c

21 Wed
2nd ♋

☽♋ ⚻ ☿♒	1:32 am		
☽♋ △ ♆♓	1:38 am		☽ v/c
☽ enters ♌	8:40 am	**5:40 am**	
☽♌ ☍ ♀♒	10:37 am	**7:37 am**	
☽♌ ⚻ ☉♓	1:53 pm	**10:53 am**	
☽♌ ☍ ♀♒	10:03 pm	**7:03 pm**	
☽♌ ☍ ♂♒	10:13 pm	**7:13 pm**	
♀♒ ☌ ♂♒		**11:14 pm**	
☽♌ ⚻ ♄♓		**11:28 pm**	

22 Thu
2nd ♌

♀♒ ☌ ♂♒	2:14 am		
☽♌ ⚻ ♄♓	2:28 am		
☽♌ □ ♃♉	4:39 am	**1:39 am**	
☽♌ △ ♅♈	6:17 pm	**3:17 pm**	
☽♌ □ ♅♉	11:18 pm	**8:18 pm**	☽ v/c
☿ enters ♓		**11:29 pm**	

☿ enters ♓ 2:29 am
☽ ♌ ⚻ ♆ ♓ 1:36 pm **10:36 am**
☽ enters ♍ 8:38 pm **5:38 pm**
☽♍ ⚻ ♀ ≈ 10:46 pm **7:46 pm**
☽♍ ☍ ☿ ♓ 11:52 pm **8:52 pm**

FRI 23
2nd ♌

☽♍ ☍ ☉ ♓ 7:30 am **4:30 am**
☽♍ ⚻ ♂ ≈ 2:39 pm **11:39 am**
☽♍ ☍ ♄ ♓ 3:24 pm **12:24 pm**
☽♍ ⚻ ♀ ≈ 5:18 pm **2:18 pm**
☽♍ △ ♃ ♉ 5:49 pm **2:49 pm**
♀≈ □ ♃ ♉ 11:01 pm **8:01 pm**

SAT 24
2nd ♍
○ Full Moon 5 ♍ 23

☽♍ ⚻ ♅ ♈ 7:05 am **4:05 am**
☽♍ △ ♅ ♉ 12:04 pm **9:04 am**
☽♍ ☍ ♆ ♓   **11:35 pm** ☽ v/c

SUN 25
3rd ♍

Eastern Standard Time (EST) plain / **Pacific Standard Time (PST) bold**

		JANUARY							FEBRUARY							MARCH			
S	M	T	W	T	F	S	S	M	T	W	T	F	S	S	M	T	W	T	F	S
	1	2	3	4	5	6					1	2	3						1	2
7	8	9	10	11	12	13	4	5	6	7	8	9	10	3	4	5	6	7	8	9
14	15	16	17	18	19	20	11	12	13	14	15	16	17	10	11	12	13	14	15	16
21	22	23	24	25	26	27	18	19	20	21	22	23	24	17	18	19	20	21	22	23
28	29	30	31				25	26	27	28	29			24	25	26	27	28	29	30
														31						

February

26 Mon
3rd ♍

OP: After Moon enters Libra today until v/c Moon on Tuesday. Another long OP good for clarity, communication, and social connections, or even romance!

☽♍ ☍ ♆ ♓	2:35 am		☽ v/c
☽ enters ♎	9:29 am	**6:29 am**	
☽♎ △ ♀ ≈	11:47 am	**8:47 am**	
☽♎ ⚻ ☿ ♓	11:54 pm	**8:54 pm**	
☽♎ ⚻ ☉ ♓		**11:06 pm**	

27 Tue
3rd ♎

☽♎ ⚻ ☉ ♓	2:06 am		
♂≈ □ ♃ ♉	3:30 am	**12:30 am**	
☽♎ ⚻ ♄ ♓	4:59 am	**1:59 am**	
☽♎ ⚻ ♃ ♉	7:38 am	**4:38 am**	
☽♎ △ ♂ ≈	7:51 am	**4:51 am**	
☽♎ △ ♀ ≈	1:22 pm	**10:22 am**	☽ v/c
☽♎ ☍ ♅ ♈	8:16 pm	**5:16 pm**	
☽♎ ⚻ ♅ ♉		**10:06 pm**	

28 Wed
3rd ♎

☽♎ ⚻ ♅ ♉	1:06 am		
☉♓ ☌ ☿ ♓	3:43 am	**12:43 am**	
☿♓ ☌ ♄ ♓	10:08 am	**7:08 am**	
☽♎ ⚻ ♆ ♓	3:32 pm	**12:32 pm**	
☉♓ ☌ ♄ ♓	4:25 pm	**1:25 pm**	
☽ enters ♏	10:09 pm	**7:09 pm**	
☽♏ □ ♀ ≈		**9:33 pm**	

29 Thu
3rd ♏
Leap Day

☽♏ □ ♀ ≈	12:33 am		
☿♓ ✶ ♃ ♉	4:53 am	**1:53 am**	
☽♏ △ ♄ ♓	5:52 pm	**2:52 pm**	
☽♏ △ ☉ ♓	7:53 pm	**4:53 pm**	
☽♏ ☍ ♃ ♉	8:40 pm	**5:40 pm**	
☽♏ △ ☿ ♓	11:18 pm	**8:18 pm**	
☽♏ □ ♂ ≈		**9:08 pm**	

☽♏ □ ♂♒ 12:08 am
☉♓ ✶ ♃♉ 7:15 am **4:15 am**
☽♏ □ ♀♒ 8:09 am **5:09 am**
☽♏ ⊼ ♅♈ 8:19 am **5:19 am**
♀♒ ✶ ♅♈ 9:58 am **6:58 am**
☽♏ ☍ ♅♉ 12:53 pm **9:53 am**

☽♏ △ ♆♓ 11:47 pm ☽ v/c

FRI 1
3rd ♏

OP: After Moon opposes Uranus today until v/c Moon today or on Saturday. Wait two hours after the opposition to avoid anxiety and use this watery OP to process emotions and attune to your inner world. Participate and get together with others who share your values and ideals.

☽♏ △ ♆♓ 2:47 am ☽ v/c
☽ enters ♐ 8:56 am **5:56 am**
☽♐ ✶ ♀♒ 11:20 am **8:20 am**

SAT 2
3rd ♏

☽♐ □ ♄♓ 4:12 am **1:12 am**
☽♐ ⊼ ♃♉ 7:04 am **4:04 am**
♀♒ □ ♅♉ 8:17 am **5:17 am**
☽♐ □ ☉♓ 10:23 am **7:23 am**
☽♐ ✶ ♂♒ 1:11 pm **10:11 am**
☽♐ △ ♅♈ 5:28 pm **2:28 pm**
☽♐ □ ☿♓ 6:39 pm **3:39 pm**
☽♐ ⊼ ♅♉ 9:39 pm **6:39 pm**
☽♐ ✶ ♀♒ 11:01 pm **8:01 pm**

SUN 3
3rd ♐
◗ 4th Quarter 13 ♐ 32

Eastern Standard Time (EST) plain / **Pacific Standard Time (PST) bold**

FEBRUARY								MARCH								APRIL					
S	M	T	W	T	F	S		S	M	T	W	T	F	S		S	M	T	W	T	F	S
				1	2	3							1	2			1	2	3	4	5	6
4	5	6	7	8	9	10		3	4	5	6	7	8	9		7	8	9	10	11	12	13
11	12	13	14	15	16	17		10	11	12	13	14	15	16		14	15	16	17	18	19	20
18	19	20	21	22	23	24		17	18	19	20	21	22	23		21	22	23	24	25	26	27
25	26	27	28	29				24	25	26	27	28	29	30		28	29	30				
								31														

March

4 Mon
4th ♐

OP: After Moon enters Capricorn today until v/c Moon on **Wednesday.** Long OP great for high productivity and constructive work.

☽♐ □ ♆♓ 10:41 am **7:41 am** ☽ v/c
☿♓ ⚹ ♅♉ 3:24 pm **12:24 pm**
☽ enters ♑ 4:15 pm **1:15 pm**

5 Tue
4th ♑

☽♑ ⚹ ♄♓ 10:38 am **7:38 am**
☽♑ △ ♃♉ 1:30 pm **10:30 am**
☽♑ ⚹ ☉♓ 8:01 pm **5:01 pm**
☽♑ □ ♇♈ 10:40 pm **7:40 pm**
☽♑ △ ♅♉ **11:28 pm**

6 Wed
4th ♑

☽♑ △ ♅♉ 2:28 am
☽♑ ⚹ ☿♓ 7:54 am **4:54 am**
☽♑ ⚹ ♆♓ 2:35 pm **11:35 am** ☽ v/c
♂≈ ⚹ ♇♈ 6:04 pm **3:04 pm**
☽ enters ≈ 7:38 pm **4:38 pm**
☽≈ ☌ ♀≈ 9:54 pm **6:54 pm**

7 Thu
4th ≈

☽≈ □ ♃♉ 4:08 pm **1:08 pm**
☽≈ ⚹ ♇♈ **9:18 pm**
☽≈ ☌ ♂≈ **10:51 pm**

☽≈ ⚹ ♅♈ 12:18 am
☽≈ ☌ ♂≈ 1:51 am
☽≈ □ ♅♉ 3:50 am **12:50 am**
☿♓ ☌ ♆♓ 10:06 am **7:06 am**
☽≈ ☌ ♀≈ 1:56 pm **10:56 am** ☽ v/c
☽ enters ♓ 8:03 pm **5:03 pm**

FRI 8
4th ≈

OP: After Moon squares Uranus until v/c Moon. A friendly Friday morning to socialize and spend time with others.

☽♓ ☌ ♄♓ 1:23 pm **10:23 am**
☽♓ ⚹ ♃♉ 4:24 pm **1:24 pm**
♂≈ □ ♅♉ 5:55 pm **2:55 pm**
☉♓ ⚹ ♅♉ 6:01 pm **3:01 pm**
☿ enters ♈ 11:03 pm **8:03 pm**

SAT 9
4th ♓

☽♓ ⚹ ♅♉ 4:22 am **12:22 am**
☽♓ ☌ ☉♓ 5:00 am **1:00 am**
☽♓ ☌ ♆♓ 3:45 pm **12:45 pm** ☽ v/c
☿♈ ⚹ ♀≈ 6:21 pm **3:21 pm**
☽ enters ♈ 8:19 pm **5:19 pm**
☽♈ ⚹ ♀≈ 10:38 pm **7:38 pm**
☽♈ ☌ ☿♈ 11:15 pm **8:15 pm**

SUN 10
4th ♓
● New Moon 20 ♓ 17
DAYLIGHT SAVING TIME BEGINS AT 2:00 A.M.
RAMADAN BEGINS AT SUNDOWN

OP: This Cazimi Moon is usable ½ hour before and ½ hour after the Sun-Moon conjunction. If you have something important to start around now, this is a great time to do it.

OP: After Moon conjoins Mercury today until v/c Moon on Tuesday. Channel your energy and enthusiasm into your new ventures under this positive New Moon.

Eastern Standard Time (EST) becomes Eastern Daylight Time (EDT) March 10 (plain)
Pacific Standard Time (PST) becomes Pacific Daylight Time (PDT) March 10 (bold)

FEBRUARY						
S	M	T	W	T	F	S
				1	2	3
4	5	6	7	8	9	10
11	12	13	14	15	16	17
18	19	20	21	22	23	24
25	26	27	28	29		

MARCH						
S	M	T	W	T	F	S
					1	2
3	4	5	6	7	8	9
10	11	12	13	14	15	16
17	18	19	20	21	22	23
24	25	26	27	28	29	30
31						

APRIL						
S	M	T	W	T	F	S
	1	2	3	4	5	6
7	8	9	10	11	12	13
14	15	16	17	18	19	20
21	22	23	24	25	26	27
28	29	30				

March

11 Mon
1st ♈

♀ enters ♓	5:50 pm	**2:50 pm**
☽♈ ☌ ⚷♈		**9:41 pm**

12 Tue
1st ♈

☽♈ ☌ ⚷♈	12:41 am	
☽♈ ✶ ♂♒	7:08 am	**4:08 am** ☽ v/c
☽ enters ♉	8:28 pm	**5:28 pm**
☽♉ ✶ ♀♓	10:56 pm	**7:56 pm**
☽♉ □ ♇♒	10:57 pm	**7:57 pm**

13 Wed
1st ♉

☽♉ ✶ ♄♓	3:30 pm	**12:30 pm**
☽♉ ☌ ♃♉	7:13 pm	**4:13 pm**

14 Thu
1st ♉

OP: After Moon sextiles the Sun until Moon enters Gemini. (Taurus is one of the four signs in which the v/c Moon is a good thing. See page 79.) An excellent OP for the arts, romance, or even earthy, practical matters.

☽♉ ☌ ♅♉	6:00 am	**3:00 am**
☽♉ □ ♂♒	12:01 pm	**9:01 am**
☽♉ ✶ ☉♓	1:57 pm	**10:57 am**
☽♉ ✶ ♆♓	6:29 pm	**3:29 pm** ☽ v/c
☽ enters ♊	11:16 pm	**8:16 pm**
☽♊ △ ♇♒		**11:00 pm**

Fri 15
1st ♊

☽♊ △ ♇♒ 2:00 am
☽♊ □ ♀♓ 6:59 am **3:59 am**
☽♊ ⚹ ☿♈ 6:11 pm **3:11 pm**
☽♊ □ ♄♓ 8:06 pm **5:06 pm**

Sat 16
1st ♊
◐ 2nd Quarter 27 ♊ 04 (Pacific)

☽♊ ⚹ ⚷♈ 7:33 am **4:33 am**
☽♊ △ ♂♒ 9:02 pm **6:02 pm**
☽♊ □ ☉♓ **9:11 pm**
☽♊ □ ♆♓ **9:43 pm** ☽ v/c

Sun 17
1st ♊
◐ 2nd Quarter 27 ♊ 04 (Eastern)
St. Patrick's Day

☽♊ □ ☉♓ 12:11 am
☽♊ □ ♆♓ 12:43 am ☽ v/c
☽ enters ♋ 5:40 am **2:40 am**
☉♓ ☌ ♆♓ 7:22 am **4:22 am**
☽♋ ⚻ ♇♒ 8:42 am **5:42 am**
☽♋ △ ♀♓ 7:55 pm **4:55 pm**

Eastern Daylight Time (EDT) plain / **Pacific Daylight Time (PDT) bold**

FEBRUARY

S	M	T	W	T	F	S
				1	2	3
4	5	6	7	8	9	10
11	12	13	14	15	16	17
18	19	20	21	22	23	24
25	26	27	28	29		

MARCH

S	M	T	W	T	F	S
					1	2
3	4	5	6	7	8	9
10	11	12	13	14	15	16
17	18	19	20	21	22	23
24	25	26	27	28	29	30
31						

APRIL

S	M	T	W	T	F	S
	1	2	3	4	5	6
7	8	9	10	11	12	13
14	15	16	17	18	19	20
21	22	23	24	25	26	27
28	29	30				

MARCH

Mercury Note: Mercury enters its Storm (moving less than 40 minutes of arc per day) on Thursday, as it slows down before going retrograde. The Storm acts like the retrograde. Not favorable to start new projects—just follow through with the items that are already on your plate. Write down new ideas with date and time they occurred.

18 MON
2nd ♋

OP: After Moon squares Mercury today until Moon enters Leo on Tuesday. You have more than 24 hours to take advantage of this great waxing Moon OP! Your last chance before Mercury enters its Storm and turns retrograde.

☽♋ △ ♄♓	4:29 am	**1:29 am**
☽♋ ⚹ ♃♉	9:24 am	**6:24 am**
☽♋ □ ☿♈	10:29 am	**7:29 am**
☽♋ □ ♅♈	4:24 pm	**1:24 pm**
☽♋ ⚹ ♅♉	8:20 pm	**5:20 pm**

19 TUE
2nd ♋

SPRING EQUINOX
OSTARA
SUN ENTERS ARIES
INTERNATIONAL ASTROLOGY DAY

☽♋ ⚻ ♂♒	10:20 am	**7:20 am**
☽♋ △ ♆♓	10:30 am	**7:30 am**
☽♋ △ ☉♓	2:52 pm	**11:52 am** ☽ v/c
☽ enters ♌	3:33 pm	**12:33 pm**
☽♌ ☍ ♀♒	6:49 pm	**3:49 pm**
☉ enters ♈	11:06 pm	**8:06 pm**

20 WED
2nd ♌

☽♌ ⚻ ♀♓	1:13 pm	**10:13 am**
☿♈ ♂ ♅♈	1:27 pm	**10:27 am**
☽♌ ⚻ ♄♓	4:02 pm	**1:02 pm**
☽♌ □ ♃♉	9:35 pm	**6:35 pm**

21 THU
2nd ♌

☽♌ △ ♅♈	4:07 am	**1:07 am**
☽♌ △ ☿♈	5:57 am	**2:57 am**
☽♌ □ ♅♉	8:07 am	**5:07 am**
☉♈ ⚹ ♀♒	4:03 pm	**1:03 pm**
♀♓ ♂ ♄♓	7:09 pm	**4:09 pm**
☽♌ ⚻ ♆♓	10:42 pm	**7:42 pm**
☽♌ ☍ ♂♒		**11:34 pm** ☽ v/c

☽♌ ☌ ♂♒	2:34 am	☽ v/c
☽ enters ♍	3:42 am **12:42 am**	
☽♍ ⚻ ♀♒	7:09 am **4:09 am**	
☽♍ ⚻ ☉♈	8:30 am **5:30 am**	
♂ enters ♓	7:47 pm **4:47 pm**	

FRI 22
2nd ♌

☽♍ ☌ ♄♓	5:17 am **2:17 am**	
☽♍ ☌ ♀♓	8:54 am **5:54 am**	
☽♍ △ ♃♉	11:22 am **8:22 am**	
☽♍ ⚻ ♅♈	5:13 pm **2:13 pm**	
☽♍ △ ♅♉	9:10 pm **6:10 pm**	
☽♍ ⚻ ☿♈	**10:37 pm**	

SAT 23
2nd ♍
PURIM BEGINS AT SUNDOWN

☽♍ ⚻ ☿♈	1:37 am	
☽♍ ☌ ♆♓	11:49 am **8:49 am** ☽ v/c	
♀♓ ⚹ ♃♉	12:37 pm **9:37 am**	
☽ enters ♎	4:37 pm **1:37 pm**	
☽♎ ⚻ ♂♓	7:47 pm **4:47 pm**	
☽♎ △ ♀♒	8:11 pm **5:11 pm**	

SUN 24
2nd ♍
PALM SUNDAY

Eastern Daylight Time (EDT) plain / **Pacific Daylight Time (PDT) bold**

FEBRUARY							MARCH							APRIL						
S	M	T	W	T	F	S	S	M	T	W	T	F	S	S	M	T	W	T	F	S
				1	2	3						1	2		1	2	3	4	5	6
4	5	6	7	8	9	10	3	4	5	6	7	8	9	7	8	9	10	11	12	13
11	12	13	14	15	16	17	10	11	12	13	14	15	16	14	15	16	17	18	19	20
18	19	20	21	22	23	24	17	18	19	20	21	22	23	21	22	23	24	25	26	27
25	26	27	28	29			24	25	26	27	28	29	30	28	29	30				
							31													

25 Mon
2nd ♎︎
Lunar Eclipse | ○ Full Moon 5 ♎︎ 07

☽♎︎ ☍ ☉♈︎	3:00 am	**12:00 am**
☽♎︎ ⚻ ♄♓︎	6:45 pm	**3:45 pm**
☽♎︎ ⚻ ♃♉︎		**10:15 pm**

26 Tue
3rd ♎︎

☽♎︎ ⚻ ♃♉︎	1:15 am	
☽♎︎ ⚻ ♀♓︎	4:47 am	**1:47 am**
☽♎︎ ☍ ♀♈︎	6:16 am	**3:16 am**
☽♎︎ ⚻ ♅♉︎	10:06 am	**7:06 am**
☽♎︎ ☍ ☿♈︎	7:09 pm	**4:09 pm** ☽ v/c
☽♎︎ ⚻ ♆♓︎		**9:31 pm**

27 Wed
3rd ♎︎

☽♎︎ ⚻ ♆♓︎	12:31 am	
☽ enters ♏︎	5:03 am	**2:03 am**
☽♏︎ □ ♀≈	8:37 am	**5:37 am**
☽♏︎ △ ♂♓︎	12:18 pm	**9:18 am**
☽♏︎ ⚻ ☉♈︎	8:35 pm	**5:35 pm**

28 Thu
3rd ♏︎

OP: After Moon opposes Uranus today until v/c Moon on Friday. Good for romance and deep emotional experiences, but we're between two eclipses and Mercury is slow, so keep it flexible.

☽♏︎ △ ♄♓︎	7:11 am	**4:11 am**
♀♓︎ ⚹ ♅♉︎	9:58 am	**6:58 am**
☽♏︎ ☍ ♃♉︎	1:59 pm	**10:59 am**
☽♏︎ ⚻ ♀♈︎	6:06 pm	**3:06 pm**
☽♏︎ ☍ ♅♉︎	9:46 pm	**6:46 pm**
☽♏︎ △ ♀♓︎	11:02 pm	**8:02 pm**

☽♏ ⚺ ☿♈ 9:10 am **6:10 am**

☽♏ △ ♆♓ 11:40 am **8:40 am** ☽ v/c
☽ enters ♐ 3:52 pm **12:52 pm**
☽♐ ⚹ ♀≈ 7:23 pm **4:23 pm**
☽♐ □ ♂♓ **11:43 pm**

FRI 29
3rd ♏
GOOD FRIDAY

☽♐ □ ♂♓ 2:43 am
☽♐ △ ☉♈ 11:44 am **8:44 am**
☽♐ □ ♄♓ 5:29 pm **2:29 pm**
☽♐ ⚺ ♃♉ **9:26 pm**

SAT 30
3rd ♐

☽♐ ⚺ ♃♉ 12:26 am
☽♐ △ ♅♈ 3:39 am **12:39 am**
☽♐ ⚺ ♅♉ 7:06 am **4:06 am**
☽♐ □ ♀♓ 2:06 pm **11:06 am**
☽♐ △ ☿♈ 6:54 pm **3:54 pm**
☽♐ □ ♆♓ 8:16 pm **5:16 pm** ☽ v/c
☽ enters ♑ **9:05 pm**

SUN 31
3rd ♐
EASTER

Eastern Daylight Time (EDT) plain / **Pacific Daylight Time (PDT) bold**

FEBRUARY						
S	M	T	W	T	F	S
				1	2	3
4	5	6	7	8	9	10
11	12	13	14	15	16	17
18	19	20	21	22	23	24
25	26	27	28	29		

MARCH						
S	M	T	W	T	F	S
					1	2
3	4	5	6	7	8	9
10	11	12	13	14	15	16
17	18	19	20	21	22	23
24	25	26	27	28	29	30
31						

APRIL						
S	M	T	W	T	F	S
	1	2	3	4	5	6
7	8	9	10	11	12	13
14	15	16	17	18	19	20
21	22	23	24	25	26	27
28	29	30				

APRIL

Mercury Note: Mercury goes retrograde on Monday, April 1, and remains so until April 25, after which it will still be in its Storm until May 4. Projects initiated during this entire period may not work out as planned. It's best to use this time for reviews, editing, escrows, and so forth.

1 MON

3rd ♐

◖ 4th Quarter 12 ♑ 52

APRIL FOOLS' DAY

MERCURY RETROGRADE

☽ enters ♑	12:05 am	
☽♑ ⚹ ♂♓	1:49 pm	**10:49 am**
☿℞	6:14 pm	**3:14 pm**
☽♑ □ ☉♈	11:15 pm	**8:15 pm**
☽♑ ⚹ ♄♓		**9:46 pm**

2 TUE

4th ♑

OP: After Moon squares Mercury today or on Wednesday until v/c Moon today or on Wednesday. Short OP good for anything, from practical matters to deep romance.

☽♑ ⚹ ♄♓	12:46 am	
☽♑ △ ♃♉	7:44 am	**4:44 am**
☽♑ □ ♅♈	10:08 am	**7:08 am**
☽♑ △ ♅♉	1:20 pm	**10:20 am**
☽♑ □ ☿♈		**9:11 pm**
☽♑ ⚹ ♀♓		**9:58 pm**
☽♑ ⚹ ♆♓		**10:40 pm** ☽ v/c

3 WED

4th ♑

☽♑ □ ☿♈	12:11 am	
☽♑ ⚹ ♀♓	12:58 am	
☽♑ ⚹ ♆♓	1:40 am	☽ v/c
☽ enters ♒	5:08 am	**2:08 am**
☽♒ ♂ ♀♒	8:23 am	**5:23 am**
♀♓ ♂ ♆♓	9:10 am	**6:10 am**

4 THU

4th ♒

OP: After Moon squares Uranus today until v/c Moon today or on Friday. Great afternoon for brainstorming and innovative ideas.

☽♒ ⚹ ☉♈	6:45 am	**3:45 am**
☽♒ □ ♃♉	11:43 am	**8:43 am**
☽♒ ⚹ ♅♈	1:25 pm	**10:25 am**
☽♒ □ ♅♉	4:24 pm	**1:24 pm**
♀ enters ♈		**9:00 pm**
☽♒ ⚹ ☿♈		**10:40 pm** ☽ v/c

♀ enters ♈	12:00 am	
☽≈ ✶ ☿♈	1:40 am	☽ v/c
☽ enters ♓	7:13 am	**4:13 am**
☽♓ ♂ ♂♓		**10:08 pm**

Fri 5
4th ≈

☽♓ ♂ ♂♓	1:08 am	
☽♓ ♂ ♄♓	6:10 am	**3:10 am**
☽♓ ✶ ♃♉	1:13 pm	**10:13 am**
♀♈ ✶ ♇≈	1:46 pm	**10:46 am**
☽♓ ✶ ♅♉	5:11 pm	**2:11 pm**

Sat 6
4th ♓

OP: After Moon sextiles Jupiter today until Moon enters Aries on Sunday. (See "Translating Darkness" on page 82.) Great time to relax and have fun, as it's during the Last Quarter Moon and Mercury is retrograde.

☽♓ ♂ ♆♓	4:27 am	**1:27 am** ☽ v/c
☽ enters ♈	7:25 am	**4:25 am**
☽♈ ✶ ♇≈	10:31 am	**7:31 am**
☽♈ ♂ ♀♈	12:22 pm	**9:22 am**

Sun 7
4th ♓

Eastern Daylight Time (EDT) plain / **Pacific Daylight Time (PDT) bold**

	MARCH							APRIL							MAY					
S	M	T	W	T	F	S	S	M	T	W	T	F	S	S	M	T	W	T	F	S
					1	2		1	2	3	4	5	6				1	2	3	4
3	4	5	6	7	8	9	7	8	9	10	11	12	13	5	6	7	8	9	10	11
10	11	12	13	14	15	16	14	15	16	17	18	19	20	12	13	14	15	16	17	18
17	18	19	20	21	22	23	21	22	23	24	25	26	27	19	20	21	22	23	24	25
24	25	26	27	28	29	30	28	29	30					26	27	28	29	30	31	
31																				

8 MON
4th ♈

Solar Eclipse | ● New Moon 19 ♈ 24

☽♈ ♂ ☉♈	2:21 pm	**11:21 am**
☽♈ ♂ ♋♈	2:21 pm	**11:21 am**
☉♈ ♂ ♋♈	2:28 pm	**11:28 am**
☽♈ ♂ ☿♈	10:39 pm	**7:39 pm** ☽ v/c

9 TUE
1st ♈

RAMADAN ENDS

☽ enters ♉	7:23 am	**4:23 am**
☽♉ □ ♇≈	10:35 am	**7:35 am**

10 WED
1st ♉

OP: After Moon conjoins Uranus today until Moon enters Gemini on Thursday. Keep it real during this OP with Moon in Taurus and focus on practical matters.

☽♉ ✳ ♂♓	6:49 am	**3:49 am**
☽♉ ✳ ♄♓	7:16 am	**4:16 am**
☽♉ ♂ ♃♉	3:19 pm	**12:19 pm**
♂♓ ♂ ♄♓	4:36 pm	**1:36 pm**
☽♉ ♂ ♅♉	6:18 pm	**3:18 pm**

11 THU
1st ♉

☽♉ ✳ ♆♓	6:04 am	**3:04 am** ☽ v/c
☽ enters ♊	8:59 am	**5:59 am**
☽♊ △ ♇≈	12:23 pm	**9:23 am**
☉♈ ♂ ☿♈	7:03 pm	**4:03 pm**
☽♊ ✳ ♀♈	11:47 pm	**8:47 pm**

Fri 12
1st ♊

☽♊ □ ♄♓	10:39 am	**7:39 am**
☽♊ □ ♂♓	12:51 pm	**9:51 am**
☽♊ ⚹ ⚷♈	7:07 pm	**4:07 pm**
☽♊ ⚹ ☿♈	10:43 pm	**7:43 pm**
☽♊ ⚹ ☉♈		**11:35 pm**

Sat 13
1st ♊

☽♊ ⚹ ☉♈	2:35 am	
☽♊ □ ♆♓	10:46 am	**7:46 am** ☽ v/c
☽ enters ♋	1:45 pm	**10:45 am**
☽♋ ⚻ ♇♒	5:26 pm	**2:26 pm**

Sun 14
1st ♋

☽♋ □ ♀♈	11:24 am	**8:24 am**
☽♋ △ ♄♓	5:48 pm	**2:48 pm**
☽♋ △ ♂♓	11:17 pm	**8:17 pm**
☽♋ □ ⚷♈		**11:42 pm**

Eastern Daylight Time (EDT) plain / **Pacific Daylight Time (PDT) bold**

MARCH

S	M	T	W	T	F	S
					1	2
3	4	5	6	7	8	9
10	11	12	13	14	15	16
17	18	19	20	21	22	23
24	25	26	27	28	29	30
31						

APRIL

S	M	T	W	T	F	S
	1	2	3	4	5	6
7	8	9	10	11	12	13
14	15	16	17	18	19	20
21	22	23	24	25	26	27
28	29	30				

MAY

S	M	T	W	T	F	S
			1	2	3	4
5	6	7	8	9	10	11
12	13	14	15	16	17	18
19	20	21	22	23	24	25
26	27	28	29	30	31	

15 Mon

1st ♋

● 2nd Quarter 26 ♋ 18

OP: After Moon squares the Sun until Moon enters Leo. (Cancer is one of the four signs in which the v/c Moon is a good thing. See page 79.) Mercury is retrograde, so use this time to review and edit ongoing projects or reconnect with people from the past.

☽♋ □ ⚷♈	2:42 am		
☽♋ □ ☿♈	3:12 am	**12:12 am**	
☽♋ ✶ ♃♉	4:05 am	**1:05 am**	
☽♋ ✶ ♅♉	6:01 am	**3:01 am**	
☿♈ ♂ ⚷♈	11:23 am	**8:23 am**	
☽♋ □ ☉♈	3:13 pm	**12:13 pm**	
☽♋ △ ♆♓	7:22 pm	**4:22 pm**	☽ v/c
☽ enters ♌	10:24 pm	**7:24 pm**	
☽♌ ☍ ♀≈		**11:23 pm**	

16 Tue

2nd ♌

☽♌ ☍ ♀≈	2:23 am		

17 Wed

2nd ♌

OP: After Moon squares Uranus today until v/c Moon on Thursday. Self-motivation, creative activity, and building rapport with others will produce good results during this short OP.

☽♌ △ ♀♈	4:03 am	**1:03 am**
☽♌ ⊼ ♄♓	4:42 am	**1:42 am**
☽♌ △ ☿♈	11:01 am	**8:01 am**
☽♌ △ ⚷♈	1:53 pm	**10:53 am**
☽♌ ⊼ ♂♓	2:04 pm	**11:04 am**
☽♌ □ ♃♉	4:11 pm	**1:11 pm**
☽♌ □ ♅♉	5:20 pm	**2:20 pm**

18 Thu

2nd ♌

☽♌ ⊼ ♆♓	7:12 am	**4:12 am**	
☽♌ △ ☉♈	8:02 am	**5:02 am**	☽ v/c
☽ enters ♍	10:10 am	**7:10 am**	
☽♍ ⊼ ♀≈	2:20 pm	**11:20 am**	

Fri 19
2nd ♍
Sun enters Taurus

☿♈ ☌ ♀♈	4:59 am	**1:59 am**
☉ enters ♉	10:00 am	**7:00 am**
♂♓ ⚹ ♃♉	11:28 am	**8:28 am**
☽♍ ☍ ♄♓	5:53 pm	**2:53 pm**
♂♓ ⚹ ♅♉	7:56 pm	**4:56 pm**
☽♍ ⚻ ☿♈	9:10 pm	**6:10 pm**
☽♍ ⚻ ♀♈	11:47 pm	**8:47 pm**
☽♍ ⚻ ⚷♈		**11:59 pm**

Sat 20
2nd ♍

☽♍ ⚻ ⚷♈	2:59 am	
☽♍ △ ♃♉	6:14 am	**3:14 am**
☽♍ △ ♅♉	6:28 am	**3:28 am**
☽♍ ☍ ♂♓	7:09 am	**4:09 am**
☽♍ ☍ ♆♓	8:20 pm	**5:20 pm** ☽ v/c
♃♉ ☌ ♅♉	10:27 pm	**7:27 pm**
☽ enters ♎	11:08 pm	**8:08 pm**
☽♎ ⚻ ☉♉		**11:28 pm**

Sun 21
2nd ♎

☽♎ ⚻ ☉♉	2:28 am	
☽♎ △ ♇♒	3:20 am	**12:20 am**
♀♈ ☌ ⚷♈	7:49 am	**4:49 am**
☉♉ □ ♇♒	1:02 pm	**10:02 am**

Eastern Daylight Time (EDT) plain / **Pacific Daylight Time (PDT) bold**

MARCH

S	M	T	W	T	F	S
					1	2
3	4	5	6	7	8	9
10	11	12	13	14	15	16
17	18	19	20	21	22	23
24	25	26	27	28	29	30
31						

APRIL

S	M	T	W	T	F	S
	1	2	3	4	5	6
7	8	9	10	11	12	13
14	15	16	17	18	19	20
21	22	23	24	25	26	27
28	29	30				

MAY

S	M	T	W	T	F	S
			1	2	3	4
5	6	7	8	9	10	11
12	13	14	15	16	17	18
19	20	21	22	23	24	25
26	27	28	29	30	31	

APRIL

Mercury Note: Mercury goes direct on Thursday, April 25, but remains in its Storm, moving slowly, until May 4.

22 MON
2nd ♎︎
EARTH DAY
PASSOVER BEGINS AT SUNDOWN

☽ ♎︎ ⚻ ♄ ♓︎	7:08 am	**4:08 am**
☽ ♎︎ ☍ ☿ ♈︎	8:10 am	**5:10 am**
☽ ♎︎ ☍ ♀ ♈︎	3:54 pm	**12:54 pm**
☽ ♎︎ ⚻ ♅ ♉︎	7:18 pm	**4:18 pm**
☽ ♎︎ ☍ ♀ ♈︎	7:24 pm	**4:24 pm** ☽ v/c
☽ ♎︎ ⚻ ♃ ♉︎	7:58 pm	**4:58 pm**
☽ ♎︎ ⚻ ♂ ♓︎	11:51 pm	**8:51 pm**

23 TUE
2nd ♎︎
○ Full Moon 4 ♏︎ 18

☽ ♎︎ ⚻ ♆ ♓︎	8:45 am	**5:45 am**
☽ enters ♏︎	11:20 am	**8:20 am**
☽ ♏︎ □ ♇ ♒︎	3:27 pm	**12:27 pm**
☽ ♏︎ ☍ ☉ ♉︎	7:49 pm	**4:49 pm**

24 WED
3rd ♏︎

☽ ♏︎ ⚻ ☿ ♈︎	6:41 pm	**3:41 pm**
☽ ♏︎ △ ♄ ♓︎	6:52 pm	**3:52 pm**

25 THU
3rd ♏︎
MERCURY DIRECT
OP: After Moon opposes Jupiter until v/c Moon. Take advantage of Mercury stationing direct during this OP to plan and chart a new path.

☽ ♏︎ ⚻ ♀ ♈︎	3:09 am	**12:09 am**
☽ ♏︎ ☍ ♅ ♉︎	6:26 am	**3:26 am**
☽ ♏︎ ☍ ♃ ♉︎	7:55 am	**4:55 am**
☿ D	8:54 am	**5:54 am**
☽ ♏︎ ⚻ ♀ ♈︎	12:42 pm	**9:42 am**
☽ ♏︎ △ ♂ ♓︎	2:25 pm	**11:25 am**
☽ ♏︎ △ ♆ ♓︎	7:17 pm	**4:17 pm** ☽ v/c
☽ enters ♐︎	9:37 pm	**6:37 pm**
☽ ♐︎ ⚹ ♇ ♒︎		**10:36 pm**

☽♐ ⚹ ♀≈ 1:36 am
☽♐ ⊼ ☉♉ 10:36 am **7:36 am**

Fri 26
3rd ♐

☽♐ △ ☿♈ 3:59 am **12:59 am**
☽♐ □ ♄♓ 4:21 am **1:21 am**
☽♐ △ ♃♈ 12:10 pm **9:10 am**
☽♐ ⊼ ♅♉ 3:18 pm **12:18 pm**
☽♐ ⊼ ♆♉ 5:30 pm **2:30 pm**
☽♐ □ ♂♓ **11:15 pm**
☽♐ △ ♀♈ **11:56 pm**

Sat 27
3rd ♐

☽♐ □ ♂♓ 2:15 am
☽♐ △ ♀♈ 2:56 am
☽♐ □ ♆♓ 3:31 am **12:31 am** ☽ v/c
☽ enters ♑ 5:37 am **2:37 am**
☽♑ △ ☉♉ 10:28 pm **7:28 pm**
♂♓ ♂ ♆♓ **9:31 pm**

Sun 28
3rd ♐

·

Eastern Daylight Time (EDT) plain / **Pacific Daylight Time (PDT) bold**

		MARCH								APRIL							MAY			
S	M	T	W	T	F	S	S	M	T	W	T	F	S	S	M	T	W	T	F	S
					1	2		1	2	3	4	5	6				1	2	3	4
3	4	5	6	7	8	9	7	8	9	10	11	12	13	5	6	7	8	9	10	11
10	11	12	13	14	15	16	14	15	16	17	18	19	20	12	13	14	15	16	17	18
17	18	19	20	21	22	23	21	22	23	24	25	26	27	19	20	21	22	23	24	25
24	25	26	27	28	29	30	28	29	30					26	27	28	29	30	31	
31																				

29 Mon
3rd ♑

OP: After Moon squares Mercury today until v/c Moon on Tuesday. Very positive OP ideal for constructive and innovative projects, but Mercury is slow and the Moon is waning, so it is preferable to focus on work started before late March.

♂♓ ♂ ♆♓	12:31 am		
♀ enters ♉	7:31 am	**4:31 am**	
☽♑ ⚹ ♄♓	11:28 am	**8:28 am**	
☽♑ □ ☿♈	11:45 am	**8:45 am**	
☽♑ □ ☊♈	6:49 pm	**3:49 pm**	
☽♑ △ ♅♉	9:49 pm	**6:49 pm**	
☽♑ △ ♃♉		**9:39 pm**	

30 Tue
3rd ♑
Passover ends

☽♑ △ ♃♉	12:39 am		
☽♑ ⚹ ♆♓	9:25 am	**6:25 am**	
☽♑ ⚹ ♂♓	11:19 am	**8:19 am**	☽ v/c
☽ enters ♒	11:20 am	**8:20 am**	
♂ enters ♈	11:33 am	**8:33 am**	
☽♒ □ ♀♉	2:04 pm	**11:04 am**	
☽♒ ♂ ♀♒	3:00 pm	**12:00 pm**	
♀♉ □ ♀♒		**9:30 pm**	

1 Wed
3rd ♒
◑ 4th Quarter 11 ♒ 35
Beltane

♀♉ □ ♀♒	12:30 am		
☽♒ □ ☉♉	7:27 am	**4:27 am**	
☽♒ ⚹ ☿♈	5:48 pm	**2:48 pm**	
☽♒ ⚹ ☊♈	11:12 pm	**8:12 pm**	
☽♒ □ ♅♉		**11:06 pm**	

2 Thu
4th ♒
Pluto retrograde

☽♒ □ ♅♉	2:06 am		
☽♒ □ ♃♉	5:28 am	**2:28 am**	☽ v/c
♀℞	1:46 pm	**10:46 am**	
☽ enters ♓	2:52 pm	**11:52 am**	
☽♓ ⚹ ♀♉	10:21 pm	**7:21 pm**	

Mercury Note: Mercury finally leaves its Storm on Sunday. Look over your notes on any ideas that occurred to you while Mercury was retrograde or slow. How do they look now?

♂♈⚹♀♒	5:06 am	**2:06 am**
☽♓⚹☉♉	1:55 pm	**10:55 am**
☽♓☌♄♓	7:05 pm	**4:05 pm**

FRI 3
4th ♓
ORTHODOX GOOD FRIDAY

☽♓⚹♅♉	4:28 am	**1:28 am**
☽♓⚹♃♉	8:22 am	**5:22 am**
☽♓☌♆♓	3:06 pm	**12:06 pm** ☽ v/c
☽ enters ♈	4:41 pm	**1:41 pm**
☽♈⚹♀♒	8:08 pm	**5:08 pm**
☽♈☌♂♈	10:17 pm	**7:17 pm**

SAT 4
4th ♓
OP: After Moon sextiles Uranus until Moon enters Aries. This OP is favorable for the innovative arts, meditation, and helping others.

☽♈☌☿♈	**10:57 pm** ☽ v/c
☽♈☌♀♈	**11:59 pm**

SUN 5
4th ♈
CINCO DE MAYO
ORTHODOX EASTER

Eastern Daylight Time (EDT) plain / **Pacific Daylight Time (PDT) bold**

		APRIL							MAY							JUNE			
S	M	T	W	T	F	S	S	M	T	W	T	F	S	S	M	T	W	T	F	S
	1	2	3	4	5	6				1	2	3	4							1
7	8	9	10	11	12	13	5	6	7	8	9	10	11	2	3	4	5	6	7	8
14	15	16	17	18	19	20	12	13	14	15	16	17	18	9	10	11	12	13	14	15
21	22	23	24	25	26	27	19	20	21	22	23	24	25	16	17	18	19	20	21	22
28	29	30					26	27	28	29	30	31		23	24	25	26	27	28	29
														30						

May

6 Mon
4th ♈

☽♈ ☌ ☿♈	1:57 am		☽ v/c
☽♈ ☌ ♅♈	2:59 am		
☽ enters ♉	5:42 pm	2:42 pm	
☽♉ □ ♇≈	9:08 pm	6:08 pm	
☿♈ ☌ ♅♈	10:27 pm	7:27 pm	
☉ ⚹ ♄♓		10:42 pm	

7 Tue
4th ♉
● New Moon 18 ♉ 02

OP: This Cazimi Moon is usable ½ hour before and ½ hour after the Sun-Moon conjunction. If you have something important to start around now, this is a great time to do it.

☉♉ ⚹ ♄♓	1:42 am	
☽♉ ☌ ♀♉	10:05 am	7:05 am
☽♉ ⚹ ♄♓	10:02 pm	7:02 pm
☽♉ ☌ ☉♉	11:22 pm	8:22 pm

8 Wed
1st ♉

☽♉ ☌ ♅♉	7:19 am	4:19 am	
☽♉ ☌ ♃♉	12:30 pm	9:30 am	
☽♉ ⚹ ♆♓	5:55 pm	2:55 pm	☽ v/c
☽ enters ♊	7:20 pm	4:20 pm	
☽♊ △ ♇≈	10:52 pm	7:52 pm	

9 Thu
1st ♊

☽♊ ⚹ ♂♈	6:47 am	3:47 am
☽♊ □ ♄♓		10:03 pm

☽Ⅱ □ ♄♓	1:03 am	
☽Ⅱ ⚹ ⚷♈	7:43 am	**4:43 am**
☽Ⅱ ⚹ ☿♈	1:13 pm	**10:13 am**
☽Ⅱ □ ♆♓	9:49 pm	**6:49 pm** ☽ v/c
☽ enters ♋	11:13 pm	**8:13 pm**
☽♋ ⚻ ♀≈		**11:57 pm**

Fri 10
1st Ⅱ

☽♋ ⚻ ♀≈	2:57 am	
☽♋ □ ♂♈	2:36 pm	**11:36 am**

Sat 11
1st ♋

☽♋ ⚹ ♀♉	3:57 am	**12:57 am**
☽♋ △ ♄♓	7:11 am	**4:11 am**
☽♋ □ ⚷♈	2:13 pm	**11:13 am**
☽♋ ⚹ ☉♉	4:34 pm	**1:34 pm**
☽♋ ⚹ ♅♉	5:29 pm	**2:29 pm**
☽♋ ⚹ ♃♉		**9:52 pm**
☽♋ □ ☿♈		**9:56 pm**

Sun 12
1st ♋
Mother's Day

Eastern Daylight Time (EDT) plain / **Pacific Daylight Time (PDT) bold**

APRIL							MAY							JUNE						
S	M	T	W	T	F	S	S	M	T	W	T	F	S	S	M	T	W	T	F	S
	1	2	3	4	5	6				1	2	3	4							1
7	8	9	10	11	12	13	5	6	7	8	9	10	11	2	3	4	5	6	7	8
14	15	16	17	18	19	20	12	13	14	15	16	17	18	9	10	11	12	13	14	15
21	22	23	24	25	26	27	19	20	21	22	23	24	25	16	17	18	19	20	21	22
28	29	30					26	27	28	29	30	31		23	24	25	26	27	28	29
														30						

MAY

13 MON
1st ♋

OP: After Moon squares Mercury on Sunday or today until Moon enters Leo today. A good time to try something new and break out of the routine, aided by the Sun-Uranus conjunction.

☽♋ ⚹ ♃♉	12:52 am	
☽♋ □ ☿♈	12:56 am	
☽♋ △ ♆♓	5:13 am	**2:13 am** ☽ v/c
☉♉ ☌ ♅♉	5:14 am	**2:14 am**
☽ enters ♌	6:36 am	**3:36 am**
☽♌ ☍ ♇≈	10:35 am	**7:35 am**
♀♉ ⚹ ♄♓	3:45 pm	**12:45 pm**
☽♌ △ ♂♈		**11:49 pm**

14 TUE
1st ♌

☽♌ △ ♂♈	2:49 am	
☽♌ ⚻ ♄♓	5:06 am	**2:06 pm**
☽♌ □ ♀♉	7:47 pm	**4:47 pm**
☽♌ △ ⚷♈		**9:29 pm**

15 WED
1st ♌
◐ 2nd Quarter 25 ♌ 08

☽♌ △ ⚷♈	12:29 am	
☽♌ □ ♅♉	3:58 am	**12:58 am**
☽♌ □ ☉♉	7:48 am	**4:48 am**
☽♌ □ ♃♉	12:41 pm	**9:41 am** ☽ v/c
☿ enters ♉	1:05 pm	**10:05 am**
☽♌ ⚻ ♆♓	4:12 pm	**1:12 pm**
☽ enters ♍	5:33 pm	**2:33 pm**
☽♍ △ ☿♉	6:04 pm	**3:04 pm**
☽♍ ⚻ ♇≈	9:42 pm	**6:42 pm**

16 THU
2nd ♍

☽♍ ⚻ ♂♈	6:48 pm	**3:48 pm**

☿ ♉ □ ♀ ♒	3:44 am **12:44 am**	
☽ ♍ ☌ ♄ ♓	5:48 am **2:48 am**	
☽ ♍ ⊼ ♅ ♈	1:17 pm **10:17 am**	
☽ ♍ △ ♀ ♉	3:15 pm **12:15 pm**	
☽ ♍ △ ♅ ♉	4:53 pm **1:53 pm**	
☽ ♍ △ ☉ ♉	**10:53 pm**	
☽ ♍ △ ♃ ♉	**11:42 pm**	

FRI 17
2nd ♍

☽ ♍ △ ☉ ♉	1:53 am	
☽ ♍ △ ♃ ♉	2:42 am	
☽ ♍ ☌ ♆ ♓	5:09 am **2:09 am** ☽ v/c	
☽ enters ♎	6:23 am **3:23 am**	
♀ ♉ ☌ ♅ ♉	7:41 am **4:41 am**	
☽ ♎ △ ♀ ♒	10:32 am **7:32 am**	
☽ ♎ ⊼ ☿ ♉	2:29 pm **11:29 am**	
☉ ♉ ☌ ♃ ♉	2:45 pm **11:45 am**	

SAT 18
2nd ♍

☽ ♎ ☌ ♂ ♈	11:48 am **8:48 am** ☽ v/c	
☉ ♉ ⚹ ♆ ♓	6:45 pm **3:45 pm**	
☽ ♎ ⊼ ♄ ♓	6:52 pm **3:52 pm**	
☽ ♎ ☌ ♅ ♈	**11:09 pm**	

SUN 19
2nd ♎

Eastern Daylight Time (EDT) plain / **Pacific Daylight Time (PDT) bold**

	APRIL							MAY							JUNE					
S	M	T	W	T	F	S	S	M	T	W	T	F	S	S	M	T	W	T	F	S
	1	2	3	4	5	6			1	2	3	4								1
7	8	9	10	11	12	13	5	6	7	8	9	10	11	2	3	4	5	6	7	8
14	15	16	17	18	19	20	12	13	14	15	16	17	18	9	10	11	12	13	14	15
21	22	23	24	25	26	27	19	20	21	22	23	24	25	16	17	18	19	20	21	22
28	29	30					26	27	28	29	30	31		23	24	25	26	27	28	29
														30						

MAY

20 MON
2nd ♎
VICTORIA DAY (CANADA)
SUN ENTERS GEMINI

☽⚹ ☍ ⚷ ♈	2:09 am	
☽⚹ ⚻ ♅ ♉	5:43 am	**2:43 am**
☉ enters ♊	8:59 am	**5:59 am**
☽⚹ ⚻ ♀ ♉	10:41 am	**7:41 am**
☽⚹ ⚻ ♃ ♉	4:11 pm	**1:11 pm**
☽⚹ ⚻ ♆ ♓	5:29 pm	**2:29 pm**
☽ enters ♏	6:34 pm	**3:34 pm**
☽♏ ⚻ ☉ ♊	7:23 pm	**4:23 pm**
☽♏ □ ♀ ♒	10:34 pm	**7:34 pm**

21 TUE
2nd ♏

☽♏ ☍ ☿ ♉	10:18 am	**7:18 am**
☽♏ ⚻ ♂ ♈		**11:49 pm**

22 WED
2nd ♏

☽♏ ⚻ ♂ ♈	2:49 am	
☽♏ △ ♄ ♓	6:03 am	**3:03 am**
☉♊ △ ♀ ♒	11:14 am	**8:14 am**
☽♏ ⚻ ⚷ ♈	12:56 pm	**9:56 am**
☽♏ ☍ ♅ ♉	4:24 pm	**1:24 pm**

23 THU
2nd ♏
○ Full Moon 2 ♐ 55
OP: After Moon opposes Jupiter until v/c Moon. Just a few min-utes to do something meaningful.

☽♏ ☍ ♀ ♉	3:07 am	**12:07 am**
☽♏ ☍ ♃ ♉	3:13 am	**12:13 am**
☽♏ △ ♆ ♓	3:28 am	**12:28 am** ☽ v/c
☽ enters ♐	4:24 am	**1:24 am**
♀♉ ♂ ♃ ♉	4:29 am	**1:29 am**
♀♉ ⚹ ♆ ♓	6:50 am	**3:50 am**
☽♐ ⚹ ♀ ♒	8:10 am	**5:10 am**
☽♐ ☍ ☉ ♊	9:53 am	**6:53 am**
♀ enters ♊	4:30 pm	**1:30 pm**
♃♉ ⚹ ♆ ♓	5:44 pm	**2:44 pm**

☽♐ ⊼ ☿ ♉	3:05 am	**12:05 am**	
☽♐ □ ♄ ♓	2:29 pm	**11:29 am**	
☽♐ △ ♂ ♈	2:36 am	**11:36 am**	
☽♐ △ ♄ ♈	9:01 pm	**6:01 pm**	
☽♐ ⊼ ♅ ♉		**9:21 pm**	

FRI 24
3rd ♐

☽♐ ⊼ ♅ ♉	12:21 am		
♀♊ △ ♀ ♒	7:16 am	**4:16 am**	
☽♐ □ ♆ ♓	10:47 am	**7:47 am** ☽ v/c	
☽♐ ⊼ ♃ ♉	11:28 am	**8:28 am**	
☽ enters ♑	11:36 am	**8:36 am**	
☽♑ ⊼ ♀ ♊	3:58 pm	**12:58 pm**	
♃ enters ♊	7:15 pm	**4:15 pm**	
☽♑ ⊼ ☉ ♊	9:06 pm	**6:06 pm**	

SAT 25
3rd ♐

☽♑ △ ☿ ♉	4:49 pm	**1:49 pm**	
☽♑ ✶ ♄ ♓	8:33 pm	**5:33 pm**	
☽♑ □ ♂ ♈	11:37 pm	**8:37 pm**	
☽♑ □ ♄ ♈		**11:49 pm**	

SUN 26
3rd ♑

OP: After Moon squares Mars today until v/c Moon on Monday. This OP is versatile, good for battles and contests or practical matters.

Eastern Daylight Time (EDT) plain / **Pacific Daylight Time (PDT) bold**

APRIL							MAY							JUNE						
S	M	T	W	T	F	S	S	M	T	W	T	F	S	S	M	T	W	T	F	S
	1	2	3	4	5	6				1	2	3	4							1
7	8	9	10	11	12	13	5	6	7	8	9	10	11	2	3	4	5	6	7	8
14	15	16	17	18	19	20	12	13	14	15	16	17	18	9	10	11	12	13	14	15
21	22	23	24	25	26	27	19	20	21	22	23	24	25	16	17	18	19	20	21	22
28	29	30					26	27	28	29	30	31		23	24	25	26	27	28	29
														30						

May

27 Mon
3rd ♑
Memorial Day

☽♑ □ ♅ ♈	2:49 am	
☽♑ △ ♅ ♉	6:05 am	**3:05 am**
☽♑ ⚹ ♆ ♓	4:02 pm	**1:02 pm** ☽ v/c
☽ enters ♒	4:45 pm	**1:45 pm**
☽♒ △ ♃ ♊	5:32 pm	**2:32 pm**
☽♒ ☌ ♀ ♒	8:10 pm	**5:10 pm**
♀♉ ⚹ ♄ ♓	11:22 pm	**8:22 pm**
☽♒ △ ♀ ♊		**11:10 pm**

28 Tue
3rd ♒

☽♒ △ ♀ ♊	2:10 am	
☽♒ △ ☉ ♊	5:54 am	**2:54 am**

29 Wed
3rd ♒

☽♒ □ ☿ ♉	4:36 am	**1:36 am**
☽♒ ⚹ ♂ ♈	6:46 am	**3:46 am**
☽♒ ⚹ ♅ ♈	7:06 am	**4:06 am**
☽♒ □ ♅ ♉	10:20 am	**7:20 am** ☽ v/c
♂♈ ☌ ♅ ♈	1:08 pm	**10:08 am**
☽ enters ♓	8:33 pm	**5:33 pm**
☽♓ □ ♃ ♊	10:12 pm	**7:12 pm**

30 Thu
3rd ♓
◗ 4th Quarter 9 ♓ 46

☽♓ □ ♀ ♊	10:43 am	**7:43 am**
☽♓ □ ☉ ♊	1:13 pm	**10:13 am**
☿♉ ☌ ♅ ♉		**10:54 pm**

☿♉ ♂ ♅♉ 1:54 am
☽♓ ♂ ♄♓ 4:24 am **1:24 am**
☽♓ ⚹ ♅♉ 1:36 pm **10:36 am**
☽♓ ⚹ ☿♉ 3:19 pm **12:19 pm**
☽♓ ♂ ♆♓ 10:55 pm **7:55 pm** ☽ v/c
☽ enters ♈ 11:28 pm **8:28 pm**
☽♈ ⚹ ♃♊ **10:57 pm**
☽♈ ⚹ ♀≈ **11:41 pm**

FRI 31
4th ♓

OP: After Moon sextiles Uranus until Moon enters Aries. Use this time for innovative artistic activities, mind expansion, and clearing out emotional baggage.

☽♈ ⚹ ♃♊ 1:57 am
☽♈ ⚹ ♀≈ 2:41 am
☽♈ ⚹ ♀♊ 6:15 pm **3:15 pm**
☽♈ ⚹ ☉♊ 7:35 pm **4:35 pm**

SAT 1
4th ♈

☽♈ ♂ ♗♈ 1:03 pm **10:03 am**
☽♈ ♂ ♂♈ 6:04 pm **3:04 pm** ☽ v/c
♃♊ △ ♀≈ 8:13 pm **5:13 pm**
☿♉ ⚹ ♆♓ 11:57 pm **8:57 pm**
☽ enters ♉ **10:55 pm**

SUN 2
4th ♈

Eastern Daylight Time (EDT) plain / **Pacific Daylight Time (PDT) bold**

		APRIL								MAY								JUNE			
S	M	T	W	T	F	S		S	M	T	W	T	F	S		S	M	T	W	T	F	S
	1	2	3	4	5	6						1	2	3	4								1
7	8	9	10	11	12	13		5	6	7	8	9	10	11		2	3	4	5	6	7	8
14	15	16	17	18	19	20		12	13	14	15	16	17	18		9	10	11	12	13	14	15
21	22	23	24	25	26	27		19	20	21	22	23	24	25		16	17	18	19	20	21	22
28	29	30						26	27	28	29	30	31			23	24	25	26	27	28	29
																30						

3 MON
4th ♈

☽ enters ♉	1:55 am	
☿ enters ♊	3:37 am	**12:37 am**
☽♉ □ ♇≈	5:05 am	**2:05 am**
☿♊ △ ♇≈		**11:12 pm**

4 TUE
4th ♉

OP: After Moon conjoins Uranus today until Moon enters Gemini on Wednesday. This Last Quarter Moon OP is a good time to get organized, let go of what is no longer necessary, and finish up projects.

☿♊ △ ♇≈	2:12 am	
☿♊ ♂ ♃♊	6:23 am	**3:23 am**
☽♉ ✶ ♄♓	9:46 am	**6:46 am**
☉♊ ♂ ♀♊	11:32 am	**8:32 am**
☽♉ ♂ ♅♉	7:04 pm	**4:04 pm**

5 WED
4th ♉

☽♉ ✶ ♆♓	4:09 am	**1:09 am** ☽ v/c
☽ enters ♊	4:36 am	**1:36 am**
☽♊ △ ♇≈	7:46 am	**4:46 am**
☽♊ ♂ ♃♊	8:49 am	**5:49 am**
☽♊ ♂ ☿♊	12:46 pm	**9:46 am**

6 THU
4th ♊
● New Moon 16 ♊ 18

☽♊ ♂ ☉♊	8:38 am	**5:38 am**
☽♊ ♂ ♀♊	9:36 am	**6:36 am**
☽♊ □ ♄♓	1:19 pm	**10:19 am**
☽♊ ✶ ♅♈	7:28 pm	**4:28 pm**

☽♊ ✶ ♂♈	6:22 am	**3:22 am**	
☽♊ □ ♆♓	8:16 am	**5:16 am**	☽ v/c
☽ enters ♋	8:41 am	**5:41 am**	
☽♋ ⊼ ♇♒	11:55 am	**8:55 am**	

FRI 7
1st ♊

OP: After Moon enters Cancer today until Moon enters Leo on Sunday. Long OP while the Moon goes through the entire sign of Cancer, great for finding or expressing love after your emotions are renewed.

♀♊ □ ♄♓	4:25 am	**1:25 am**
☽♋ △ ♄♓	7:08 pm	**4:08 pm**
♂ enters ♉		**9:35 pm**
☽♋ □ ⚷♈		**10:39 pm**

SAT 8
1st ♋

♂ enters ♉	12:35 am		
☽♋ □ ⚷♈	1:39 am		
☽♋ ✶ ♅♉	5:26 am	**2:26 am**	
☉♊ □ ♄♓	6:36 am	**3:36 am**	
☽♋ △ ♆♓	3:05 pm	**12:05 pm**	☽ v/c
☽ enters ♌	3:29 pm	**12:29 pm**	
☽♌ □ ♂♉	4:24 pm	**1:24 pm**	
☽♌ ☍ ♇♒	6:50 pm	**3:50 pm**	
☽♌ ✶ ♃♊	10:09 pm	**7:09 pm**	

SUN 9
1st ♋

Eastern Daylight Time (EDT) plain / **Pacific Daylight Time (PDT) bold**

MAY

S	M	T	W	T	F	S
			1	2	3	4
5	6	7	8	9	10	11
12	13	14	15	16	17	18
19	20	21	22	23	24	25
26	27	28	29	30	31	

JUNE

S	M	T	W	T	F	S
						1
2	3	4	5	6	7	8
9	10	11	12	13	14	15
16	17	18	19	20	21	22
23	24	25	26	27	28	29
30						

JULY

S	M	T	W	T	F	S
	1	2	3	4	5	6
7	8	9	10	11	12	13
14	15	16	17	18	19	20
21	22	23	24	25	26	27
28	29	30	31			

10 Mon
1st ♌

☽♌ ⚹ ☿ Ⅱ 10:35 pm **7:35 pm**

11 Tue
1st ♌
Shavuot begins at sundown

♀Ⅱ ⚹ ♅ ♈ 3:12 am **12:12 am**
☽♌ ⚻ ♄ ♓ 4:14 am **1:14 am**
☽♌ ⚹ ☉ Ⅱ 7:58 am **4:58 am**
♂♉ □ ♀≈ 9:21 am **6:21 am**
☽♌ △ ♅ ♈ 11:10 am **8:10 am**
☽♌ ⚹ ♀ Ⅱ 12:02 pm **9:02 am**
☽♌ □ ♅ ♉ 3:16 pm **12:16 pm** ☽ v/c
☽♌ ⚻ ♆ ♓   **10:17 pm**
☽ enters ♍   **10:39 pm**

12 Wed
1st ♌

☽♌ ⚻ ♆ ♓ 1:17 am
☽ enters ♍ 1:39 am
☽♍ ⚻ ♀≈ 5:07 am **2:07 am**
☽♍ △ ♂♉ 6:26 am **3:26 am**
☿Ⅱ □ ♄ ♓ 6:47 am **3:47 am**
☽♍ □ ♃ Ⅱ 9:49 am **6:49 am**
☉Ⅱ ⚹ ♅ ♈   **11:24 pm**

13 Thu
1st ♍
◐ 2nd Quarter 23 ♍ 39 (Pacific)

☉Ⅱ ⚹ ♅ ♈ 2:24 am
☽♍ ☍ ♄ ♓ 4:18 am **1:18 pm**
☿Ⅱ ⚹ ♅ ♈ 10:02 pm **7:02 pm**
☽♍ ⚻ ♅ ♈ 11:31 pm **8:31 pm**
☽♍ □ ☿ Ⅱ 11:51 pm **8:51 pm**
☽♍ □ ☉ Ⅱ   **10:18 pm**

Fri 14

1st ♍

◐ 2nd Quarter 23 ♍ 39 (Eastern)

Flag Day

☽♍ □ ☉♊	1:18 am		
☽♍ △ ♅♉	3:50 am	**12:50 am**	
☽♍ □ ♀♊	7:13 am	**4:13 am**	
☉♊ ☌ ☿♊	12:33 pm	**9:33 am**	
☽♍ ☍ ♆♓	1:54 pm	**10:54 am**	☽ v/c
☽ enters ♎	2:12 pm	**11:12 am**	
☽♎ △ ♇♒	5:39 pm	**2:39 pm**	
☽♎ ⚻ ♂♉	11:08 pm	**8:08 pm**	
☽♎ △ ♃♊	11:44 pm	**8:44 pm**	

OP: After Moon enters Libra today until v/c Moon on Sunday or Monday. An excellent waxing Moon OP for commerce, arts, networking, and partying.

Sat 15

2nd ♎

Sun 16

2nd ♎

Father's Day

☽♎ ⚻ ♄♓	5:14 am	**2:14 am**	
☽♎ ☍ ⚷♈	12:24 pm	**9:24 am**	
☽♎ ⚻ ♅♉	4:45 pm	**1:45 pm**	
☽♎ △ ☉♊	7:14 pm	**4:14 pm**	
♀♊ □ ♆♓	11:46 pm	**8:46 pm**	
☽♎ △ ☿♊		**11:05 pm**	☽ v/c
♀ enters ♋		**11:20 pm**	
☽♎ ⚻ ♆♓		**11:22 pm**	
☽ enters ♏		**11:38 pm**	
☽♏ △ ♀♋		**11:40 pm**	

Eastern Daylight Time (EDT) plain / **Pacific Daylight Time (PDT) bold**

MAY

S	M	T	W	T	F	S
			1	2	3	4
5	6	7	8	9	10	11
12	13	14	15	16	17	18
19	20	21	22	23	24	25
26	27	28	29	30	31	

JUNE

S	M	T	W	T	F	S
						1
2	3	4	5	6	7	8
9	10	11	12	13	14	15
16	17	18	19	20	21	22
23	24	25	26	27	28	29
30						

JULY

S	M	T	W	T	F	S
	1	2	3	4	5	6
7	8	9	10	11	12	13
14	15	16	17	18	19	20
21	22	23	24	25	26	27
28	29	30	31			

June

17 Mon
2nd ♎

☽♎ △ ☿♊	2:05 am		☽ v/c
♀ enters ♋	2:20 am		
☽♎ ⚻ ♆♓	2:22 am		
☽ enters ♏	2:38 am		
☽♏ △ ♀♋	2:40 am		
☿♊ □ ♆♓	3:41 am	**12:41 am**	
☿ enters ♋	5:07 am	**2:07 am**	
☽♏ □ ♇♒	5:54 am	**2:54 am**	
☿♋ ☌ ♀♋	8:43 am	**5:43 am**	
☽♏ ⚻ ♃♊	1:02 pm	**10:02 am**	
☽♏ ☍ ♂♉	3:10 pm	**12:10 pm**	
☿♋ ⚻ ♇♒	11:13 pm	**8:13 pm**	

18 Tue
2nd ♏

♀♋ ⚻ ♇♒	10:12 am	**7:12 am**
☽♏ △ ♄♓	4:19 pm	**1:19 pm**
☽♏ ⚻ ⚷♈	11:12 pm	**8:12 pm**

19 Wed
2nd ♏

Juneteenth

OP: After Moon opposes Uranus until v/c Moon. Short OP filled with intense emotions. Good for deep thinking and reflection.

☽♏ ☍ ♅♉	3:24 am	**12:24 am**	
☽♏ ⚻ ☉♊	10:15 am	**7:15 am**	
☽♏ △ ♆♓	12:19 pm	**9:19 am**	☽ v/c
☽ enters ♐	12:32 pm	**9:32 am**	
☽♐ ⚹ ♇♒	3:32 pm	**12:32 pm**	
☽♐ ⚻ ♀♋	6:41 pm	**3:41 pm**	
☽♐ ☍ ♃♊	11:22 pm	**8:22 pm**	
☽♐ ⚻ ☿♋	11:40 pm	**8:40 pm**	

20 Thu
2nd ♐

Summer Solstice

Litha

Sun enters Cancer

☽♐ ⚻ ♂♉	3:47 am	**12:47 am**
☉♊ □ ♆♓	2:12 pm	**11:12 am**
☉ enters ♋	4:51 pm	**1:51 pm**
☽♐ □ ♄♓		**9:08 pm**

☽♐ □ ♄♓ 12:08 am
☽♐ △ ♅♈ 6:41 am **3:41 am**
☽♐ ⊼ ♅♉ 10:44 am **7:44 am**
☿♋ ✶ ♂♉ 12:23 pm **9:23 am**
☽♐ □ ♆♓ 6:58 pm **3:58 pm** ☽ v/c
☽ enters ♑ 7:08 pm **4:08 pm**
☽♑ ☌ ☉♋ 9:08 pm **6:08 pm**

Fri 21
2nd ♐
○ Full Moon 1 ♑ 07

☽♑ ⊼ ♃♊ 6:18 am **3:18 am**
☽♑ ☌ ♀♋ 6:20 am **3:20 am**
☉♋ ⊼ ♇≈ 8:01 am **5:01 am**
☽♑ △ ♂♉ 12:37 pm **9:37 am**
☽♑ ☌ ☿♋ 3:25 pm **12:25 pm**

Sat 22
3rd ♑

☽♑ ✶ ♄♓ 5:02 am **2:02 am**
☽♑ □ ♅♈ 11:21 am **8:21 am**
☽♑ △ ♅♉ 3:20 pm **12:20 pm**
☽♑ ✶ ♆♓ 11:05 pm **8:05 pm** ☽ v/c
☽ enters ≈ 11:14 pm **8:14 pm**
☽≈ ☌ ♀≈ **10:50 pm**

Sun 23
3rd ♑

Eastern Daylight Time (EDT) plain / **Pacific Daylight Time (PDT) bold**

		MAY							JUNE							JULY				
S	M	T	W	T	F	S	S	M	T	W	T	F	S	S	M	T	W	T	F	S
			1	2	3	4							1		1	2	3	4	5	6
5	6	7	8	9	10	11	2	3	4	5	6	7	8	7	8	9	10	11	12	13
12	13	14	15	16	17	18	9	10	11	12	13	14	15	14	15	16	17	18	19	20
19	20	21	22	23	24	25	16	17	18	19	20	21	22	21	22	23	24	25	26	27
26	27	28	29	30	31		23	24	25	26	27	28	29	28	29	30	31			
							30													

June

24 Mon
3rd ♒

☽♒ ☌ ♇♒	1:50 am	
☽♒ ⚻ ☉♋	4:57 am	**1:57 am**
☽♒ △ ♃♊	10:52 am	**7:52 am**
☽♒ ⚻ ♀♋	3:00 pm	**12:00 pm**
☽♒ □ ♂♉	6:58 pm	**3:58 pm**

25 Tue
3rd ♒

☽♒ ⚻ ☿♋	3:27 am	**12:27 am**	
☽♒ ⚹ ⚷♈	2:31 pm	**11:31 am**	
☽♒ □ ♅♉	6:30 pm	**3:30 pm**	☽ v/c
☽ enters ♓		**11:08 pm**	

26 Wed
3rd ♒

☽ enters ♓	2:08 am	
☽♓ △ ☉♋	11:26 am	**8:26 am**
☿♋ △ ♄♓	2:10 pm	**11:10 am**
☽♓ □ ♃♊	2:27 pm	**11:27 am**
☽♓ △ ♀♋	10:33 pm	**7:33 pm**
☽♓ ⚹ ♂♉		**9:26 pm**

27 Thu
3rd ♓

OP: After Moon conjoins Saturn today until Moon enters Aries on Friday. This is a good opportunity for connections as well as expressing love and compassion.

☽♓ ⚹ ♂♉	12:26 am	
☽♓ ☌ ♄♓	10:57 am	**7:57 am**
☽♓ △ ☿♋	2:11 pm	**11:11 am**
☽♓ ⚹ ♅♉	9:23 pm	**6:23 pm**

☽♓ ☌ ♆♓	4:45 am	**1:45 am** ☽ v/c
☽ enters ♈	4:52 am	**1:52 am**
☽♈ ⚹ ♀≈	7:18 am	**4:18 am**
☿♋ □ ♂♈	1:58 pm	**10:58 am**
☽♈ □ ☉♋	5:53 pm	**2:53 pm**
☽♈ ⚹ ♃Ⅱ	6:03 pm	**3:03 pm**
♀♋ ⚹ ♂♉		**9:49 pm**

FRI 28
3rd ♓
◑ 4th Quarter 7 ♈ 40

♀♋ ⚹ ♂♉	12:49 am	
☽♈ □ ♀♋	6:16 am	**3:16 am**
♄℞	3:07 pm	**12:07 pm**
☽♈ ☌ ♂♈	8:25 pm	**5:25 pm**
☿♋ ⚹ ♅♉	10:20 pm	**7:20 pm**
☽♈ □ ☿♋		**9:56 pm** ☽ v/c

SAT 29
4th ♈
SATURN RETROGRADE

☽♈ □ ☿♋	12:56 am	☽ v/c
☽ enters ♉	8:00 am	**5:00 am**
☽♉ □ ♀≈	10:23 am	**7:23 am**
☽♉ ⚹ ☉♋		**9:57 pm**

SUN 30
4th ♈

Eastern Daylight Time (EDT) plain / **Pacific Daylight Time (PDT) bold**

		MAY								JUNE								JULY			
S	M	T	W	T	F	S		S	M	T	W	T	F	S		S	M	T	W	T	F	S
			1	2	3	4								1			1	2	3	4	5	6
5	6	7	8	9	10	11		2	3	4	5	6	7	8		7	8	9	10	11	12	13
12	13	14	15	16	17	18		9	10	11	12	13	14	15		14	15	16	17	18	19	20
19	20	21	22	23	24	25		16	17	18	19	20	21	22		21	22	23	24	25	26	27
26	27	28	29	30	31			23	24	25	26	27	28	29		28	29	30	31			
								30													

July

1 Mon
4th ♉
Canada Day

☽♉ ⚹ ☉♋	12:57 am	
☽♉ ☌ ♂♉	12:19 pm	**9:19 am**
☽♉ ⚹ ♀♋	2:42 pm	**11:42 am**
☽♉ ⚹ ♄♓	5:28 pm	**2:28 pm**

2 Tue
4th ♉
Neptune retrograde
OP: After Moon conjoins Uranus until Moon enters Gemini.
Seize this opportunity to connect with your intuition and complete unfinished tasks.

☽♉ ☌ ♅♉	4:29 am	**1:29 am**
♆℞	6:40 am	**3:40 am**
☿♋ △ ♆♓	7:53 am	**4:53 am**
☿ enters ♌	8:50 am	**5:50 am**
☽♉ ⚹ ♆♓	11:43 am	**8:43 am** ☽ v/c
☽ enters ♊	11:50 am	**8:50 am**
☽♊ ⚹ ☿♌	12:16 pm	**9:16 am**
☽♊ △ ♀≈	2:11 pm	**11:11 am**
♀♋ △ ♄♓	9:41 pm	**6:41 pm**

3 Wed
4th ♊

☽♊ ☌ ♃♊	3:05 am	**12:05 am**
☿♌ ☍ ♀≈	3:27 am	**12:27 am**
☽♊ □ ♄♓	9:58 pm	**6:58 pm**

4 Thu
4th ♊
Independence Day

☽♊ ⚹ ♅♈	4:54 am	**1:54 am**
☽♊ □ ♆♓	4:44 pm	**1:44 pm** ☽ v/c
☽ enters ♋	4:51 pm	**1:51 pm**
☽♋ ⚻ ♀≈	7:11 pm	**4:11 pm**

142

♂♉ ⚹ ♄♓	3:02 pm	**12:02 pm**
☽♋ ♂ ☉♋	6:57 pm	**3:57 pm**
♀♋ □ ☿♈		**11:33 pm**

FRI 5

4th ♋

● New Moon 14 ♋ 23

OP: This Cazimi Moon is usable ½ hour before and ½ hour after the Sun-Moon conjunction. If you have something important to start around now, this is a great time to do it.

♀♋ □ ☿♈	2:33 am		
☽♋ △ ♄♓	4:10 am	**1:10 am**	
☽♋ ⚹ ♂♉	4:56 am	**1:56 am**	
☽♋ □ ☿♈	11:31 am	**8:31 am**	
☽♋ ♂ ♀♋	12:27 pm	**9:27 am**	
☽♋ ⚹ ♅♉	4:24 pm	**1:24 pm**	
☽♋ △ ♆♓	11:47 pm	**8:47 pm**	☽ v/c
☽ enters ♌	11:56 pm	**8:56 pm**	
☽♌ ♂ ♇♒		**11:16 pm**	

SAT 6

1st ♋

☽♌ ♂ ♇♒	2:16 am	
☽♌ ♂ ☿♌	4:23 pm	**1:23 pm**
☽♌ ⚹ ♃♊	6:19 pm	**3:19 pm**

SUN 7

1st ♌

ISLAMIC NEW YEAR BEGINS AT SUNDOWN

Eastern Daylight Time (EDT) plain / **Pacific Daylight Time (PDT) bold**

JUNE								JULY								AUGUST						
S	M	T	W	T	F	S		S	M	T	W	T	F	S		S	M	T	W	T	F	S
						1			1	2	3	4	5	6						1	2	3
2	3	4	5	6	7	8		7	8	9	10	11	12	13		4	5	6	7	8	9	10
9	10	11	12	13	14	15		14	15	16	17	18	19	20		11	12	13	14	15	16	17
16	17	18	19	20	21	22		21	22	23	24	25	26	27		18	19	20	21	22	23	24
23	24	25	26	27	28	29		28	29	30	31					25	26	27	28	29	30	31
30																						

8 Mon
1st ♌

♀⊗ ✶ ♅ ♉	7:04 am	**4:04 am**	
☿♌ ✶ ♃ ♊	10:26 am	**7:26 am**	
☽♌ ⊼ ♄ ♓	12:57 pm	**9:57 am**	
☽♌ □ ♂ ♉	5:18 pm	**2:18 pm**	
☽♌ △ ⚷ ♈	8:49 pm	**5:49 pm**	
☽♌ □ ♅ ♉		**11:04 pm**	☽ v/c

9 Tue
1st ♌

☽♌ □ ♅ ♉	2:04 am		☽ v/c
☽♌ ⊼ ♆ ♓	9:38 am	**6:38 am**	
☽ enters ♍	9:48 am	**6:48 am**	
☽♍ ⊼ ♀ ≈	12:08 pm	**9:08 am**	

10 Wed
1st ♍

☽♍ □ ♃ ♊	6:07 am	**3:07 am**
☉⊗ △ ♄ ♓	11:05 pm	**8:05 pm**
☽♍ ☍ ♄ ♓		**9:27 pm**
☽♍ ✶ ☉⊗		**9:34 pm**

11 Thu
1st ♍

OP: After Moon enters Libra today until v/c Moon on Saturday. Long waxing Moon OP that requires an extra effort but will give good results for projects related to beauty, arts, networking, and more.

☽♍ ☍ ♄ ♓	12:27 am		
☽♍ ✶ ☉⊗	12:34 am		
☽♍ ⊼ ⚷ ♈	8:47 am	**5:47 am**	
☽♍ △ ♂ ♉	8:51 am	**5:51 am**	
♀⊗ △ ♆ ♓	10:32 am	**7:32 am**	
♀ enters ♌	12:19 pm	**9:19 am**	
☽♍ △ ♅ ♉	2:20 pm	**11:20 am**	
☽♍ ☍ ♆ ♓	9:55 pm	**6:55 pm**	☽ v/c
☽ enters ♎	10:06 pm	**7:06 pm**	
☽♎ ✶ ♀ ♌	11:15 pm	**8:15 pm**	
☽♎ △ ♀ ≈		**9:24 pm**	

☽☌ △ ♀ ≈	12:24 am	
♀♌ ☍ ♀ ≈	10:12 am	**7:12 am**
☽☌ △ ♃ ♊	7:58 pm	**4:58 pm**

Fri **12**
1st ☌

☽☌ ✶ ☿ ♌	8:18 am	**5:18 am**
☽☌ ⊼ ♄ ♓	1:16 pm	**10:16 am**
☽☌ □ ☉☌	6:49 pm	**3:49 pm** ☽ v/c
☽☌ ☍ ♆ ♈	9:45 pm	**6:45 pm**
☽☌ ⊼ ♂ ♉		**10:35 pm**

Sat **13**
1st ☌
◐ 2nd Quarter 22 ☌ 01

☽☌ ⊼ ♂ ♉	1:35 am	
☽☌ ⊼ ♅ ♉	3:24 am	**12:24 am**
☽☌ ⊼ ♆ ♓	10:40 am	**7:40 am**
☽ enters ♏	10:53 am	**7:53 am**
☽♏ □ ♀ ≈	1:01 pm	**10:01 am**
☽♏ □ ♀ ♌	6:55 pm	**3:55 pm**

Sun **14**
2nd ☌

Eastern Daylight Time (EDT) plain / **Pacific Daylight Time (PDT) bold**

JUNE							**JULY**							**AUGUST**						
S	M	T	W	T	F	S	S	M	T	W	T	F	S	S	M	T	W	T	F	S
						1		1	2	3	4	5	6					1	2	3
2	3	4	5	6	7	8	7	8	9	10	11	12	13	4	5	6	7	8	9	10
9	10	11	12	13	14	15	14	15	16	17	18	19	20	11	12	13	14	15	16	17
16	17	18	19	20	21	22	21	22	23	24	25	26	27	18	19	20	21	22	23	24
23	24	25	26	27	28	29	28	29	30	31				25	26	27	28	29	30	31
30																				

15 Mon
2nd ♏

☿♌ ⊼ ♄♓	4:57 am	**1:57 am**
☉⊛ □ ♃♈	7:44 am	**4:44 am**
☽♏ ⊼ ♃Ⅱ	9:15 am	**6:15 am**
♂♉ ♂ ♅♉	10:05 am	**7:05 am**
☽♏ △ ♄♓		**9:45 pm**
☽♏ □ ☿♌		**11:59 pm**

16 Tue
2nd ♏

☽♏ △ ♄♓	12:45 am	
☽♏ □ ☿♌	2:59 am	
☽♏ ⊼ ♃♈	9:00 am	**6:00 am**
☽♏ △ ☉⊛	11:04 am	**8:04 am**
☽♏ ♂ ♅♉	2:31 pm	**11:31 am**
☽♏ ♂ ♂♉	4:06 pm	**1:06 pm**
☽♏ △ ♆♓	9:10 pm	**6:10 pm** ☽ v/c
☽ enters ♐	9:25 pm	**6:25 pm**
☽♐ ⚹ ♀≈	11:20 pm	**8:20 pm**

17 Wed
2nd ♐

☽♐ △ ♀♌	11:08 am	**8:08 am**
☽♐ ♂ ♃Ⅱ	7:20 pm	**4:20 pm**

18 Thu
2nd ♐

☽♐ □ ♄♓	8:49 am	**5:49 am**
☉⊛ ⚹ ♅♉	10:00 am	**7:00 am**
☽♐ △ ☿♌	4:24 pm	**1:24 pm**
☽♐ △ ♃♈	4:41 pm	**1:41 pm**
☿♌ △ ♃♈	7:57 pm	**4:57 pm**
☽♐ ⊼ ♅♉	9:56 pm	**6:56 pm**
☽♐ ⊼ ☉⊛	10:49 pm	**7:49 pm**
☽♐ ⊼ ♂♉		**11:16 pm**

☽ ♐ ☌ ♂ ♉	2:16 am	

Fri 19
2nd ♐

☽ ♐ □ ♆ ♓ 3:58 am **12:58 am** ☽ v/c
☽ enters ♑ 4:14 am **1:14 am**
☽ ♑ ☌ ♀ ♌ 10:17 pm **7:17 pm**
☽ ♑ ☌ ♃ ♊ **10:29 pm**

☽ ♑ ☌ ♃ ♊ 1:29 am
♂ ♉ ⚹ ♆ ♓ 11:17 am **8:17 am**
☽ ♑ ⚹ ♄ ♓ 1:15 pm **10:15 am**
♂ enters ♊ 4:43 pm **1:43 pm**
☽ ♑ □ ⚷ ♈ 8:49 pm **5:49 pm**
☽ ♑ ☌ ☿ ♌ **9:42 pm**
☽ ♑ △ ♅ ♉ **10:53 pm**

Sat 20
2nd ♑

☽ ♑ ☌ ☿ ♌ 12:42 am
☽ ♑ △ ♅ ♉ 1:53 am
☽ ♑ ☍ ☉ ♋ 6:17 am **3:17 am**

Sun 21
2nd ♑
○ Full Moon 29 ♑ 09

OP: After Moon opposes the Sun until v/c Moon. A short OP that works well for quick intuitive decisions. Get up early to catch it!

☽ ♑ ⚹ ♆ ♓ 7:26 am **4:26 am** ☽ v/c
☽ enters ♒ 7:43 am **4:43 am**
☽ ♒ △ ♂ ♊ 8:29 am **5:29 am**
☽ ♒ ☌ ♀ ♒ 9:14 am **6:14 am**
♀ ♌ ⚹ ♃ ♊ 4:43 pm **1:43 pm**
☿ ♌ □ ♅ ♉ 6:21 pm **3:21 pm**
☉ ♋ △ ♆ ♓ 11:25 pm **8:25 pm**
♂ ♊ △ ♀ ♒ 11:48 pm **8:48 pm**

Eastern Daylight Time (EDT) plain / **Pacific Daylight Time (PDT) bold**

		JUNE				
S	M	T	W	T	F	S
						1
2	3	4	5	6	7	8
9	10	11	12	13	14	15
16	17	18	19	20	21	22
23	24	25	26	27	28	29
30						

		JULY				
S	M	T	W	T	F	S
	1	2	3	4	5	6
7	8	9	10	11	12	13
14	15	16	17	18	19	20
21	22	23	24	25	26	27
28	29	30	31			

		AUGUST				
S	M	T	W	T	F	S
				1	2	3
4	5	6	7	8	9	10
11	12	13	14	15	16	17
18	19	20	21	22	23	24
25	26	27	28	29	30	31

22 Mon

3rd ≈

Sun enters Leo

☉ enters ♌	3:44 am	**12:44 am**	
☽≈ △ ♃ ♊	4:43 am	**1:43 am**	
☽≈ ☍ ♀♌	5:39 am	**2:39 am**	
☽≈ ✶ ⚷♈	10:44 pm	**7:44 pm**	
☉♌ ☍ ♀≈		**10:38 pm**	

23 Tue

3rd ≈

☉♌ ☍ ♀≈	1:38 am		
☽≈ □ ♅ ♉	3:47 am	**12:47 am**	
☽≈ ☍ ☿♌	5:58 am	**2:58 am** ☽ v/c	
☽ enters ♓	9:23 am	**6:23 am**	
☽♓ ⚻ ☉♌	11:27 am	**8:27 am**	
☽♓ □ ♂♊	12:36 pm	**9:36 am**	

24 Wed

3rd ♓

OP: After Moon conjoins Saturn today until Moon enters Aries on Thursday. This is a great time to hone your intuition, meditate, and help others.

☽♓ □ ♃ ♊	6:47 am	**3:47 am**	
☽♓ ⚻ ♀♌	11:36 am	**8:36 am**	
☽♓ ☌ ♄♓	4:31 pm	**1:31 pm**	

25 Thu

3rd ♓

OP: Two back-to-back OPs: The second OP starts when the Moon enters Aries today until v/c Moon on Friday. This great OP ends with the Moon enclosed between benefics, which means you are set up to succeed. This is your last chance before Mercury enters its Storm.

☽♓ ✶ ♅ ♉	5:19 am	**2:19 am**	
☽♓ ⚻ ☿♌	10:26 am	**7:26 am**	
☽♓ ☌ ♆♓	10:31 am	**7:31 am** ☽ v/c	
☽ enters ♈	10:52 am	**7:52 am**	
☿♌ ⚻ ♆♓	12:00 pm	**9:00 am**	
☽♈ ✶ ♀≈	12:13 pm	**9:13 am**	
☽♈ △ ☉♌	4:29 pm	**1:29 pm**	
☽♈ ✶ ♂♊	4:36 pm	**1:36 pm**	
☿ enters ♍	6:42 pm	**3:42 pm**	
☉♌ ✶ ♂♊	10:32 pm	**7:32 pm**	

Mercury Note: Mercury enters its Storm (moving less than 40 minutes of arc per day) on Saturday, as it slows down before going retrograde. The Storm acts like the retrograde. Not favorable to start new projects—just follow through with the items that are already on your plate. Write down new ideas with date and time they occurred.

FRI 26

3rd ♈

CHIRON RETROGRADE

☽♈ ⚹ ♃♊	9:16 am	**6:16 am**
⚷℞	9:59 am	**6:59 am**
☽♈ △ ♀♌	6:14 pm	**3:14 pm** ☽ v/c
♀♌ ⚻ ♄♓	8:07 pm	**5:07 pm**
☿♍ ⚻ ♇♒	8:49 pm	**5:49 pm**
☽♈ ☌ ⚷♈		**11:22 pm**

SAT 27

3rd ♈

◑ 4th Quarter 5 ♉ 32

☽♈ ☌ ⚷♈	2:22 am	
☽ enters ♉	1:23 pm	**10:23 am**
☽♉ □ ♇♒	2:41 pm	**11:41 am**
☽♉ △ ☿♍	3:36 pm	**12:36 pm**
☽♉ □ ☉♌	10:52 pm	**7:52 pm**

SUN 28

4th ♉

☽♉ ⚹ ♄♓	9:42 pm	**6:42 pm**
☽♉ □ ♀♌		**11:45 pm**

Eastern Daylight Time (EDT) plain / **Pacific Daylight Time (PDT) bold**

JUNE

S	M	T	W	T	F	S
						1
2	3	4	5	6	7	8
9	10	11	12	13	14	15
16	17	18	19	20	21	22
23	24	25	26	27	28	29
30						

JULY

S	M	T	W	T	F	S
	1	2	3	4	5	6
7	8	9	10	11	12	13
14	15	16	17	18	19	20
21	22	23	24	25	26	27
28	29	30	31			

AUGUST

S	M	T	W	T	F	S
				1	2	3
4	5	6	7	8	9	10
11	12	13	14	15	16	17
18	19	20	21	22	23	24
25	26	27	28	29	30	31

29 Mon
4th ♉

OP: After Moon conjoins Uranus until Moon enters Gemini. This short Last Quarter Moon OP is an excellent time to be practical and complete tasks.

☽♉ □ ♀♌	2:45 am	
☽♉ ♂ ♅♉	11:47 am	**8:47 am**
☽♉ ⚹ ♆♓	4:59 pm	**1:59 pm** ☽ v/c
☽ enters ♊	5:28 pm	**2:28 pm**
☽♊ △ ♇♒	6:43 pm	**3:43 pm**
☽♊ □ ☿♍	10:00 pm	**7:00 pm**

30 Tue
4th ♊

☽♊ ♂ ♂♊	5:01 am	**2:01 am**
☽♊ ⚹ ☉♌	7:15 am	**4:15 am**
♀♌ △ ♃♈	3:54 pm	**12:54 pm**
☽♊ ♂ ♃♊	6:45 pm	**3:45 pm**
☽♊ □ ♄♓		**11:42 pm**

31 Wed
4th ♊

OP: After Moon enters Cancer today until Moon enters Leo on Saturday. Use this exceptionally long OP for finishing up projects during the Balsamic phase of the Moon.

☽♊ □ ♄♓	2:42 am	
☽♊ ⚹ ♃♈	11:32 am	**8:32 am**
☽♊ ⚹ ♀♌	1:33 pm	**10:33 am**
☽♊ □ ♆♓	10:46 pm	**7:46 pm** ☽ v/c
☽ enters ♋	11:19 pm	**8:19 pm**
☽♋ ⚻ ♇♒		**9:31 pm**

1 Thu
4th ♋
LAMMAS

☽♋ ⚻ ♇♒	12:31 am	
☽♋ ⚹ ☿♍	5:43 am	**2:43 am**

Mercury Note: Mercury goes retrograde on Sunday, August 4 (Pacific Time), or Monday, August 5 (Eastern Time), and remains so until August 28, after which it will still be in its Storm until September 3. Projects initiated during this entire period may not work out as planned. It's best to use this time for reviews, editing, escrows, and so forth.

♀♌ □ ♅ ♉	9:27 am	**6:27 am**
☽♋ △ ♄ ♓	9:32 am	**6:32 am**
☽♋ □ ♂ ♈	6:54 pm	**3:54 pm**
☽♋ ✶ ♅ ♉		**10:17 pm**

Fri 2
4th ♋

☽♋ ✶ ♅ ♉	1:17 am	
☽♋ △ ♆ ♓	6:31 am	**3:31 am** ☽ v/c
☽ enters ♌	7:10 am	**4:10 am**
☽♌ ♂ ♀ ≈	8:19 am	**5:19 am**
☽♌ ✶ ♂ ♊		**10:54 pm**

Sat 3
4th ♋

☽♌ ✶ ♂ ♊	1:54 am	
☽♌ ♂ ☉♌	7:13 am	**4:13 am**
☽♌ ✶ ♃ ♊	12:01 pm	**9:01 am**
♀♌ ⚻ ♆ ♓	3:24 pm	**12:24 pm**
☽♌ ⚻ ♄ ♓	6:31 pm	**3:31 pm**
♀ enters ♍	10:23 pm	**7:23 pm**
☿℞		**9:56 pm**

Sun 4
4th ♌
● New Moon 12 ♌ 34
Mercury retrograde (Pacific)

Eastern Daylight Time (EDT) plain / **Pacific Daylight Time (PDT) bold**

	JULY							AUGUST							SEPTEMBER					
S	M	T	W	T	F	S	S	M	T	W	T	F	S	S	M	T	W	T	F	S
	1	2	3	4	5	6					1	2	3	1	2	3	4	5	6	7
7	8	9	10	11	12	13	4	5	6	7	8	9	10	8	9	10	11	12	13	14
14	15	16	17	18	19	20	11	12	13	14	15	16	17	15	16	17	18	19	20	21
21	22	23	24	25	26	27	18	19	20	21	22	23	24	22	23	24	25	26	27	28
28	29	30	31				25	26	27	28	29	30	31	29	30					

5 Mon
1st ♌
Mercury retrograde (Eastern)

☿R	12:56 am	
☽♌ △ ⚷♈	4:28 am	**1:28 am**
♀♍ ⊼ ♇♒	9:18 am	**6:18 am**
☽♌ □ ♅♉	11:16 am	**8:16 am** ☽ v/c
☽♌ ⊼ ♆♓	4:32 pm	**1:32 pm**
☽ enters ♍	5:17 pm	**2:17 pm**
☽♍ ⊼ ♇♒	6:22 pm	**3:22 pm**
☽♍ ♂ ♀♍	7:24 pm	**4:24 pm**
☽♍ ♂ ☿♍		**10:19 pm**

6 Tue
1st ♍

☽♍ ♂ ☿♍	1:19 am	
☽♍ □ ♂♊	4:15 pm	**1:15 pm**
☽♍ □ ♃♊		**9:08 pm**

7 Wed
1st ♍

☽♍ □ ♃♊	12:08 am	
☽♍ ☍ ♄♓	5:44 am	**2:44 am**
☉♌ ⚹ ♃♊	9:37 am	**6:37 am**
☽♍ ⊼ ⚷♈	4:16 pm	**1:16 pm**
☿♍ ♂ ♀♍	11:12 pm	**8:12 pm**
☽♍ △ ♅♉	11:27 pm	**8:27 pm**

8 Thu
1st ♍

OP: After Moon enters Libra today until v/c Moon on Friday. This is a great time to get in touch with important people and to renew your connections.

☽♍ ☍ ♆♓	4:40 am	**1:40 am** ☽ v/c
☽ enters ♎	5:31 am	**2:31 am**
☽♎ △ ♇♒	6:32 am	**3:32 am**

☽⚏△♂Ⅱ	8:40 am	**5:40 am**
☽⚏△♃Ⅱ	1:55 pm	**10:55 am**
☽⚏⚹☉♌	5:45 pm	**2:45 pm** ☽ v/c
☽⚏⚼♄♓	6:24 pm	**3:24 pm**
☉♌⚼♄♓		**10:26 pm**

FRI 9
1st ⚏

☉♌⚼♄♓	1:26 am	
☽⚏☍♅♈	5:16 am	**2:16 am**
☽⚏⚼♅♉	12:36 pm	**9:36 am**
☽⚏⚼♆♓	5:37 pm	**2:37 pm**
☽ enters ♏	6:34 pm	**3:34 pm**
☽♏□♀≈	7:27 pm	**4:27 pm**
☽♏⚹☿♍	11:42 pm	**8:42 pm**

SAT 10
1st ⚏

☽♏⚹♀♍	10:40 am	**7:40 am**
☽♏⚼♂Ⅱ		**9:48 pm**

SUN 11
1st ♏

Eastern Daylight Time (EDT) plain / **Pacific Daylight Time (PDT) bold**

		JULY				
S	M	T	W	T	F	S
	1	2	3	4	5	6
7	8	9	10	11	12	13
14	15	16	17	18	19	20
21	22	23	24	25	26	27
28	29	30	31			

		AUGUST				
S	M	T	W	T	F	S
				1	2	3
4	5	6	7	8	9	10
11	12	13	14	15	16	17
18	19	20	21	22	23	24
25	26	27	28	29	30	31

		SEPTEMBER				
S	M	T	W	T	F	S
1	2	3	4	5	6	7
8	9	10	11	12	13	14
15	16	17	18	19	20	21
22	23	24	25	26	27	28
29	30					

August

12 Mon

1st ♏
◐ 2nd Quarter 20 ♏ 24

☽♏ ⚻ ♂♊	12:48 am	
☽♏ ⚻ ♃♊	3:14 am	**12:14 am**
☽♏ △ ♄♓	6:29 am	**3:29 am**
☽♏ □ ☉♌	11:19 am	**8:19 am**
☽♏ ⚻ ⚷♈	5:12 pm	**2:12 pm**
☽♏ ☍ ♅♉		**9:24 pm**

13 Tue

2nd ♏

☽♏ ☍ ♅♉	12:24 am	
☽♏ △ ♆♓	5:01 am	**2:01 am** ☽ v/c
☽ enters ♐	6:01 am	**3:01 am**
☽♐ ⚹ ♇♒	6:45 am	**3:45 am**
☽♐ □ ☿♍	8:09 am	**5:09 am**

14 Wed

2nd ♐

☽♐ □ ♀♍	3:33 am	**12:33 am**
☿♍ ⚻ ♇♒	9:03 am	**6:03 am**
♂♊ ☌ ♃♊	11:22 am	**8:22 am**
☽♐ ☍ ♃♊	1:35 pm	**10:35 am**
☽♐ ☍ ♂♊	1:40 pm	**10:40 am**
☽♐ □ ♄♓	3:38 pm	**12:38 pm**
☿ enters ♌	8:16 pm	**5:16 pm**
☽♐ △ ☉♌		**9:57 pm**
☽♐ △ ⚷♈		**10:52 pm**

15 Thu

2nd ♐

OP: After Moon squares Neptune until Moon enters Capricorn. (Sagittarius is one of the four signs in which the v/c Moon is a good thing. See page 79.) You can apply this fluid energy to both work and fun.

OP: Two back-to-back OPs: The second OP starts when the Moon enters Capricorn today until v/c Moon on Saturday. Take advantage of this long OP useful for practical matters that have to do with existing projects since Mercury is retrograde.

☽♐ △ ☉♌	12:57 am	
☽♐ △ ⚷♈	1:52 am	
☽♐ ⚻ ♅♉	8:42 am	**5:42 am**
☽♐ □ ♆♓	12:50 pm	**9:50 am**
☽♐ △ ☿♌	12:52 pm	**9:52 am** ☽ v/c
☉♌ △ ⚷♈	1:12 pm	**10:12 am**
☿♌ ⚻ ♆♓	1:19 pm	**10:19 am**
☽ enters ♑	1:51 pm	**10:51 am**
♂♊ □ ♄♓		**10:30 pm**

♂Ⅱ □ ♄⯑	1:30 am	
☽♈ △ ♀♍	3:08 pm	**12:08 pm**
☽♈ ⯑ ♃Ⅱ	7:45 pm	**4:45 pm**
☽♈ ✶ ♄⯑	8:49 pm	**5:49 pm**
☽♈ ⯑ ♂Ⅱ	9:51 pm	**6:51 pm**

FRI 16
2nd ♑

☽♈ □ ♅♈	6:30 am	**3:30 am**
☽♈ ⯑ ☉♌	9:33 am	**6:33 am**
☽♈ △ ♅♉	12:59 pm	**9:59 am**
☽♈ ⯑ ☿♌	1:57 pm	**10:57 am**
☽♈ ✶ ♆⯑	4:43 pm	**1:43 pm** ☽ v/c
☽ enters ♒	5:45 pm	**2:45 pm**
☽♒ ♂ ♀♒	6:13 pm	**3:13 pm**

SAT 17
2nd ♑

☿♌ □ ♅♉	5:47 am	**2:47 am**
☉♌ ♂ ☿♌	9:58 pm	**6:58 pm**
☽♒ ⯑ ♀♍	10:05 pm	**7:05 pm**
☽♒ △ ♃Ⅱ	10:22 pm	**7:22 pm**
♀♍ □ ♃Ⅱ		**10:53 pm**
☽♒ △ ♂Ⅱ		**11:08 pm**

SUN 18
2nd ♒

Eastern Daylight Time (EDT) plain / **Pacific Daylight Time (PDT) bold**

	JULY								AUGUST								SEPTEMBER				
S	M	T	W	T	F	S		S	M	T	W	T	F	S		S	M	T	W	T	F	S
	1	2	3	4	5	6						1	2	3		1	2	3	4	5	6	7
7	8	9	10	11	12	13		4	5	6	7	8	9	10		8	9	10	11	12	13	14
14	15	16	17	18	19	20		11	12	13	14	15	16	17		15	16	17	18	19	20	21
21	22	23	24	25	26	27		18	19	20	21	22	23	24		22	23	24	25	26	27	28
28	29	30	31					25	26	27	28	29	30	31		29	30					

19 Mon
2nd ≈
○ Full Moon 27 ≈ 15

♀♏ □ ♃ Ⅱ	1:53 am	
☽≈ △ ♂ Ⅱ	2:08 am	
♀♏ ♂ ♄ ⅹ	4:30 am	**1:30 am**
☽≈ ✳ ♄ ♈	8:01 am	**5:01 am**
☽≈ ♂ ☿ ♌	12:32 pm	**9:32 am**
☉♌ □ ♅ ♉	12:45 pm	**9:45 am**
☽≈ □ ♅ ♉	2:19 pm	**11:19 am**
☽≈ ♂ ☉♌	2:26 pm	**11:26 am** ☽ v/c
♃ Ⅱ □ ♄ ⅹ	5:46 pm	**2:46 pm**
☽ enters ⅹ	6:52 pm	**3:52 pm**

20 Tue
3rd ⅹ

☽ⅹ ♂ ♄ ⅹ	10:45 pm	**7:45 pm**
☽ⅹ □ ♃ Ⅱ	11:10 pm	**8:10 pm**
☽ⅹ ♂ ♀♏		**11:44 pm**

21 Wed
3rd ⅹ

OP: After Moon sextiles Uranus until Moon enters Aries. Good for anything, especially the arts and healing.

☽ⅹ ♂ ♀♏	2:44 am	
☽ⅹ □ ♂ Ⅱ	4:34 am	**1:34 am**
☽ⅹ ⊼ ☿ ♌	10:15 am	**7:15 am**
☽ⅹ ✳ ♅ ♉	2:32 pm	**11:32 am**
☉♌ ⊼ ♆ ⅹ	5:29 pm	**2:29 pm**
☽ⅹ ♂ ♆ ⅹ	5:54 pm	**2:54 pm** ☽ v/c
☽ⅹ ⊼ ☉♌	5:56 pm	**2:56 pm**
☽ enters ♈	7:02 pm	**4:02 pm**
☽♈ ✳ ♀≈	7:21 pm	**4:21 pm**

22 Thu
3rd ♈

SUN ENTERS VIRGO

OP: Another two back-to-back OPs: The second OP starts when the Moon enters Aries on Wednesday until v/c Moon on Friday. This OP is versatile, good for competition and sports, the dramatic arts, writing, and creativity.

☉ enters ♍	10:55 am	**7:55 am**
☉♍ ⊼ ♀≈	3:34 pm	**12:34 pm**
♀♏ □ ♂ Ⅱ	11:20 pm	**8:20 pm**
☽♈ ✳ ♃ Ⅱ		**9:05 pm**

☽♈ ✶ ♃♊	12:05 am	
☽♈ ✶ ♂♊	7:21 am	**4:21 am**
☽♈ ⊼ ♀♍	7:43 am	**4:43 am**
☿♌ △ ♅♈	8:21 am	**5:21 am**
☽♈ △ ☿♌	8:44 am	**5:44 am** ☽ v/c
☽♈ ☌ ♅♈	8:45 am	**5:45 am**
♀♍ ⊼ ♅♈	7:57 pm	**4:57 pm**
☽ enters ♉	8:00 pm	**5:00 pm**
☽♉ □ ♀≈	8:17 pm	**5:17 pm**
☽♉ △ ☉♍	10:22 pm	**7:22 pm**
☿♌ ✶ ♂♊		**9:31 pm**

Fri 23
3rd ♈

☿♌ ✶ ♂♊	12:31 am	
♂♊ ✶ ♅♈	2:33 pm	**11:33 am**
☽♉ ✶ ♄♓		**9:46 pm**

Sat 24
3rd ♉

☽♉ ✶ ♄♓	12:46 am	
☽♉ □ ☿♌	9:25 am	**6:25 am**
☽♉ △ ♀♍	3:03 pm	**12:03 pm**
☽♉ ☌ ♅♉	6:15 pm	**3:15 pm**
☽♉ ✶ ♆♓	9:40 pm	**6:40 pm** ☽ v/c
☽ enters ♊	11:04 pm	**8:04 pm**
☽♊ △ ♀≈	11:17 pm	**8:17 pm**

Sun 25
3rd ♉

OP: After Moon squares Mercury until Moon enters Gemini.
With Mercury still retrograde and the Moon in Taurus, use this
OP for practical projects.

Eastern Daylight Time (EDT) plain / **Pacific Daylight Time (PDT) bold**

	JULY							AUGUST							SEPTEMBER					
S	M	T	W	T	F	S	S	M	T	W	T	F	S	S	M	T	W	T	F	S
	1	2	3	4	5	6					1	2	3	1	2	3	4	5	6	7
7	8	9	10	11	12	13	4	5	6	7	8	9	10	8	9	10	11	12	13	14
14	15	16	17	18	19	20	11	12	13	14	15	16	17	15	16	17	18	19	20	21
21	22	23	24	25	26	27	18	19	20	21	22	23	24	22	23	24	25	26	27	28
28	29	30	31				25	26	27	28	29	30	31	29	30					

August

Mercury Note: Mercury goes direct on Wednesday, August 28, but remains in its Storm, moving slowly, until September 3.

26 Mon
3rd ♊
◑ 4th Quarter 3 ♊ 38

☽♊ □ ☉♍	5:26 am	**2:26 am**

27 Tue
4th ♊

♀♍ △ ♅ ♉	3:24 am	**12:24 am**
☽♊ □ ♄ ♓	5:02 am	**2:02 am**
☽♊ ♂ ♃ ♊	7:50 am	**4:50 am**
☽♊ ⚹ ☿ ♌	1:17 pm	**10:17 am**
☽♊ ⚹ ♇ ♈	4:11 pm	**1:11 pm**
☽♊ ♂ ♂ ♊	8:00 pm	**5:00 pm**
☽ □ ♀ ♍		**10:50 pm**

28 Wed
4th ♊
Mercury direct

OP: After Moon enters Cancer today until Moon enters Leo on Friday. Very good opportunity to implement changes and return to projects that were stuck during Mercury's retrograde period.

☽♊ □ ♀ ♍	1:50 am	
☽♊ □ ♆ ♓	3:14 am	**12:14 am** ☽ v/c
☽ enters ♋	4:47 am	**1:47 am**
☽♋ ⊼ ♀ ≈	4:56 am	**1:56 am**
☽♋ ⚹ ☉♍	3:50 pm	**12:50 pm**
♀♍ ♂ ♆ ♓	4:25 pm	**1:25 pm**
☿ D	5:14 pm	**2:14 pm**

29 Thu
4th ♋

♀ enters ♎	9:23 am	**6:23 am**
♀♎ △ ♀ ≈	10:32 am	**7:32 am**
☽♋ △ ♄ ♓	11:57 am	**8:57 am**
☽♋ □ ♇ ♈	11:50 pm	**8:50 pm**

Fri 30
4th ♋

☽♋ ⚹ ♅♉ 7:54 am **4:54 am**
☽♋ △ ♆♓ 11:24 am **8:24 am** ☽ v/c
☽ enters ♌ 1:09 pm **10:09 am**
☽♌ ☍ ♇♒ 1:14 pm **10:14 am**
☽♌ ⚹ ♀♎ 4:10 pm **1:10 pm**

Sat 31
4th ♌

☽♌ ⚻ ♄♓ 9:18 pm **6:18 pm**
☽♌ ⚹ ♃♊ **11:10 pm**

Sun 1
4th ♌
Uranus retrograde

☽♌ ⚹ ♃♊ 2:10 am
☽♌ ☌ ☿♌ 8:36 am **5:36 am**
☽♌ △ ⚷♈ 9:51 am **6:51 am**
♅℞ 11:18 am **8:18 am**
☽♌ □ ♅♉ 6:22 pm **3:22 pm**
♇ enters ♑ 8:10 pm **5:10 pm**
☽♌ ⚹ ♂♊ 8:25 pm **5:25 pm** ☽ v/c
☽♌ ⚻ ♆♓ 9:52 pm **6:52 pm**
☽♌ ⚻ ♇♑ 11:48 pm **8:48 pm**
☽ enters ♍ 11:48 pm **8:48 pm**

Eastern Daylight Time (EDT) plain / **Pacific Daylight Time (PDT) bold**

JULY

S	M	T	W	T	F	S
	1	2	3	4	5	6
7	8	9	10	11	12	13
14	15	16	17	18	19	20
21	22	23	24	25	26	27
28	29	30	31			

AUGUST

S	M	T	W	T	F	S
				1	2	3
4	5	6	7	8	9	10
11	12	13	14	15	16	17
18	19	20	21	22	23	24
25	26	27	28	29	30	31

SEPTEMBER

S	M	T	W	T	F	S
1	2	3	4	5	6	7
8	9	10	11	12	13	14
15	16	17	18	19	20	21
22	23	24	25	26	27	28
29	30					

September

Mercury Note: Mercury finally leaves its Storm on Wednesday. Look over your notes on any ideas that occurred to you while Mercury was retrograde or slow. How do they look now?

2 Mon
4th ♍︎
● New Moon 11 ♍︎ 04
Labor Day (US)
Labour Day (Canada)

☿♌︎ △ ⚷♈︎	9:46 am	**6:46 am**
☽♍︎ ☌ ☉♍︎	9:56 pm	**6:56 pm**
♂♊︎ □ ♆♓︎		**9:10 pm**

3 Tue
1st ♍︎

♂♊︎ □ ♆♓︎	12:10 am	
☽♍︎ ☍ ♄♓︎	8:37 am	**5:37 am**
☽♍︎ □ ♃♊︎	2:34 pm	**11:34 am**
☽♍︎ ⚻ ⚷♈︎	9:45 pm	**6:45 pm**

4 Wed
1st ♍︎

☽♍︎ △ ⛢♉︎	6:37 am	**3:37 am**
☽♍︎ ☍ ♆♓︎	10:05 am	**7:05 am**
☽♍︎ □ ♂♊︎	12:00 pm	**9:00 am**
☽♍︎ △ ♀♑︎	12:06 pm	**9:06 am** ☽ v/c
☽ enters ♎︎	12:12 pm	**9:12 am**
♂♊︎ ⚻ ♀♑︎	1:59 pm	**10:59 am**
♂ enters ♋︎	3:46 pm	**12:46 pm**

5 Thu
1st ♎︎

☽♎︎ ☌ ♀♎︎	5:12 am	**2:12 am**
☽♎︎ ⚻ ♄♓︎	9:11 pm	**6:11 pm**

☽︎♎︎ △ ♃ ♊︎	4:08 am	**1:08 am**
☽︎♎︎ ☌ ♅ ♈︎	10:39 am	**7:39 am**
☽︎♎︎ ✶ ☿ ♌︎	7:11 pm	**4:11 pm**
☽︎♎︎ ⚻ ♅ ♉︎	7:42 pm	**4:42 pm**
☽︎♎︎ ⚻ ♆ ♓︎	11:04 pm	**8:04 pm**
☿♌︎ ☐ ♅ ♉︎		**9:21 pm**
☽︎♎︎ ☐ ♀ ♑︎		**10:08 pm** ☽ v/c
☽ enters ♏︎		**10:18 pm**

Fri 6
1st ♎︎

☿♌︎ ☐ ♅ ♉︎	12:21 am	
☽︎♎︎ ☐ ♀ ♑︎	1:08 am	☽ v/c
☽ enters ♏︎	1:18 am	
☽♏︎ △ ♂ ♋︎	4:24 am	**1:24 am**
☉♍︎ ☌ ♄ ♓︎		**9:35 pm**

Sat 7
1st ♎︎

☉♍︎ ☌ ♄ ♓︎	12:35 am	
☿♌︎ ⚻ ♆ ♓︎	6:52 am	**3:52 am**
☽♏︎ △ ♄ ♓︎	9:37 am	**6:37 am**
☽♏︎ ✶ ☉♍︎	10:29 am	**7:29 am**
☽♏︎ ⚻ ♃ ♊︎	5:20 pm	**2:20 pm**
☽♏︎ ⚻ ♅ ♈︎	11:01 pm	**8:01 pm**
☿♌︎ ⚻ ♀ ♑︎		**9:55 pm**
☿ enters ♍︎		**11:50 pm**

Sun 8
1st ♏︎

Eastern Daylight Time (EDT) plain / **Pacific Daylight Time (PDT) bold**

AUGUST						
S	M	T	W	T	F	S
				1	2	3
4	5	6	7	8	9	10
11	12	13	14	15	16	17
18	19	20	21	22	23	24
25	26	27	28	29	30	31

SEPTEMBER						
S	M	T	W	T	F	S
1	2	3	4	5	6	7
8	9	10	11	12	13	14
15	16	17	18	19	20	21
22	23	24	25	26	27	28
29	30					

OCTOBER						
S	M	T	W	T	F	S
		1	2	3	4	5
6	7	8	9	10	11	12
13	14	15	16	17	18	19
20	21	22	23	24	25	26
27	28	29	30	31		

September

9 Mon
1st ♏

OP: After Moon trines Neptune until v/c Moon. This is a good, fluid time when emotions run deep and imagination is fertile.

☿♌ ⊼ ♀♑	12:55 am	
☿ enters ♍	2:50 am	
☽♏ ☍ ♅♉	7:58 am	**4:58 am**
☽♏ △ ♆♓	11:07 am	**8:07 am**
☽♏ ✶ ♀♑	1:11 pm	**10:11 am** ☽ v/c
☽ enters ♐	1:26 pm	**10:26 am**
☽♐ □ ☿♍	2:50 pm	**11:50 am**
☽♐ ⊼ ♂♋	7:28 pm	**4:28 pm**

10 Tue
1st ♐

◗ 2nd Quarter 19 ♐ 00 (Pacific)

☽♐ ✶ ♀♎	6:48 pm	**3:48 pm**
☽♐ □ ♄♓	8:02 pm	**5:02 pm**
☽♐ □ ☉♍		**11:06 pm**

11 Wed
1st ♐

◗ 2nd Quarter 19 ♐ 00 (Eastern)

☽♐ □ ☉♍	2:06 am	
☽♐ ☍ ♃♊	4:07 am	**1:07 am**
♀♎ ⊼ ♄♓	6:52 am	**3:52 am**
☽♐ △ ♅♈	8:55 am	**5:55 am**
☽♐ ⊼ ♅♉	5:28 pm	**2:28 pm**
☽♐ □ ♆♓	8:21 pm	**5:21 pm** ☽ v/c
☽ enters ♑	10:38 pm	**7:38 pm**
☿♍ ✶ ♂♋	11:42 pm	**8:42 pm**

12 Thu
2nd ♑

☉♍ □ ♃♊	6:53 am	**3:53 am**
☽♑ ☍ ♂♋	6:56 am	**3:56 am**
☽♑ △ ☿♍	7:36 am	**4:36 am**
☽♑ ✶ ♄♓		**11:53 pm**

162

☽♑ ✶ ♄♓ 2:53 am	**Fri 13**
☽♑ □ ♀♎ 7:30 am **4:30 am**	2nd ♑
☽♑ ⊼ ♃♊ 11:02 am **8:02 am**	
☽♑ △ ☉♍ 1:01 pm **10:01 am**	
☽♑ □ ♅♈ 3:01 pm **12:01 pm**	
☽♑ △ ♅♉ 11:04 pm **8:04 pm**	
☽♑ ✶ ♆♓ **10:40 pm**	

☽♑ ✶ ♆♓ 1:40 am	**Sat 14**
☽♑ ☌ ♀♑ 3:35 am **12:35 am** ☽ v/c	2nd ♑
☽ enters ♒ 3:53 am **12:53 am**	
☽♒ ⊼ ♂♋ 1:52 pm **10:52 am**	
☉♍ ⊼ ♅♈ 4:22 pm **1:22 pm**	
☽♒ ⊼ ☿♍ 7:21 pm **4:21 pm**	
♀♎ △ ♃♊ **10:34 pm**	

♀♎ △ ♃♊ 1:34 am	**Sun 15**
☽♒ △ ♃♊ 2:05 pm **11:05 am**	2nd ♒
☽♒ △ ♀♎ 3:09 pm **12:09 pm**	
☽♒ ✶ ♅♈ 5:24 pm **2:24 pm**	
☽♒ ⊼ ☉♍ 7:15 pm **4:15 pm**	
☽♒ □ ♅♉ **10:04 pm** ☽ v/c	

Eastern Daylight Time (EDT) plain / **Pacific Daylight Time (PDT) bold**

AUGUST							**SEPTEMBER**							**OCTOBER**						
S	M	T	W	T	F	S	S	M	T	W	T	F	S	S	M	T	W	T	F	S
				1	2	3	1	2	3	4	5	6	7			1	2	3	4	5
4	5	6	7	8	9	10	8	9	10	11	12	13	14	6	7	8	9	10	11	12
11	12	13	14	15	16	17	15	16	17	18	19	20	21	13	14	15	16	17	18	19
18	19	20	21	22	23	24	22	23	24	25	26	27	28	20	21	22	23	24	25	26
25	26	27	28	29	30	31	29	30						27	28	29	30	31		

September

16 Mon
2nd ≈

☽≈ □ ♅ ♉	1:04 am		☽ v/c
☽ enters ♓	5:39 am	**2:39 am**	
☽♓ △ ♂♋	5:03 pm	**2:03 pm**	
♀⚷ ⚶ ☄ ♈	5:29 pm	**2:29 pm**	
☽♓ ⚷ ☿ ♍		**11:55 pm**	

17 Tue
2nd ♓
Lunar Eclipse | ○ Full Moon 25 ♓ 41

☽♓ ⚷ ☿ ♍	2:55 am	
☽♓ ♂ ♄ ♓	6:11 am	**3:11 am**
☽♓ □ ♃ ♊	2:30 pm	**11:30 am**
☽♓ ⊼ ♀⚷	7:31 pm	**4:31 pm**
☽♓ ⚷ ☉♍	10:34 pm	**7:34 pm**
☽♓ ⚹ ♅ ♉		**9:53 pm**

18 Wed
3rd ♓

☽♓ ⚹ ♅ ♉	12:53 am		
☽♓ ♂ ♆♓	3:10 am	**12:10 am**	
☿♍ ⚷ ♄♓	4:50 am	**1:50 am**	
☽♓ ⚹ ♇♑	5:02 am	**2:02 am**	☽ v/c
☽ enters ♈	5:24 am	**2:24 am**	
☽♈ □ ♂♋	6:27 pm	**3:27 pm**	

19 Thu
3rd ♈

☽♈ ⊼ ☿♍	8:57 am	**5:57 am**
☉♍ △ ♅ ♉	10:04 am	**7:04 am**
☽♈ ⚹ ♃ ♊	2:11 pm	**11:11 am**
☽♈ ♂ ⚷♈	4:44 pm	**1:44 pm**
☽♈ ⚷ ♀⚷	11:14 pm	**8:14 pm**
☽♈ ⊼ ☉♍		**10:26 pm**

☽♈ ⊼ ☉♍	1:26 am	
☽♈ □ ☿♑	4:39 am	**1:39 am** ☽ v/c
☽ enters ♉	5:03 am	**2:03 am**
♀♎ ⊼ ♅♉	1:36 pm	**10:36 am**
☉♍ ☍ ♆♓	8:17 pm	**5:17 pm**
☽♉ ⚹ ♂♋	8:18 pm	**5:18 pm**

Fri 20
3rd ♈

☿♍ □ ♃♊	4:50 am	**1:50 am**
☽♉ ⚹ ♄♓	5:28 am	**2:28 am**
☽♉ △ ☿♍	4:30 pm	**1:30 pm**
♀♎ ⊼ ♆♓	4:53 pm	**1:53 pm**
☿♍ ⊼ ⚷♈	10:59 pm	**7:59 pm**
☽♉ ♂ ♅♉		**10:29 pm**
☉♍ △ ♀♑		**11:12 pm**

Sat 21
3rd ♉
UN International Day of Peace

☽♉ ♂ ♅♉	1:29 am	
☉♍ △ ♀♑	2:12 am	
☽♉ ⚹ ♆♓	3:50 am	**12:50 am**
☽♉ ⊼ ♀♎	4:53 am	**1:53 am**
☽♉ △ ♀♑	5:57 am	**2:57 am**
☽♉ △ ☉♍	6:14 am	**3:14 am** ☽ v/c
☽ enters ♊	6:24 am	**3:24 am**
☉ enters ♎	8:44 am	**5:44 am**
♀♎ □ ♀♑	5:15 pm	**2:15 pm**
♀ enters ♏	10:36 pm	**7:36 pm**

Sun 22
3rd ♉
Fall Equinox
Mabon
Sun enters Libra

OP: After Moon sextiles Neptune until Moon enters Gemini. Productive time during the wee hours of the morning. Keep it practical since we are between eclipses.

Eastern Daylight Time (EDT) plain / **Pacific Daylight Time (PDT) bold**

	AUGUST								SEPTEMBER								OCTOBER				
S	M	T	W	T	F	S		S	M	T	W	T	F	S		S	M	T	W	T	F	S
				1	2	3		1	2	3	4	5	6	7				1	2	3	4	5
4	5	6	7	8	9	10		8	9	10	11	12	13	14		6	7	8	9	10	11	12
11	12	13	14	15	16	17		15	16	17	18	19	20	21		13	14	15	16	17	18	19
18	19	20	21	22	23	24		22	23	24	25	26	27	28		20	21	22	23	24	25	26
25	26	27	28	29	30	31		29	30							27	28	29	30	31		

23 Mon
3rd ♊

☽♊ □ ♄♓	7:58 am	**4:58 am**
☽♊ ☌ ♃♊	6:39 pm	**3:39 pm**
☽♊ ⚹ ⚷♈	8:45 pm	**5:45 pm**

24 Tue
3rd ♊
◐ 4th Quarter 2 ♋ 12

☽♊ □ ☿♍	4:13 am	**1:13 am**
☽♊ □ ♆♓	7:59 am	**4:59 am** ☽ v/c
☽♊ ⊼ ♀♑	10:19 am	**7:19 am**
☽ enters ♋	10:50 am	**7:50 am**
☿♍ △ ♅♉	1:27 pm	**10:27 am**
☽♋ △ ♀♏	2:30 pm	**11:30 am**
☽♋ □ ☉♎	2:50 pm	**11:50 am**

25 Wed
4th ♋

☿♍ ☍ ♆♓	7:07 am	**4:07 am**
☽♋ ☌ ♂♋	8:40 am	**5:40 am**
☽♋ △ ♄♓	1:52 pm	**10:52 am**
☿♍ △ ♀♑		**9:14 pm**

26 Thu
4th ♋

☿♍ △ ♀♑	12:14 am	
☽♋ □ ⚷♈	3:37 am	**12:37 am**
☿ enters ♎	4:09 am	**1:09 am**
☽♋ ⚹ ♅♉	1:02 pm	**10:02 am**
☽♋ △ ♆♓	3:38 pm	**12:38 pm**
☽♋ ☍ ♀♑	6:12 pm	**3:12 pm** ☽ v/c
☽ enters ♌	6:47 pm	**3:47 pm**
☽♌ ⚹ ☿♎	9:18 pm	**6:18 pm**

☽♌ ⚹ ☉♎ 3:51 am **12:51 am**
☽♌ □ ♀♏ 4:47 am **1:47 am**
☽♌ ⊼ ♄♓ 11:04 pm **8:04 pm**

Fri 27
4th ♌

☽♌ ⚹ ♃♊ 12:05 pm **9:05 am**
☽♌ △ ♗♈ 1:38 pm **10:38 am**
☽♌ □ ♅♉ 11:36 pm **8:36 pm** ☽ v/c
☽♌ ⊼ ♆♓ **11:16 pm**

Sat 28
4th ♌

☽♌ ⊼ ♆♓ 2:16 am
☽♌ ⊼ ♀♑ 5:03 am **2:03 am**
☽ enters ♍ 5:42 am **2:42 am**
☽♍ ⚹ ♀♏ 10:49 pm **7:49 pm**
♂♋ △ ♄♓ **9:06 pm**

Sun 29
4th ♌

Eastern Daylight Time (EDT) plain / **Pacific Daylight Time (PDT) bold**

AUGUST							SEPTEMBER							OCTOBER						
S	M	T	W	T	F	S	S	M	T	W	T	F	S	S	M	T	W	T	F	S
				1	2	3	1	2	3	4	5	6	7			1	2	3	4	5
4	5	6	7	8	9	10	8	9	10	11	12	13	14	6	7	8	9	10	11	12
11	12	13	14	15	16	17	15	16	17	18	19	20	21	13	14	15	16	17	18	19
18	19	20	21	22	23	24	22	23	24	25	26	27	28	20	21	22	23	24	25	26
25	26	27	28	29	30	31	29	30						27	28	29	30	31		

30 Mon
4th ♍

♂⊗ △ ♄ ⌘	12:06 am	
☽♍ ☌ ♄ ⌘	10:38 am	**7:38 am**
☽♍ ✶ ♂⊗	11:11 am	**8:11 am**
☉♎ ☌ ☿♎	5:09 pm	**2:09 pm**
☽♍ □ ♃ ♊		**9:30 pm**
☽♍ ⊼ ⚷ ♈		**10:42 pm**

1 Tue
4th ♍

☽♍ □ ♃ ♊	12:30 am	
☽♍ ⊼ ⚷ ♈	1:42 am	
☽♍ △ ♅ ♉	12:00 pm	**9:00 am**
☽♍ ☍ ♆ ⌘	2:42 pm	**11:42 am**
☽♍ △ ♀ ♑	5:39 pm	**2:39 pm** ☽ v/c
☽ enters ♎	6:20 pm	**3:20 pm**

2 Wed
4th ♎

Solar Eclipse | ● New Moon 10 ♎ 04
Rosh Hashanah begins at sundown

☽♎ ☌ ☉♎	2:49 pm	**11:49 am**
☽♎ ☌ ☿♎	6:22 pm	**3:22 pm**
☽♎ ⊼ ♄ ⌘	11:17 pm	**8:17 pm**

3 Thu
1st ♎

☽♎ □ ♂⊗	3:00 am	**12:00 am**
☽♎ △ ♃ ♊	1:40 pm	**10:40 am**
☽♎ ☍ ⚷ ♈	2:32 pm	**11:32 am**
☽♎ ⊼ ♅ ♉		**9:56 pm**
☿♎ ⊼ ♄ ⌘		**11:46 pm**

☽︎⚷︎♅︎☌︎	12:56 am	
☿︎⚷︎♄︎⚹︎	2:46 am	
☽︎⚷︎♆︎⚹︎	3:37 am	**12:37 am**
☽︎☐︎♀︎♑︎	6:40 am	**3:40 am** ☽ v/c
☽ enters ♏︎	7:22 am	**4:22 am**
♀︎♏︎△♄︎⚹︎	1:04 pm	**10:04 am**

FRI 4
1st ♎︎

☽︎♏︎△♄︎⚹︎	11:46 am	**8:46 am**
☽︎♏︎☌♀︎♏︎	2:28 pm	**11:28 am**
☽︎♏︎△♂︎♋︎	6:27 pm	**3:27 pm**
☽︎♏︎⚷︎♃︎♊︎		**11:19 pm**
☿︎♎︎☐︎♂︎♋︎		**11:37 pm**
☽︎♏︎⚷︎♅︎♈︎		**11:52 pm**

SAT 5
1st ♏︎

☽︎♏︎⚷︎♃︎♊︎	2:19 am	
☿︎♎︎☐︎♂︎♋︎	2:37 am	
☽︎♏︎⚷︎♅︎♈︎	2:52 am	
☽︎♏︎☌♅︎☌︎	1:09 pm	**10:09 am**
☉︎♎︎⚷︎♄︎♄︎	2:28 pm	**11:28 am**
☽︎♏︎△♆︎⚹︎	3:47 pm	**12:47 pm**
☽︎♏︎⚹︎♀︎♑︎	6:52 pm	**3:52 pm** ☽ v/c
☽ enters ♐︎	7:34 pm	**4:34 pm**

SUN 6
1st ♏︎

OP: After Moon opposes Uranus until v/c Moon. Take advantage of the only Opportunity Period for weeks. Good for everything from deep romance to hard work.

Eastern Daylight Time (EDT) plain / **Pacific Daylight Time (PDT) bold**

SEPTEMBER								OCTOBER								NOVEMBER					
S	M	T	W	T	F	S		S	M	T	W	T	F	S		S	M	T	W	T	F	S
1	2	3	4	5	6	7				1	2	3	4	5							1	2
8	9	10	11	12	13	14		6	7	8	9	10	11	12		3	4	5	6	7	8	9
15	16	17	18	19	20	21		13	14	15	16	17	18	19		10	11	12	13	14	15	16
22	23	24	25	26	27	28		20	21	22	23	24	25	26		17	18	19	20	21	22	23
29	30							27	28	29	30	31				24	25	26	27	28	29	30

7 Mon
1st ♐

☽♐ □ ♄ ♓	10:50 pm	**7:50 pm**
☽♐ ⚹ ☉ ♎		**10:49 pm**

8 Tue
1st ♐

☽♐ ⚹ ☉ ♎	1:49 am	
♀♏ △ ♂ ♋	6:22 am	**3:22 am**
☽♐ ⚻ ♂ ♋	8:02 am	**5:02 am**
☿♎ △ ♃ ♊	8:23 am	**5:23 am**
☿♎ ☍ ♅ ♈	10:36 am	**7:36 am**
☽♐ ☍ ♃ ♊	1:10 pm	**10:10 am**
☽♐ △ ♅ ♈	1:27 pm	**10:27 am**
☽♐ ⚹ ☿ ♎	1:54 pm	**10:54 am**
☽♐ ⚻ ♅ ♉	11:23 pm	**8:23 pm**
☽♐ □ ♆ ♓		**10:54 pm** ☽ v/c

9 Wed
1st ♐
JUPITER RETROGRADE

☽♐ □ ♆ ♓	1:54 am	☽ v/c
♃ ℞	3:05 am	**12:05 am**
☽ enters ♑	5:38 am	**2:38 am**

10 Thu
1st ♑
◑ 2nd Quarter 17 ♑ 58

☽♑ ⚹ ♄ ♓	7:16 am	**4:16 am**
♀♏ ⚻ ♃ ♊	11:44 am	**8:44 am**
♀♏ ⚻ ♅ ♈	12:57 pm	**9:57 am**
☽♑ □ ☉ ♎	2:55 pm	**11:55 am**
☽♑ ☍ ♂ ♋	6:22 pm	**3:22 pm**
☽♑ ⚻ ♃ ♊	9:02 pm	**6:02 pm**
☽♑ □ ♅ ♈	9:07 pm	**6:07 pm**
☽♑ ⚹ ♀♏	9:58 pm	**6:58 pm**

Fri 11
2nd ♑
Yom Kippur begins at sundown
Pluto direct

☽♑ □ ☿♎	5:35 am	**2:35 am**
☽♑ △ ♅♉	6:31 am	**3:31 am**
☽♑ ⚹ ♆♓	8:54 am	**5:54 am**
☽♑ ☌ ♇♑	11:53 am	**8:53 am** ☽ v/c
☽ enters ♒	12:31 pm	**9:31 am**
☿♎ ⚻ ♅♉	1:11 pm	**10:11 am**
♇D	8:34 pm	**5:34 pm**

Sat 12
2nd ♒

♃♊ ⚹ ⚷♈	3:31 am	**12:31 am**
☿♎ ⚻ ♆♓	8:41 am	**5:41 am**
☽♒ △ ☉♎	11:39 pm	**8:39 pm**
☽♒ ⚻ ♂♋		**9:44 pm**
☽♒ ⚹ ⚷♈		**10:19 pm**
☽♒ △ ♃♊		**10:22 pm**

Sun 13
2nd ♒

☽♒ ⚻ ♂♋	12:44 am	
☽♒ ⚹ ⚷♈	1:19 am	
☽♒ △ ♃♊	1:22 am	
☽♒ □ ♀♏	7:08 am	**4:08 am**
☿♎ □ ♇♑	10:03 am	**7:03 am**
☽♒ □ ♅♉	10:11 am	**7:11 am** ☽ v/c
☿ enters ♏	3:23 pm	**12:23 pm**
☽ enters ♓	3:55 pm	**12:55 pm**
☽♓ △ ☿♏	3:59 pm	**12:59 pm**
♂♋ □ ⚷♈	4:36 pm	**1:36 pm**
☉♎ ☍ ⚷♈	10:28 pm	**7:28 pm**
☉♎ △ ♃♊	11:52 pm	**8:52 pm**

Eastern Daylight Time (EDT) plain / **Pacific Daylight Time (PDT) bold**

SEPTEMBER

S	M	T	W	T	F	S
1	2	3	4	5	6	7
8	9	10	11	12	13	14
15	16	17	18	19	20	21
22	23	24	25	26	27	28
29	30					

OCTOBER

S	M	T	W	T	F	S
		1	2	3	4	5
6	7	8	9	10	11	12
13	14	15	16	17	18	19
20	21	22	23	24	25	26
27	28	29	30	31		

NOVEMBER

S	M	T	W	T	F	S
					1	2
3	4	5	6	7	8	9
10	11	12	13	14	15	16
17	18	19	20	21	22	23
24	25	26	27	28	29	30

14 Mon
2nd ♓︎

Indigenous Peoples' Day
Thanksgiving Day (Canada)

OP: After Moon squares Jupiter today or on Tuesday until v/c Moon on Tuesday. Great for artistic activities, romance, or anything you want to see grow.

☉︎⚏□♂︎♋︎	4:15 am	**1:15 am**	
☽︎♓︎ ♂ ♄♓︎	2:09 pm	**11:09 am**	
♀︎♏︎ ☍♅♉︎	6:22 pm	**3:22 pm**	
☽︎♓︎ □ ♃♊︎		**11:38 pm**	

15 Tue
2nd ♓︎

☽︎♓︎ □ ♃♊︎	2:38 am		
☽︎♓︎ △ ♂♋︎	3:41 am	**12:41 am**	
☽︎♓︎ ⚻ ☉︎⚏	4:34 am	**1:34 am**	
☽︎♓︎ ⚹ ♅♉︎	10:59 am	**7:59 am**	
☽︎♓︎ △ ♀︎♏︎	12:28 pm	**9:28 am**	
☽︎♓︎ ♂ ♆♓︎	1:09 pm	**10:09 am**	
☽︎♓︎ ⚹ ♀︎♑︎	4:00 pm	**1:00 pm**	☽︎ v/c
☽︎ enters ♈︎	4:34 pm	**1:34 pm**	
♀︎♏︎ △♆♓︎	8:49 pm	**5:49 pm**	
☽︎♈︎ ⚻ ☿♏︎	10:22 pm	**7:22 pm**	

16 Wed
2nd ♈︎

Sukkot begins at sundown

☽︎♈︎ ♂ ♇♈︎		**10:56 pm**	
☽︎♈︎ ⚹ ♃♊︎		**11:09 pm**	

17 Thu
2nd ♈︎

○ Full Moon 24 ♈︎ 35

☽︎♈︎ ♂ ♇♈︎	1:56 am		
☽︎♈︎ ⚹ ♃♊︎	2:09 am		
☽︎♈︎□♂♋︎	4:44 am	**1:44 am**	
☽︎♈︎ ☍ ☉︎⚏	7:26 am	**4:26 am**	
♀︎♏︎ ⚹ ♀︎♑︎	8:30 am	**5:30 am**	
☽︎♈︎ □ ♀︎♑︎	3:26 pm	**12:26 pm**	☽︎ v/c
♀︎ enters ♐︎	3:28 pm	**12:28 pm**	
☽︎ enters ♉︎	4:00 pm	**1:00 pm**	
☽︎♉︎ ⚻ ♀︎♐︎	4:02 pm	**1:02 pm**	

Fri 18
3rd ♉

☽♉ ☍ ☿♏ 3:15 am **12:15 am**
☽♉ ⚹ ♄♓ 1:13 pm **10:13 am**
☉♎ ⚻ ♅♉ **11:40 pm**

Sat 19
3rd ♉

☉♎ ⚻ ♅♉ 2:40 am
☽♉ ⚹ ♂♋ 6:00 am **3:00 am**
☽♉ ☌ ♅♉ 10:11 am **7:11 am**
☽♉ ⚻ ☉♎ 10:44 am **7:44 am**
☽♉ ⚹ ♆♓ 12:28 pm **9:28 am**
☽♉ △ ♇♑ 3:33 pm **12:33 pm** ☽ v/c
☽ enters ♊ 4:07 pm **1:07 pm**
☽♊ ☍ ♀♐ 8:30 pm **5:30 pm**

OP: After Moon conjoins Uranus until Moon enters Gemini. Good weekend hours for either work or play; especially good for innovative artistic endeavors.

Sun 20
3rd ♊

☽♊ ⚻ ☿♏ 9:39 am **6:39 am**
☉♎ ⚻ ♆♓ 11:44 am **8:44 am**
☽♊ □ ♄♓ 2:07 pm **11:07 am**

Eastern Daylight Time (EDT) plain / **Pacific Daylight Time (PDT) bold**

SEPTEMBER

S	M	T	W	T	F	S
1	2	3	4	5	6	7
8	9	10	11	12	13	14
15	16	17	18	19	20	21
22	23	24	25	26	27	28
29	30					

OCTOBER

S	M	T	W	T	F	S
		1	2	3	4	5
6	7	8	9	10	11	12
13	14	15	16	17	18	19
20	21	22	23	24	25	26
27	28	29	30	31		

NOVEMBER

S	M	T	W	T	F	S
					1	2
3	4	5	6	7	8	9
10	11	12	13	14	15	16
17	18	19	20	21	22	23
24	25	26	27	28	29	30

21 MON
3rd ♊

OP: After Moon squares Neptune until v/c Moon. Wait some time after the square for clarity and use this short period to do the right thing; especially positive for networking and communication.

☽♊ ⚹ ♅♈	3:06 am	**12:06 am**
☽♊ ☌ ♃♊	3:25 am	**12:25 am**
☽♊ □ ♆♓	2:50 pm	**11:50 am**
☽♊ △ ☉♎	5:00 pm	**2:00 pm** ☽ v/c
☽♊ ⊼ ♇♑	6:15 pm	**3:15 pm**
☽ enters ♋	6:50 pm	**3:50 pm**
☿♏ △ ♄♓		**11:35 pm**

22 TUE
3rd ♋
SUN ENTERS SCORPIO

☿♏ △ ♄♓	2:35 am	
☽♋ ⊼ ♀♐	4:30 am	**1:30 am**
☉♎ □ ♇♑	10:15 am	**7:15 am**
☉ enters ♏	6:15 pm	**3:15 pm**
☽♋ △ ♄♓	6:17 pm	**3:17 pm**
☽♋ △ ☿♏	8:22 pm	**5:22 pm**

23 WED
3rd ♋
SUKKOT ENDS

☽♋ □ ♅♈	8:15 am	**5:15 am**
☽♋ ☌ ♂♋	5:20 pm	**2:20 pm**
☽♋ ⚹ ♅♉	6:16 pm	**3:16 pm**
☽♋ △ ♆♓	9:00 pm	**6:00 pm**
☽♋ ☍ ♇♑		**9:47 pm** ☽ v/c
☽ enters ♌		**10:24 pm**

24 THU
3rd ♋
◑ 4th Quarter 1 ♌ 24

☽♋ ☍ ♇♑	12:47 am	☽ v/c
☽ enters ♌	1:24 am	
☽♌ □ ☉♏	4:03 am	**1:03 am**
☽♌ △ ♀♐	5:43 pm	**2:43 pm**
♂♋ ⚹ ♅♉	8:13 pm	**5:13 pm**
☽♌ ⊼ ♄♓		**11:27 pm**

Fri 25
4th ♌

☽♌ ⚻ ♄♓ 2:27 am
☽♌ □ ☿♏ 12:41 pm **9:41 am**
☽♌ △ ⚷♈ 5:22 pm **2:22 pm**
☽♌ ⚹ ♃♊ 5:42 pm **2:42 pm**

Sat 26
4th ♌

☽♌ □ ♅♉ 4:04 am **1:04 am** ☽ v/c
☽♌ ⚻ ♆♓ 7:02 am **4:02 am**
☽♌ ⚻ ♇♑ 11:11 am **8:11 am**
☽ enters ♍ 11:47 am **8:47 am**
☽♍ ⚹ ☉♏ 7:54 pm **4:54 pm**
☿♏ ⚻ ⚷♈ **11:24 pm**

Sun 27
4th ♍

☿♏ ⚻ ⚷♈ 2:24 am
☿♏ ⚻ ♃♊ 4:50 am **1:50 am**
☽♍ □ ♀♐ 11:39 am **8:39 am**
☽♍ ☍ ♄♓ 1:56 pm **10:56 am**

Eastern Daylight Time (EDT) plain / **Pacific Daylight Time (PDT) bold**

SEPTEMBER

S	M	T	W	T	F	S
1	2	3	4	5	6	7
8	9	10	11	12	13	14
15	16	17	18	19	20	21
22	23	24	25	26	27	28
29	30					

OCTOBER

S	M	T	W	T	F	S
		1	2	3	4	5
6	7	8	9	10	11	12
13	14	15	16	17	18	19
20	21	22	23	24	25	26
27	28	29	30	31		

NOVEMBER

S	M	T	W	T	F	S
					1	2
3	4	5	6	7	8	9
10	11	12	13	14	15	16
17	18	19	20	21	22	23
24	25	26	27	28	29	30

October

28 Mon

4th ♍

OP: After Moon opposes Neptune until v/c Moon. Excellent for cleaning up and getting organized during the Last Quarter Moon.

☽♍ ⚻ ⚷♈	5:20 am	**2:20 am**
☽♍ □ ♃♊	5:37 am	**2:37 am**
♂♋ △ ♆♓	8:31 am	**5:31 am**
☽♍ ⚹ ☿♏	9:16 am	**6:16 am**
♀♐ □ ♄♓	9:35 am	**6:35 am**
☽♍ △ ♅♉	4:23 pm	**1:23 pm**
☽♍ ☍ ♆♓	7:31 pm	**4:31 pm**
☽♍ ⚹ ♂♋	7:55 pm	**4:55 pm**
☽♍ △ ♇♑	11:54 pm	**8:54 pm** ☽ v/c
☽ enters ♎		**9:30 pm**

29 Tue

4th ♍

☽ enters ♎	12:30 am	
☽♎ ⚻ ♄♓		**11:50 pm**

30 Wed

4th ♎

☽♎ ⚻ ♄♓	2:50 am	
☽♎ ⚹ ♀♐	7:39 am	**4:39 am**
☽♎ ☍ ⚷♈	6:13 pm	**3:13 pm**
☿♏ ☍ ♅♉	6:15 pm	**3:15 pm**
☽♎ △ ♃♊	6:22 pm	**3:22 pm**

31 Thu

4th ♎

Halloween

Samhain

☽♎ ⚻ ♅♉	5:15 am	**2:15 am**
☽♎ ⚻ ♆♓	8:27 am	**5:27 am**
☽♎ □ ♂♋	10:57 am	**7:57 am**
☽♎ □ ♇♑	12:57 pm	**9:57 am** ☽ v/c
☽ enters ♏	1:29 pm	**10:29 am**
☿♏ △ ♆♓	8:33 pm	**5:33 pm**

☽♏ ☌ ☉♏	8:47 am	**5:47 am**
☽♏ △ ♄ ⅄	3:20 pm	**12:20 pm**

FRI 1
4th ♏
● New Moon 9 ♏ 35
ALL SAINTS' DAY

♃Ⅱ ⚹ ♆♈	4:12 am	**1:12 am**
☿♏ △ ♂♋	4:21 am	**1:21 am**
☽♏ ⚻ ♃Ⅱ	6:18 am	**3:18 am**
☽♏ ⚻ ♆♈	6:19 am	**3:19 am**
☿♏ ⚹ ♀♑	11:03 am	**8:03 am**
☿ enters ♐	3:18 pm	**12:18 pm**
☽♏ ☍ ♅♉	5:06 pm	**2:06 pm**
☽♏ △ ♆♓	8:20 pm	**5:20 pm**
☽♏ △ ♂♋		**9:40 pm**
☽♏ ⚹ ♀♑		**9:51 pm** ☽ v/c
☽ enters ♐		**10:19 pm**
☽♐ ☌ ☿♐		**11:37 pm**

SAT 2
1st ♏

☽♏ △ ♂♋	12:40 am	
☽♏ ⚹ ♀♑	12:51 am	☽ v/c
☽ enters ♐	1:19 am	
☽♐ ☌ ☿♐	1:37 am	
♂♋ ☍ ♀♑	6:37 am	**3:37 am**
♀♐ ☍ ♃Ⅱ	10:25 am	**7:25 am**
♀♐ △ ♆♈	11:22 am	**8:22 am**
♂ enters ♌	11:10 pm	**8:10 pm**
☽♐ □ ♄♓		**10:19 pm**

SUN 3
1st ♏
DAYLIGHT SAVING TIME ENDS AT 2:00 A.M.

Eastern Daylight Time (EDT) becomes Eastern Standard Time (EST) November 3 (plain)
Pacific Daylight Time (PDT) becomes Pacific Standard Time (PST) November 3 (bold)

SEPTEMBER						
S	M	T	W	T	F	S
1	2	3	4	5	6	7
8	9	10	11	12	13	14
15	16	17	18	19	20	21
22	23	24	25	26	27	28
29	30					

OCTOBER						
S	M	T	W	T	F	S
		1	2	3	4	5
6	7	8	9	10	11	12
13	14	15	16	17	18	19
20	21	22	23	24	25	26
27	28	29	30	31		

NOVEMBER						
S	M	T	W	T	F	S
					1	2
3	4	5	6	7	8	9
10	11	12	13	14	15	16
17	18	19	20	21	22	23
24	25	26	27	28	29	30

November

4 Mon
1st ♐

☽♐ □ ♄♓	1:19 am	
☉♏△♄♓	12:36 pm	**9:36 am**
☽♐ ☍ ♃♊	3:32 pm	**12:32 pm**
☽♐ △ ⚷♈	3:44 pm	**12:44 pm**
☽♐ ☌ ♀♐	6:51 pm	**3:51 pm**
☽♐ ⚻ ♅♉		**11:10 pm**

5 Tue
1st ♐

Election Day (general)

☽♐ ⚻ ♅♉	2:10 am		
☽♐ □ ♆♓	5:23 am	**2:23 am**	☽ v/c
☽ enters ♑	10:17 am	**7:17 am**	
☽♑ ⚻ ♂♌	11:15 am	**8:15 am**	

6 Wed
1st ♑

☽♑ ⚹ ♄♓	10:17 am	**7:17 am**
☽♑ ⚹ ☉♏	2:11 pm	**11:11 am**
☽♑ ⚻ ♃♊	11:38 pm	**8:38 pm**
☽♑ □ ⚷♈		**9:01 pm**

7 Thu
1st ♑

☽♑ □ ⚷♈	12:01 am		
☽♑ △ ♅♉	10:01 am	**7:01 am**	
☽♑ ⚹ ♆♓	1:12 pm	**10:12 am**	
☽♑ ☌ ♇♑	5:38 pm	**2:38 pm**	☽ v/c
☽ enters ♒	5:58 pm	**2:58 pm**	
☽♒ ☍ ♂♌	8:15 pm	**5:15 pm**	
♀♐ ⚻ ♅♉	9:20 pm	**6:20 pm**	

☽≈ ⚹ ☿ ♐ 7:52 am **4:52 am**
☽≈ □ ☉♏ **9:55 pm**

1st ≈
◐ 2nd Quarter 17 ≈ 20 (Pacific)

☽≈ □ ☉♏ 12:55 am
☽≈ △ ♃ ♊ 5:12 am **2:12 am**
☽≈ ⚹ ♄ ♈ 5:47 am **2:47 am**
♀♐ □ ♆♓ 8:15 am **5:15 am**
☽≈ □ ♅ ♉ 3:17 pm **12:17 pm**

☽≈ ⚹ ♀ ♐ 7:23 pm **4:23 pm** ☽ v/c
☽ enters ♓ 11:00 pm **8:00 pm**
☽♓ ⚻ ♂♌ **11:21 pm**

1st ≈
◐ 2nd Quarter 17 ≈ 20 (Eastern)
OP: After Moon squares Uranus until v/c Moon. During this short but very positive OP, you're able to succeed at anything, from inspired creativity to romance.

☽♓ ⚻ ♂♌ 2:21 am
☽♓ □ ☿ ♐ 5:20 pm **2:20 pm**
☽♓ ☌ ♄♓ 8:39 pm **5:39 pm**

2nd ♓

Eastern Standard Time (EST) plain / **Pacific Standard Time (PST) bold**

		OCTOBER							NOVEMBER							DECEMBER				
S	M	T	W	T	F	S	S	M	T	W	T	F	S	S	M	T	W	T	F	S
		1	2	3	4	5						1	2	1	2	3	4	5	6	7
6	7	8	9	10	11	12	3	4	5	6	7	8	9	8	9	10	11	12	13	14
13	14	15	16	17	18	19	10	11	12	13	14	15	16	15	16	17	18	19	20	21
20	21	22	23	24	25	26	17	18	19	20	21	22	23	22	23	24	25	26	27	28
27	28	29	30	31			24	25	26	27	28	29	30	29	30	31				

11 Mon
2nd ♓

Remembrance Day (Canada)

OP: After Moon squares Jupiter today until Moon enters Aries today or on Tuesday. Intuition is heightened, so use it to start new projects that spark your interest.

☉♏ ☌ ♃ ♊	6:08 am	**3:08 am**
☽♓ □ ♃ ♊	8:07 am	**5:07 am**
☽♓ △ ☉♏	8:17 am	**5:17 am**
♀ enters ♑	1:26 pm	**10:26 am**
☉♏ ☌ ♅ ♈	4:41 pm	**1:41 pm**
☽♓ ⚹ ♅ ♉	5:56 pm	**2:56 pm**
☽♓ ☌ ♆♓	9:01 pm	**6:01 pm**
☽♓ ⚹ ♀♑		**10:13 pm** ☽ v/c
☽ enters ♈		**10:26 pm**
☽♈ □ ♀♑		**11:29 pm**

12 Tue
2nd ♓

☽♓ ⚹ ♀♑	1:13 am	☽ v/c
☽ enters ♈	1:26 am	
☽♈ □ ♀♑	2:29 am	
☽♈ △ ♂♌	5:37 am	**2:37 am**
☿♐ □ ♄♓	8:22 am	**5:22 am**
☽♈ △ ☿♐	11:19 pm	**8:19 pm**

13 Wed
2nd ♈

☽♈ ⚹ ♃ ♊	8:51 am	**5:51 am**
☽♈ ☌ ♅ ♈	9:49 am	**6:49 am**
☽♈ ☌ ☉♏	12:54 pm	**9:54 am**
☽♈ □ ♀♑		**10:50 pm** ☽ v/c
☽ enters ♉		**10:59 pm**

14 Thu
2nd ♈

☽♈ □ ♀♑	1:50 am	☽ v/c
☽ enters ♉	1:59 am	
♀♑ ☌ ♂♌	3:02 am	**12:02 am**
☽♉ □ ♂♌	6:57 am	**3:57 am**
☽♉ △ ♀♑	7:13 am	**4:13 am**
☽♉ ⚹ ♄♓	10:18 pm	**7:18 pm**

☽♉ ⊼ ☿♐	3:20 am	**12:20 am**
♄D	9:20 am	**6:20 am**
☽♉ ☌ ☉♏	4:28 pm	**1:28 pm**
☽♉ ☌ ♅♉	6:32 pm	**3:32 pm**
☽♉ ⚹ ♆♓	9:43 pm	**6:43 pm**
☽♉ △ ♀♑		**11:03 pm** ☽ v/c
☽ enters ♊		**11:09 pm**

FRI 15

2nd ♉

○ Full Moon 24 ♉ 01
SATURN DIRECT

OP: After Moon conjoins Uranus today until Moon enters Gemini today or on Saturday. Wait two hours after the conjunction to gain stability and take advantage of this OP so close to the Full Moon for a good panoramic view and making sound decisions.

☽♉ △ ♀♑	2:03 am	☽ v/c
☽ enters ♊	2:09 am	
☽♊ ⚹ ♂♌	8:00 am	**5:00 am**
☽♊ ⊼ ♀♑	11:41 am	**8:41 am**
☉♏ ☌ ♅♉	9:45 pm	**6:45 pm**
☽♊ □ ♄♓	10:52 pm	**7:52 pm**

SAT 16

3rd ♉

☽♊ ☌ ☿♐	7:41 am	**4:41 am**
☽♊ ☌ ♃♊	9:07 am	**6:07 am**
☽♊ ⚹ ♁♈	10:37 am	**7:37 am**
☽♊ ⊼ ☉♏	9:27 pm	**6:27 pm**
☽♊ □ ♆♓	11:09 pm	**8:09 pm** ☽ v/c

SUN 17

3rd ♊

	OCTOBER							NOVEMBER							DECEMBER					
S	M	T	W	T	F	S	S	M	T	W	T	F	S	S	M	T	W	T	F	S
		1	2	3	4	5						1	2	1	2	3	4	5	6	7
6	7	8	9	10	11	12	3	4	5	6	7	8	9	8	9	10	11	12	13	14
13	14	15	16	17	18	19	10	11	12	13	14	15	16	15	16	17	18	19	20	21
20	21	22	23	24	25	26	17	18	19	20	21	22	23	22	23	24	25	26	27	28
27	28	29	30	31			24	25	26	27	28	29	30	29	30	31				

November

Mercury Note: Mercury enters its Storm (moving less than 40 minutes of arc per day) on Thursday, as it slows down before going retrograde. The Storm acts like the retrograde. Not favorable to start new projects—just follow through with the items that are already on your plate. Write down new ideas with date and time they occurred.

18 Mon
3rd ♊

OP: After Moon opposes Venus today until Moon enters Leo on Wednesday. This OP is your last chance before Mercury turns retrograde. Use this family-oriented energy suitable for any project you're involved with.

☽♊ ⊼ ♀♈	3:47 am	**12:47 am**	
☽ enters ⊙	3:50 am	**12:50 am**	
☿♐ ☍ ♃♊	3:55 am	**12:55 am**	
☽⊙ ☍ ♀♈	6:35 pm	**3:35 pm**	
☉♏ △ ♆♓	9:07 pm	**6:07 pm**	
☽⊙ △ ♄♓		**10:48 pm**	

19 Tue
3rd ⊙

☽⊙ △ ♄♓	1:48 am	
☿♐ △ ♀♈	6:29 am	**3:29 am**
☽⊙ □ ♀♈	2:13 pm	**11:13 am**
☽⊙ ⊼ ☿♐	2:43 pm	**11:43 am**
♀ enters ♒	3:29 pm	**12:29 pm**
☽⊙ ⚹ ♅♉	11:56 pm	**8:56 pm**

20 Wed
3rd ⊙

☽⊙ △ ♆♓	3:46 am	**12:46 am**	
☽⊙ △ ☉♏	6:20 am	**3:20 am**	☽ v/c
☽ enters ♌	8:51 am	**5:51 am**	
☽♌ ☍ ♀♒	8:52 am	**5:52 am**	
☽♌ ☌ ♂♌	5:15 pm	**2:15 pm**	

21 Thu
3rd ♌

SUN ENTERS SAGITTARIUS

☽♌ ⊼ ♀♈	6:20 am	**3:20 am**
☽♌ ⊼ ♄♓	8:36 am	**5:36 am**
☉ enters ♐	2:56 pm	**11:56 am**
☉♐ ⚹ ♀♒	3:49 pm	**12:49 pm**
☽♌ ⚹ ♃♊	7:21 pm	**4:21 pm**
☽♌ △ ♀♈	9:49 pm	**6:49 pm**
☽♌ △ ☿♐		**10:36 pm**

☽♌ △ ☿ ♐ 1:36 am
♀♑ ✶ ♄ ⅹ 6:55 am **3:55 am**
☽♌ □ ♅ ♉ 8:15 am **5:15 am** ☽ v/c
☽♌ ⊼ ♆ ⅹ 12:31 pm **9:31 am**
☽ enters ♍ 6:01 pm **3:01 pm**
☽♍ ⊼ ♀≈ 6:08 pm **3:08 pm**
☽♍ □ ☉♐ 8:28 pm **5:28 pm**

Fri 22
3rd ♌
◑ 4th Quarter 1 ♍ 15

☽♍ ☍ ♄ⅹ 7:24 pm **4:24 pm**
☽♍ △ ♀♑ 11:21 pm **8:21 pm**

Sat 23
4th ♍

☽♍ □ ♃ ♊ 6:04 am **3:04 am**
☽♍ ⊼ ♂♈ 9:07 am **6:07 am**
☽♍ □ ☿♐ 3:10 pm **12:10 pm**
☽♍ △ ♅♉ 7:59 pm **4:59 pm**
☽♍ ☍ ♆ⅹ **9:35 pm** ☽ v/c

Sun 24
4th ♍

Eastern Standard Time (EST) plain / **Pacific Standard Time (PST) bold**

		OCTOBER							NOVEMBER							DECEMBER				
S	M	T	W	T	F	S	S	M	T	W	T	F	S	S	M	T	W	T	F	S
		1	2	3	4	5						1	2	1	2	3	4	5	6	7
6	7	8	9	10	11	12	3	4	5	6	7	8	9	8	9	10	11	12	13	14
13	14	15	16	17	18	19	10	11	12	13	14	15	16	15	16	17	18	19	20	21
20	21	22	23	24	25	26	17	18	19	20	21	22	23	22	23	24	25	26	27	28
27	28	29	30	31			24	25	26	27	28	29	30	29	30	31				

November

Mercury Note: Mercury goes retrograde on Monday, November 25, and remains so until December 15, after which it will still be in its Storm until December 20. Projects initiated during this entire period may not work out as planned. It's best to use this time for reviews, editing, escrows, and so forth.

25 Mon
4th ♍
Mercury retrograde

☽♍ ☍ ♆ ♅	12:35 am		☽ v/c
☽ enters ♎	6:20 am	**3:20 am**	
☽ ♎ △ ♀ ≈	6:33 am	**3:33 am**	
☽ ♎ ⚹ ☉ ♐	2:32 pm	**11:32 am**	
☽ ♎ ⚹ ♂ ♌	5:18 pm	**2:18 pm**	
☿ ℞	9:42 pm	**6:42 pm**	

26 Tue
4th ♎

OP: After Moon squares Venus today until v/c Moon on Wednesday. Excellent OP for communication and artistic activities, but with the waning Moon and Mercury retrograde, it's better to review existing projects than to start new ones.

☽ ♎ ⊼ ♄ ♓	8:25 am	**5:25 am**
♀♑ ⊼ ♃ ♊	1:08 pm	**10:08 am**
☽ ♎ △ ♃ ♊	6:27 pm	**3:27 pm**
☽ ♎ □ ♀ ♑	7:06 pm	**4:06 pm**
☽ ♎ ☍ ♅ ♈	10:02 pm	**7:02 pm**

27 Wed
4th ♎

☉♐ △ ♂ ♌	3:06 am	**12:06 am**	
☽ ♎ ⚹ ☿ ♐	4:14 am	**1:14 am**	☽ v/c
☽ ♎ ⊼ ♅ ♉	8:51 am	**5:51 am**	
☽ ♎ ⊼ ♆ ♓	1:36 pm	**10:36 am**	
☽ enters ♏	7:21 pm	**4:21 pm**	
☽♏ □ ♀ ≈	7:40 pm	**4:40 pm**	
♀♑ □ ♅ ♈	11:58 pm	**8:58 pm**	

28 Thu
4th ♏
Thanksgiving Day (US)

☽♏ □ ♂ ♌	6:49 am	**3:49 am**
☽♏ △ ♄ ♓	9:07 pm	**6:07 pm**

☽♏ ⚻ ♃♊	6:08 am	**3:08 am**
☽♏ ⚻ ♂♈	10:07 am	**7:07 am**
☽♏ ⚹ ♀♑	1:51 pm	**10:51 am**
☽♏ ☍ ♅♉	8:32 pm	**5:32 pm**
☽♏ △ ♆♓		**10:19 pm** ☽ v/c

Fri 29
4th ♏

☽♏ △ ♆♓	1:19 am	☽ v/c
☽ enters ♐	6:53 am	**3:53 am**
☽♐ ⚹ ♀≈	7:18 am	**4:18 am**
☽♐ △ ♂♌	6:23 pm	**3:23 pm**
☽♐ ☌ ☉♐		**10:21 pm**

Sat 30
4th ♏
● New Moon 9 ♐ 33 (Pacific)

☽♐ ☌ ☉♐	1:21 am	
☽♐ □ ♄♓	7:49 am	**4:49 am**
☽♐ ☍ ♃♊	3:45 pm	**12:45 pm**
☽♐ △ ♂♈	8:05 pm	**5:05 pm**
☽♐ ☌ ☿♐	8:29 pm	**5:29 pm**
☿♐ △ ♂♈		**10:16 pm**

Sun 1
4th ♐
● New Moon 9 ♐ 33 (Eastern)

Eastern Standard Time (EST) plain / **Pacific Standard Time (PST) bold**

OCTOBER

S	M	T	W	T	F	S
		1	2	3	4	5
6	7	8	9	10	11	12
13	14	15	16	17	18	19
20	21	22	23	24	25	26
27	28	29	30	31		

NOVEMBER

S	M	T	W	T	F	S
					1	2
3	4	5	6	7	8	9
10	11	12	13	14	15	16
17	18	19	20	21	22	23
24	25	26	27	28	29	30

DECEMBER

S	M	T	W	T	F	S
1	2	3	4	5	6	7
8	9	10	11	12	13	14
15	16	17	18	19	20	21
22	23	24	25	26	27	28
29	30	31				

December

2 Mon
1st ♐

OP: After Moon enters Capricorn today until v/c Moon on Wednesday. Good time for constructive work on projects you started before November 21.

☿♐ △ ♅♈	1:16 am	
☽♐ ⚻ ♅♉	6:02 am	**3:02 am**
♀♑ △ ♅♉	9:43 am	**6:43 am**
☽♐ □ ♆♓	10:47 am	**7:47 am** ☽ v/c
☽ enters ♑	4:09 pm	**1:09 pm**

3 Tue
1st ♑

☽♑ ⚻ ♂♌	3:30 am	**12:30 am**
☽♑ ✶ ♄♓	4:17 pm	**1:17 pm**
☽♑ ⚻ ♃♊	11:13 pm	**8:13 pm**

4 Wed
1st ♑

☽♑ □ ♅♈	3:52 am	**12:52 am**
☿♐ ☍ ♃♊	5:16 am	**2:16 am**
☉♐ □ ♄♓	11:18 am	**8:18 am**
☽♑ △ ♅♉	1:24 pm	**10:24 am**
♀♑ ✶ ♆♓	1:52 pm	**10:52 am**
☽♑ ✶ ♆♓	6:09 pm	**3:09 pm**
☽♑ ☌ ♀♑	6:34 pm	**3:34 pm** ☽ v/c
☽ enters ♒	11:21 pm	**8:21 pm**
☽♒ ☌ ♀♒	11:56 pm	**8:56 pm**

5 Thu
1st ♒

☽♒ ☍ ♂♌	10:28 am	**7:28 am**
☉♐ ☌ ☿♐	9:18 pm	**6:18 pm**
☽♒ ✶ ☿♐		**9:56 pm**
☽♒ ✶ ☉♐		**10:38 pm**

186

Fri 6

1st ≈

Mars retrograde

☽≈ ⚹ ☿♐	12:56 am		
☽≈ ⚹ ☉♐	1:38 am		
☽≈ △ ♃♊	4:53 am	**1:53 am**	
☽≈ ⚹ ⚷♈	9:51 am	**6:51 am**	
♂℞	6:33 pm	**3:33 pm**	
☽≈ □ ♅♉	7:01 pm	**4:01 pm**	☽ v/c
☿♐ □ ♄♓	8:53 pm	**5:53 pm**	
♀ enters ≈		**10:13 pm**	

Sat 7

1st ≈

Neptune direct

♀ enters ≈	1:13 am	
☽ enters ♓	4:49 am	**1:49 am**
♀≈ ☌ ♇≈	9:08 am	**6:08 am**
☽♓ ⚻ ♂♌	3:36 pm	**12:36 pm**
☉♐ ☍ ♃♊	3:58 pm	**12:58 pm**
♆D	6:43 pm	**3:43 pm**
☽♓ □ ☿♐		**9:58 pm**

Sun 8

1st ♓

◐ 2nd Quarter 17 ♓ 02

☽♓ □ ☿♐	12:58 am	
☽♓ ☌ ♄♓	3:43 am	**12:43 am**
☽♓ □ ♃♊	8:56 am	**5:56 am**
☽♓ □ ☉♐	10:27 am	**7:27 am**
☽♓ ⚹ ♅♉	11:00 pm	**8:00 pm**

OP: After Moon squares Sun today until Moon enters Aries on Monday. You'll have the whole day and night to use this OP for fun, adventures, mind expansion, etc.

Eastern Standard Time (EST) plain / **Pacific Standard Time (PST) bold**

NOVEMBER

S	M	T	W	T	F	S
					1	2
3	4	5	6	7	8	9
10	11	12	13	14	15	16
17	18	19	20	21	22	23
24	25	26	27	28	29	30

DECEMBER

S	M	T	W	T	F	S
1	2	3	4	5	6	7
8	9	10	11	12	13	14
15	16	17	18	19	20	21
22	23	24	25	26	27	28
29	30	31				

JANUARY 2025

S	M	T	W	T	F	S
			1	2	3	4
5	6	7	8	9	10	11
12	13	14	15	16	17	18
19	20	21	22	23	24	25
26	27	28	29	30	31	

9 Mon

2nd ♓

OP: Two back-to-back OPs: The second OP starts when the Moon enters Aries today until v/c Moon on Tuesday. An excellent time for connections and reaching out to important people, but with Mercury retrograde, be sure to double-check everything.

☽ ♓ ♂ ♆ ♓	3:45 am	**12:45 am**	☽ v/c
☽ enters ♈	8:38 am	**5:38 am**	
☽ ♈ ⚹ ♀ ♒	9:22 am	**6:22 am**	
☽ ♈ ⚹ ♀ ♒	1:33 pm	**10:33 am**	
☽ ♈ △ ♂ ♌	6:59 pm	**3:59 pm**	
☽ ♈ △ ☿ ♐		**9:19 pm**	

10 Tue

2nd ♈

☽ ♈ △ ☿ ♐	12:19 am		
☽ ♈ ⚹ ♃ ♊	11:24 am	**8:24 am**	
☉ ♐ △ ♅ ♈	12:49 pm	**9:49 am**	
☽ ♈ ♂ ♅ ♈	4:54 pm	**1:54 pm**	
☽ ♈ △ ☉ ♐	5:13 pm	**2:13 pm**	☽ v/c

11 Wed

2nd ♈

☽ enters ♉	10:55 am	**7:55 am**	
☽ ♉ □ ♀ ♒	11:43 am	**8:43 am**	
☽ ♉ □ ♀ ♒	8:01 pm	**5:01 pm**	
☽ ♉ □ ♂ ♌	8:50 pm	**5:50 pm**	
☽ ♉ ⚻ ☿ ♐	11:29 pm	**8:29 pm**	

12 Thu

2nd ♉

♀ ♒ ☍ ♂ ♌	5:46 am	**2:46 am**	
☽ ♉ ⚹ ♄ ♓	8:55 am	**5:55 am**	
☽ ♉ ⚻ ☉ ♐	10:34 pm	**7:34 pm**	
☿ ♐ ⚹ ♀ ♒		**11:45 pm**	
☽ ♉ ♂ ♅ ♉		**11:49 pm**	

Mercury Note: Mercury goes direct on Sunday, December 15, but remains in its Storm, moving slowly, until December 20.

☿✗ ✶ ♀≈	2:45 am	
☽♉ ♂ ♅♉	2:49 am	
☽♉ ✶ ♆♓	7:39 am	**4:39 am** ☽ v/c
☽ enters ♊	12:22 pm	**9:22 am**
☽♊ △ ♀≈	1:15 pm	**10:15 am**
☽♊ ✶ ♂♌	9:58 pm	**6:58 pm**
☽♊ ☍ ☿✗	11:20 pm	**8:20 pm**
☽♊ △ ♀≈		**10:40 pm**

FRI 13
2nd ♉

OP: After Moon conjoins Uranus on Thursday or today until Moon enters Gemini today. This OP is favorable for creativity and innovative work on a practical level. Same warning as for last Monday.

☽♊ △ ♀≈	1:40 am	
☽♊ □ ♄♓	10:34 am	**7:34 am**
☽♊ ♂ ♃♊	1:43 pm	**10:43 am**
☽♊ ✶ ♅♈	8:01 pm	**5:01 pm**

SAT 14
2nd ♊

☽♊ ☍ ☉✗	4:02 am	**1:02 am**
☽♊ □ ♆♓	9:32 am	**6:32 am** ☽ v/c
☉✗ ⊼ ♅♉	9:44 am	**6:44 am**
☽ enters ♋	2:21 pm	**11:21 am**
☽♋ ⊼ ♀≈	3:22 pm	**12:22 pm**
☿ D	3:56 pm	**12:56 pm**
☽♋ ⊼ ☿✗		**10:16 pm**

SUN 15
2nd ♊
○ Full Moon 23 ♊ 53
MERCURY DIRECT

OP: After Moon enters Cancer today until Moon enters Leo on Tuesday. With Mercury just turning direct, this is a good time for setting lofty goals and inspiration.

Eastern Standard Time (EST) plain / **Pacific Standard Time (PST) bold**

NOVEMBER

S	M	T	W	T	F	S
					1	2
3	4	5	6	7	8	9
10	11	12	13	14	15	16
17	18	19	20	21	22	23
24	25	26	27	28	29	30

DECEMBER

S	M	T	W	T	F	S
1	2	3	4	5	6	7
8	9	10	11	12	13	14
15	16	17	18	19	20	21
22	23	24	25	26	27	28
29	30	31				

JANUARY 2025

S	M	T	W	T	F	S
			1	2	3	4
5	6	7	8	9	10	11
12	13	14	15	16	17	18
19	20	21	22	23	24	25
26	27	28	29	30	31	

16 Mon
3rd ♋

☽♋ ⊼ ☿ ✕	1:16 am	
☽♋ ⊼ ♀ ≈	8:34 am	**5:34 am**
☽♋ △ ♄ ♓	1:34 pm	**10:34 am**
☽♋ □ ⚷ ♈	11:14 pm	**8:14 pm**

17 Tue
3rd ♋

☽♋ ✶ ⛢ ♉	8:02 am	**5:02 am**
☽♋ ⊼ ☉ ✕	11:56 am	**8:56 am**
☽♋ △ ♆ ♓	1:33 pm	**10:33 am** ☽ v/c
☽ enters ♌	6:39 pm	**3:39 pm**
☽♌ ☍ ♀ ≈	7:50 pm	**4:50 pm**

18 Wed
3rd ♌

☽♌ ☌ ♂♌	4:13 am	**1:13 am**
☽♌ △ ☿ ✕	7:15 am	**4:15 am**
☉✕ □ ♆ ♓	9:29 am	**6:29 am**
☽♌ ☍ ♀ ≈	7:10 pm	**4:10 pm**
☽♌ ⊼ ♄ ♓	7:39 pm	**4:39 pm**
☽♌ ✶ ♃ ♊	9:40 pm	**6:40 pm**

19 Thu
3rd ♌

OP: After Moon squares Uranus until v/c Moon. Good for creativity and also healthy connections and relationships, aided by the Venus-Jupiter trine.

☽♌ △ ⚷ ♈	5:44 am	**2:44 am**
☽♌ □ ⛢ ♉	3:04 pm	**12:04 pm**
☽♌ ⊼ ♆ ♓	9:10 pm	**6:10 pm**
♀≈ △ ♃ ♊	9:11 pm	**6:11 pm**
☽♌ △ ☉ ✕		**9:19 pm** ☽ v/c
☽ enters ♍		**11:37 pm**

Mercury Note: Mercury finally leaves its Storm on Saturday. Look over your notes on any ideas that occurred to you while Mercury was retrograde or slow. How do they look now?

☽♌ △ ☉♐	12:19 am	☽ v/c
☽ enters ♍	2:37 am	
☽♍ ⊼ ♀♒	4:01 am	**1:01 am**
☽♍ □ ☿♐	6:46 pm	**3:46 pm**

FRI 20
3rd ♌

☉ enters ♑	4:21 am	**1:21 am**
☽♍ ☍ ♄♓	5:39 am	**2:39 am**
☽♍ □ ♃♊	6:55 am	**3:55 am**
☽♍ ⊼ ♀♒	10:45 am	**7:45 am**
☽♍ ⊼ ♂♈	4:03 pm	**1:03 pm**
☽♍ △ ♅♉		10:50 pm

SAT 21
3rd ♍
WINTER SOLSTICE
YULE
SUN ENTERS CAPRICORN

☽♍ △ ♅♉	1:50 am	
☽♍ ☍ ♆♓	8:27 am	**5:27 am** ☽ v/c
☽ enters ♎	2:08 pm	**11:08 am**
☽♎ △ ♀♒	3:44 pm	**12:44 pm**
☽♎ □ ☉♑	5:18 pm	**2:18 pm**
☽♎ ✶ ♂♌	10:59 pm	**7:59 pm**

SUN 22
3rd ♍
◑ 4th Quarter 1 ♎ 34

OP: After Moon squares the Sun today until v/c Moon on Tuesday. This great OP ends with the Moon enclosed between benefics, forming a grand trine, which is awesome for everything joyous, just in time for the holidays.

Eastern Standard Time (EST) plain / **Pacific Standard Time (PST) bold**

NOVEMBER								DECEMBER								JANUARY 2025					
S	M	T	W	T	F	S		S	M	T	W	T	F	S		S	M	T	W	T	F	S
					1	2		1	2	3	4	5	6	7					1	2	3	4
3	4	5	6	7	8	9		8	9	10	11	12	13	14		5	6	7	8	9	10	11
10	11	12	13	14	15	16		15	16	17	18	19	20	21		12	13	14	15	16	17	18
17	18	19	20	21	22	23		22	23	24	25	26	27	28		19	20	21	22	23	24	25
24	25	26	27	28	29	30		29	30	31						26	27	28	29	30	31	

December

23 Mon
4th ♎

☽♎ ⚹ ☿ ♐	11:22 am	**8:22 am**
☽♎ ⊼ ♄ ♓	6:30 pm	**3:30 pm**
☽♎ △ ♃ ♊	6:51 pm	**3:51 pm**
♀≈ ⚹ ♅ ♈	7:46 pm	**4:46 pm**

24 Tue
4th ♎
Christmas Eve

☽♎ ☍ ♅ ♈	4:48 am	**1:48 am**	
☽♎ △ ♀ ≈	5:44 am	**2:44 am**	☽ v/c
☽♎ ⊼ ♅ ♉	2:35 pm	**11:35 am**	
♃♊ □ ♄ ♓	4:59 pm	**1:59 pm**	
☽♎ ⊼ ♆ ♓	9:28 pm	**6:28 pm**	
☉♑ ⊼ ♂ ♌		**9:00 pm**	

25 Wed
4th ♎
Christmas Day
Hanukkah begins at sundown

☉♑ ⊼ ♂ ♌	12:00 am	
☽ enters ♏	3:06 am	**12:06 am**
☽♏ □ ♀ ≈	4:51 am	**1:51 am**
☽♏ □ ♂ ♌	10:44 am	**7:44 am**
☽♏ ⚹ ☉ ♑	12:00 pm	**9:00 am**

26 Thu
4th ♏
Kwanzaa begins
Boxing Day (Canada & UK)

☽♏ ⊼ ♃ ♊	6:55 am	**3:55 am**
☽♏ △ ♄ ♓	7:31 am	**4:31 am**
☽♏ ⊼ ♅ ♈	5:12 pm	**2:12 pm**
☿♐ ☍ ♃ ♊	5:48 pm	**2:48 pm**
☽♏ □ ♀ ≈		**9:08 pm**
☿♐ □ ♄ ♓		**11:29 pm**
☽♏ ☍ ♅ ♉		**11:34 pm**

☽♏ □ ♀♒	12:08 am		
☿♐ □ ♄♓	2:29 am		
☽♏ ☍ ♅♉	2:34 am		
☽♏ △ ♆♓	9:24 am	**6:24 am**	☽ v/c
☽ enters ♐	2:46 pm	**11:46 am**	
☽♐ ✶ ♇♒	4:36 pm	**1:36 pm**	
☽♐ △ ♂♌	8:50 pm	**5:50 pm**	
♀♒ □ ♅♉		**11:42 pm**	

FRI 27
4th ♏

OP: After Moon opposes Uranus on Thursday or today until v/c Moon today. Get up early to catch this opportunity for deep thinking and good insights.

♀♒ □ ♅♉	2:42 am	
☽♐ ☍ ♃♊	4:50 pm	**1:50 pm**
☽♐ □ ♄♓	6:15 pm	**3:15 pm**
☽♐ ☌ ☿♐	10:01 pm	**7:01 pm**

SAT 28
4th ♐

☽♐ △ ⚷♈	3:07 am	**12:07 am**	
☽♐ ⚻ ♅♉	11:55 am	**8:55 am**	
☽♐ ✶ ♀♒	3:03 pm	**12:03 pm**	
⚷ D	4:13 pm	**1:13 pm**	
☽♐ □ ♆♓	6:34 pm	**3:34 pm**	☽ v/c
☽ enters ♑	11:37 pm	**8:37 pm**	

SUN 29
4th ♐
CHIRON DIRECT

Eastern Standard Time (EST) plain / **Pacific Standard Time (PST) bold**

NOVEMBER

S	M	T	W	T	F	S
					1	2
3	4	5	6	7	8	9
10	11	12	13	14	15	16
17	18	19	20	21	22	23
24	25	26	27	28	29	30

DECEMBER

S	M	T	W	T	F	S
1	2	3	4	5	6	7
8	9	10	11	12	13	14
15	16	17	18	19	20	21
22	23	24	25	26	27	28
29	30	31				

JANUARY 2025

S	M	T	W	T	F	S
			1	2	3	4
5	6	7	8	9	10	11
12	13	14	15	16	17	18
19	20	21	22	23	24	25
26	27	28	29	30	31	

30 Mon
4th ♑

● New Moon 9 ♑ 44

OP: This Cazimi Moon is usable ½ hour before and ½ hour after the Sun-Moon conjunction. If you have something important to start around now, this is a great time to do it.

☽♑ ⚻ ♂♌	4:07 am	**1:07 am**	
☽♑ ♂ ☉♑	5:27 pm	**2:27 pm**	
☽♑ ⚻ ♃♊	11:56 pm	**8:56 pm**	
☽♑ ✶ ♄♓		**11:03 pm**	
☿♐ △ ♅♈		**11:41 pm**	

31 Tue
1st ♑
New Year's Eve

☽♑ ✶ ♄♓	2:03 am		
☿♐ △ ♅♈	2:41 am		
☽♑ □ ♅♈	10:12 am	**7:12 am**	
☽♑ △ ♅♉	6:30 pm	**3:30 pm**	
☽♑ ✶ ♆♓		**10:02 pm** ☽ v/c	

1 Wed
1st ♑
New Year's Day
Kwanzaa ends

☽♑ ✶ ♆♓	1:02 am		☽ v/c
☽ enters ♒	5:50 am	**2:50 am**	
☽♒ ♂ ♀♒	7:45 am	**4:45 am**	
☽♒ ☍ ♂♌	8:53 am	**5:53 am**	

2 Thu
1st ♒
Hanukkah ends

☽♒ △ ♃♊	4:51 am	**1:51 am**	
☽♒ ✶ ♅♈	3:14 pm	**12:14 pm**	
☽♒ ✶ ☿♐	9:34 pm	**6:34 pm**	
☉♑ ⚻ ♃♊	10:18 pm	**7:18 pm**	
♀ enters ♓	10:24 pm	**7:24 pm**	
☽♒ □ ♅♉	11:13 pm	**8:13 pm** ☽ v/c	
♂♌ ☍ ♀♒		**11:21 pm**	

♂♌ ☍ ♀≈   2:21 am
☽ enters ♓ 10:21 am **7:21 am**
☽♓ ♂ ♀♓ 11:21 am **8:21 am**
☽♓ ⊼ ♂♌ 12:05 pm **9:05 am**
☿♐ ⊼ ♅♉ 2:19 pm **11:19 am**
♀♓ ⊼ ♂♌ 6:41 pm **3:41 pm**

FRI 3
1st ≈

☽♓ □ ♃Ⅱ   8:34 am **5:34 am**
☽♓ ⚹ ☉♑ 11:32 am **8:32 am**
☽♓ ♂ ♄♓ 11:56 am **8:56 am**
☉♑ ⚹ ♄♓ 5:36 pm **2:36 pm**
☽♓ ⚹ ♅♉   **11:56 pm**

SAT 4
1st ♓

☽♓ ⚹ ♅♉   2:56 am
☽♓ □ ☿♐   6:57 am **3:57 am**

☽♓ ♂ ♆♓   9:30 am **6:30 am** ☽ v/c
☽ enters ♈ 2:01 pm **11:01 am**
☽♈ △ ♂♌ 2:25 pm **11:25 am**
☽♈ ⚹ ♀≈ 4:06 pm **1:06 pm**

SUN 5
1st ♓

OP: After Moon squares Mercury until v/c Moon. This Sunday morning OP is good for play, meditation, helping others, etc.

Eastern Standard Time (EST) plain / **Pacific Standard Time (PST) bold**

DECEMBER						
S	M	T	W	T	F	S
1	2	3	4	5	6	7
8	9	10	11	12	13	14
15	16	17	18	19	20	21
22	23	24	25	26	27	28
29	30	31				

JANUARY 2025						
S	M	T	W	T	F	S
			1	2	3	4
5	6	7	8	9	10	11
12	13	14	15	16	17	18
19	20	21	22	23	24	25
26	27	28	29	30	31	

FEBRUARY 2025						
S	M	T	W	T	F	S
						1
2	3	4	5	6	7	8
9	10	11	12	13	14	15
16	17	18	19	20	21	22
23	24	25	26	27	28	

January 2024

S	M	T	W
31	1 New Year's Day Kwanzaa ends Mercury direct	2	◑
7	8	9	10
14	15 Martin Luther King Jr. Day	16	◐
21	22	23	24
28	29	30	31
4	5	6	7

Set in Eastern Standard Time

T	F	S	Notes
4	5	6	
● New Moon	12	13	
18	19	20 Sun enters Aquarius	
○ Full Moon	26	27	
1	2	3	
8	9	10	

February 2024

S	M	T	W
28	29	30	31
4	5	6	7
11	12	13	14 Valentine's Day
18 Sun enters Pisces	19 Presidents' Day	20	21
25	26	27	28
3	4	5	6

Set in Eastern Standard Time

T	F	S	Notes
1	◑	3	
8	● New Moon	10 Lunar New Year (Dragon)	
15	◐	17	
22	23	○ Full Moon	
29 Leap Day	1	2	
7	8	9	

March 2024

S	M	T	W
25	26	27	28
◑	4	5	6
● New Moon Ramadan begins at sundown Daylight Saving Time begins at 2:00 a.m.	11	12	13
◐ St. Patrick's Day	18	19 Spring Equinox/ Sun enters Aries	20
24	○ Full Moon/Lunar Eclipse	26	27
31 Easter	1	2	3

Eastern Standard Time becomes Eastern Daylight Time on March 10

T	F	S	Notes
29	1	2	
7	8	9	
14	15	16	
21	22	23	
28	29	30	
4	5	6	

April 2024

S	M	T	W
31	◖	2	3
	April Fools' Day Mercury retrograde		
7	●	9	10
	New Moon/Solar Eclipse	Ramadan ends	
14	◐	16	17
21	22	○	24
	Passover begins at sundown	Full Moon	
28	29	30	1
		Passover ends	
5	6	7	8

Set in Eastern Daylight Time

T	F	S	
4	5	6	**Notes**
11	12	13	
18	19 Sun enters Taurus	20	
25 Mercury direct	26	27	
2	3	4	
9	10	11	

May 2024

S	M	T	W
28	29	30	◑
5	6	● New Moon	8
12 Mother's Day	13	14	◐
19	20 Sun enters Gemini	21	22
26	27 Memorial Day	28	29
2	3	4	5

Set in Eastern Daylight Time

T	F	S	
2	3	4	**Notes**
9	10	11	
16	17	18	
○	24	25	
Full Moon			
◑	31	1	
6	7	8	

June 2024

S	M	T	W
26	27	28	29
2	3	4	5
9	10	11	12
16 Father's Day	17	18	19 Juneteenth
23	24	25	26
30	1	2	3

Set in Eastern Daylight Time

T	F	S	Notes
30	31	1	
● New Moon	7	8	
13	◐	15	
20 Summer Solstice/ Sun enters Cancer	○ Full Moon	22	
27	◑	29	
4	5	6	

July 2024

S	M	T	W
30	1	2	3
7	8	9	10
14	15	16	17
○ Full Moon	22 Sun enters Leo	23	24
28	29	30	31
4	5	6	7

Set in Eastern Daylight Time

T	F	S	Notes
4	●	6	
Independence Day	New Moon		
11	12	◐	
18	19	20	
25	26	◐	
1	2	3	
8	9	10	

August 2024

S	M	T	W
28	29	30	31
● New Moon	5 Mercury retrograde	6	7
11	◐	13	14
18	○ Full Moon	20	21
25	◑	27	28 Mercury direct
1	2	3	4

T	F	S	
1	2	3	**Notes**
8	9	10	
15	16	17	
22	23	24	
Sun enters Virgo			
29	30	31	
5	6	7	

September 2024

S	M	T	W
1	●	3	4
	Labor Day New Moon		
8	9	10	◗
15	16	○	18
		Full Moon/Lunar Eclipse	
22	23	◑	25
Fall Equinox/ Sun enters Libra			
29	30	1	2
6	7	8	9

Set in Eastern Daylight Time

T	F	S	
5	6	7	Notes
12	13	14	
19	20	21	
26	27	28	
3	4	5	
10	11	12	

October 2024

S	M	T	W
29	30	1	● New Moon/Solar Eclipse
6	7	8	9
13	14	15	16
20	21	22 Sun enters Scorpio	23
27	28	29	30
3	4	5	6

Set in Eastern Daylight Time

	T		F		S		Notes

T	F	S	Notes
3	4	5	
◑	11	12	
○ Full Moon	18	19	
◐	25	26	
31 Halloween	1	2	
7	8	9	

November 2024

S	M	T	W
27	28	29	30
3 Daylight Saving Time ends at 2:00 a.m.	4	5 Election Day (general)	6
10	11 Veterans Day	12	13
17	18	19	20
24	25 Mercury retrograde	26	27
1	2	3	4

Eastern Daylight Time becomes Eastern Standard Time on November 3

T	F	S	Notes
31	● New Moon	2	
7	8	◑	
14	○ Full Moon	16	
21 Sun enters Sagittarius	◐	23	
28 Thanksgiving Day	29	30	
5	6	7	

December 2024

S	M	T	W
● New Moon	2	3	4
◑	9	10	11
○ Mercury direct Full Moon	16	17	18
◐	23	24 Christmas Eve	25 Christmas Day Hanukkah begins at sundown (ends Jan. 2)
29	● New Moon	31 New Year's Eve	1
5	6	7	8

Set in Eastern Standard Time

T	F	S	Notes
5	6	7	
	Mars retrograde		
12	13	14	
19	20	21	
		Winter Solstice/ Sun enters Capricorn	
26	27	28	
Kwanzaa begins (ends Jan. 1)			
2	3	4	
9	10	11	

World Time Zones
Compared to Eastern Standard Time

(R)   EST

(S)   CST/Subtract 1 hour

(Q)   Add 1 hour

(P)   Add 2 hours

(O)   Add 3 hours

(Z)   Add 5 hours

(T)   MST/Subtract 2 hours

(U)   PST/Subtract 3 hours

(U*) Subtract 3.5 hours

(V)   Subtract 4 hours

(V*) Subtract 4.5 hours

(W) Subtract 5 hours

(X)   Subtract 6 hours

(Y)   Subtract 7 hours

(A)   Add 6 hours

(B)   Add 7 hours

(C)   Add 8 hours

(C*) Add 8.5 hours

(D)   Add 9 hours

(D*) Add 9.5 hours

(E)   Add 10 hours

(E*) Add 10.5 hours

(F)   Add 11 hours

(F*) Add 11.5 hours

(G)   Add 12 hours

(H)   Add 13 hours

(I)   Add 14 hours

(I*) Add 14.5 hours

(K)   Add 15 hours

(K*) Add 15.5 hours

(L)   Add 16 hours

(L*) Add 16.5 hours

(M) Add 17 hours

(M*) Add 18 hours

(P*) Add 2.5 hours

Eastern Standard Time = Universal Time (Greenwich Mean Time) + or − the value from the table.

World Map of Time Zones

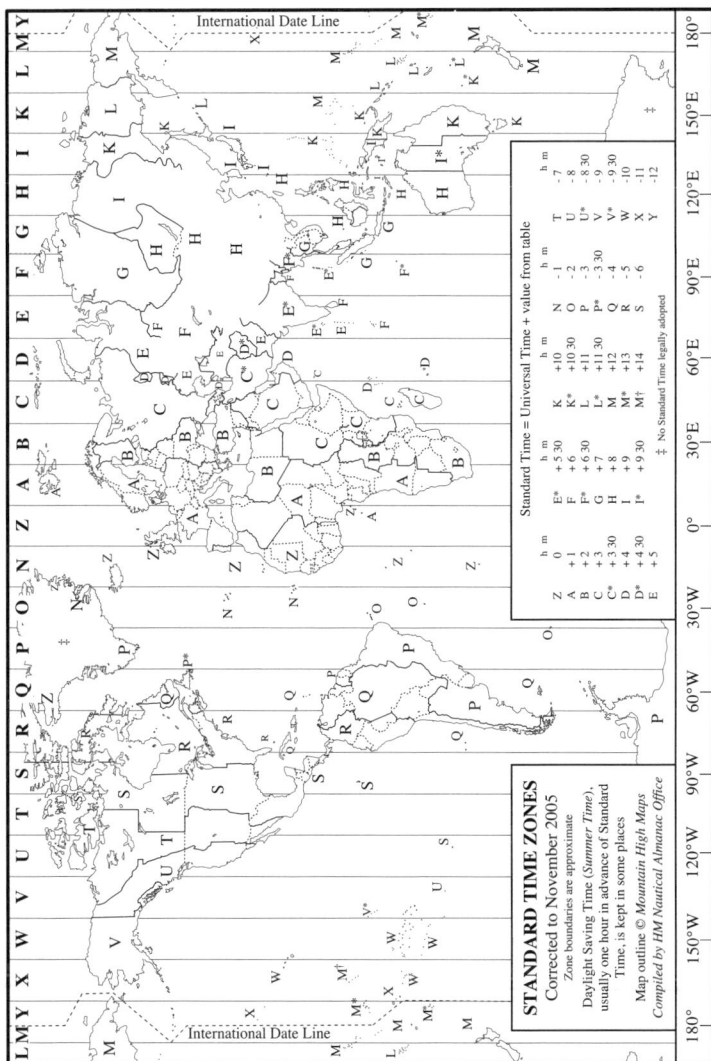

International Date Line

Standard Time = Universal Time + value from table

	h m			h m			h m
Z	0	E*	+ 5 30	K	+10	N	− 1
A	+ 1	F	+ 6	K*	+10 30	O	− 2
B	+ 2	F*	+ 6 30	L	+11	P	− 3
C	+ 3	G	+ 7	L*	+11 30	P*	− 3 30
C*	+ 3 30	H	+ 8	M	+12	Q	− 4
D	+ 4	I	+ 9	M*	+13	R	− 5
D*	+ 4 30	I*	+ 9 30	M†	+14	S	− 6
E	+ 5						

	h m
T	− 7
U	− 8
U*	− 8 30
V	− 9
V*	− 9 30
W	−10
X	−11
Y	−12

‡ No Standard Time legally adopted

STANDARD TIME ZONES

Corrected to November 2005
Zone boundaries are approximate
Daylight Saving Time (*Summer Time*),
usually one hour in advance of Standard
Time, is kept in some places
Map outline © Mountain High Maps
Compiled by HM Nautical Almanac Office

International Date Line

DATE	SID.TIME	SUN	MOON	NODE	MERCURY	VENUS	MARS	JUPITER	SATURN	URANUS	NEPTUNE	PLUTO	CERES	PALLAS	JUNO	VESTA	CHIRON
1 M	6 40 36	10 ♑ 02 20	6 ♏ 00	21 ♉ 05R	22 ♐ 17R	2 ♐ 37	27 ♐ 19	5 ♉ 35	3 ♓ 15	19 ♉ 23R	25 ♓ 05	29 ♑ 21	15 ♐ 27	17 ♏ 34	21 ♍ 19	27 ♊ 00R	15 ♈ 28
2 T	6 44 33	11 03 29	17 49	21 00	22 11D	3 50	28 03	5 35	3 20	19 22	25 05	29 23	15 51	17 57	21 24	26 45	15 28
3 W	6 48 29	12 04 38	29 37	20 58	22 14	5 03	28 48	5 36	3 25	19 21	25 06	29 25	16 15	18 20	21 29	26 30	15 28
4 Th	6 52 26	13 05 47	11 ♎ 30	20 57	22 26	6 16	29 32	5 36	3 31	19 19	25 07	29 27	16 40	18 43	21 33	26 16	15 29
5 F	6 56 22	14 06 56	23 33	20 57	22 46	7 29	0 ♑ 17	5 37	3 36	19 18	25 08	29 29	17 04	19 05	21 37	26 02	15 29
6 Sa	7 0 19	15 08 06	5 ♏ 51	20 57	23 13	8 42	1 01	5 38	3 42	19 17	25 09	29 31	17 28	19 28	21 41	25 48	15 30
7 Su	7 4 16	16 09 16	18 31	20 54	23 46	9 56	1 46	5 40	3 48	19 16	25 10	29 33	17 53	19 50	21 44	25 34	15 30
8 M	7 8 12	17 10 26	1 ♐ 35	20 49	24 26	11 09	2 31	5 41	3 53	19 15	25 11	29 35	18 17	20 12	21 46	25 21	15 31
9 T	7 12 9	18 11 36	15 06	20 42	25 10	12 22	3 16	5 43	3 59	19 14	25 13	29 37	18 41	20 34	21 48	25 08	15 32
10 W	7 16 5	19 12 46	29 05	20 31	25 59	13 36	4 01	5 45	4 05	19 13	25 14	29 39	19 05	20 56	21 50	24 56	15 32
11 Th	7 20 2	20 13 57	13 ♑ 27	20 19	26 52	14 49	4 46	5 47	4 11	19 12	25 15	29 40	19 29	21 18	21 51	24 43	15 33
12 F	7 23 58	21 15 07	28 08	20 07	27 49	16 03	5 31	5 50	4 17	19 11	25 16	29 42	19 53	21 40	21 52	24 31	15 34
13 Sa	7 27 55	22 16 16	12 ♒ 59	19 55	28 49	17 16	6 16	5 52	4 23	19 11	25 17	29 44	20 17	22 02	21 52R	24 20	15 35
14 Su	7 31 51	23 17 25	27 51	19 46	29 52	18 30	7 01	5 55	4 29	19 10	25 19	29 46	20 41	22 23	21 52	24 08	15 36
15 M	7 35 48	24 18 33	12 ♓ 36	19 39	0 ♑ 58	19 43	7 46	5 58	4 35	19 09	25 20	29 48	21 04	22 45	21 51	23 58	15 37
16 T	7 39 45	25 19 41	27 07	19 36	2 06	20 57	8 31	6 01	4 41	19 09	25 21	29 50	21 28	23 06	21 50	23 47	15 38
17 W	7 43 41	26 20 48	11 ♈ 22	19 34D	3 17	22 10	9 16	6 04	4 48	19 08	25 23	29 52	21 52	23 27	21 49	23 37	15 39
18 Th	7 47 38	27 21 54	25 18	19 34R	4 29	23 24	10 01	6 08	4 54	19 08	25 24	29 54	22 15	23 48	21 47	23 27	15 40
19 F	7 51 34	28 23 00	8 ♉ 57	19 34	5 43	24 38	10 46	6 12	5 00	19 07	25 25	29 56	22 39	24 08	21 45	23 18	15 42
20 Sa	7 55 31	29 24 04	22 20	19 32	6 59	25 51	11 32	6 15	5 07	19 07	25 27	29 58	23 02	24 29	21 42	23 09	15 43
21 Su	7 59 27	0 ♒ 25 08	5 ♊ 28	19 28	8 16	27 05	12 17	6 20	5 13	19 06	25 28	0 ♒ 00	23 26	24 50	21 38	23 01	15 44
22 M	8 3 24	1 26 11	18 24	19 21	9 35	28 19	13 02	6 24	5 19	19 06	25 30	0 02	23 49	25 10	21 35	22 53	15 45
23 T	8 7 20	2 27 13	1 ♋ 08	19 10	10 55	29 33	13 48	6 28	5 26	19 06	25 31	0 04	24 12	25 30	21 30	22 45	15 47
24 W	8 11 17	3 28 14	13 42	18 58	12 16	0 ♑ 47	14 33	6 33	5 33	19 06	25 33	0 06	24 35	25 50	21 26	22 38	15 48
25 Th	8 15 14	4 29 14	26 06	18 44	13 38	2 01	15 18	6 38	5 39	19 05	25 34	0 08	24 58	26 10	21 21	22 31	15 50
26 F	8 19 10	5 30 14	8 ♌ 21	18 31	15 01	3 14	16 04	6 43	5 46	19 05	25 36	0 10	25 21	26 30	21 15	22 25	15 52
27 Sa	8 23 7	6 31 13	20 26	18 18	16 25	4 28	16 49	6 48	5 52	19 05D	25 38	0 12	25 44	26 49	21 09	22 19	15 53
28 Su	8 27 3	7 32 10	2 ♍ 23	18 07	17 50	5 42	17 35	6 54	5 59	19 05	25 39	0 14	26 07	27 08	21 03	22 14	15 55
29 M	8 31 0	8 33 08	14 15	17 59	19 16	6 56	18 20	6 59	6 06	19 05	25 41	0 16	26 29	27 28	20 56	22 09	15 57
30 T	8 34 56	9 34 04	26 02	17 54	20 43	8 10	19 06	7 05	6 13	19 05	25 43	0 17	26 52	27 47	20 48	22 05	15 58
31 W	8 38 53	10 34 59	7 ♎ 50	17 52D	22 10	9 24	19 52	7 11	6 20	19 06	25 44	0 19	27 15	28 05	20 41	22 01	16 00

Tables are calculated for midnight Greenwich Mean Time

February 2024

DATE	SID.TIME	SUN	MOON	NODE	MERCURY	VENUS	MARS	JUPITER	SATURN	URANUS	NEPTUNE	PLUTO	CERES	PALLAS	JUNO	VESTA	CHIRON
1 Th	8 42 49	11≈35 54	19♎42	17♈51	23♑39	10♑38	20♑37	7♉17	6♓26	19♉06	25♓46	0≈23	27♐37	28♏24	20♍33R	21♊57R	16♈02
2 F	8 46 46	12 36 48	1♏42	17 52R	25 08	11 52	21 23	7 23	6 33	19 06	25 48	0 23	27 59	28 42	20 24	21 54	16 04
3 Sa	8 50 43	13 37 41	13 58	17 52	26 38	13 06	22 09	7 30	6 40	19 06	25 50	0 25	28 22	29 01	20 15	21 51	16 06
4 Su	8 54 39	14 38 34	26 33	17 51	28 09	14 20	22 55	7 36	6 47	19 07	25 51	0 27	28 44	29 19	20 06	21 49	16 08
5 M	8 58 36	15 39 26	9♐32	17 48	29 40	15 34	23 41	7 43	6 54	19 07	25 53	0 29	29 06	29 36	19 56	21 47	16 10
6 T	9 2 32	16 40 17	23 00	17 43	1≈13	16 49	24 26	7 50	7 01	19 08	25 55	0 31	29 28	29 54	19 46	21 46	16 12
7 W	9 6 29	17 41 07	6♑58	17 36	2 46	18 03	25 12	7 57	7 08	19 08	25 57	0 33	29 50	0♐11	19 35	21 45	16 14
8 Th	9 10 25	18 41 56	21 24	17 27	4 19	19 17	25 58	8 04	7 15	19 09	25 59	0 35	0♑12	0 29	19 24	21 45D	16 16
9 F	9 14 22	19 42 44	6≈14	17 18	5 54	20 31	26 44	8 11	7 22	19 10	26 01	0 36	0 33	0 46	19 13	21 45	16 19
10 Sa	9 18 19	20 43 31	21 19	17 09	7 30	21 45	27 30	8 19	7 30	19 10	26 03	0 38	0 55	1 02	19 02	21 45	16 21
11 Su	9 22 15	21 44 16	6♓31	17 01	9 06	22 59	28 16	8 27	7 37	19 11	26 05	0 40	1 16	1 19	18 50	21 46	16 23
12 M	9 26 12	22 45 00	21 38	16 56	10 43	24 13	29 02	8 35	7 44	19 12	26 07	0 42	1 38	1 35	18 38	21 48	16 25
13 T	9 30 8	23 45 42	6♈31	16 54D	12 21	25 28	29 48	8 42	7 51	19 13	26 09	0 44	1 59	1 51	18 25	21 49	16 28
14 W	9 34 5	24 46 23	21 05	16 53	13 59	26 42	0≈34	8 51	7 58	19 14	26 11	0 46	2 20	2 07	18 12	21 52	16 30
15 Th	9 38 1	25 47 02	5♉15	16 54	15 39	27 56	1 21	8 59	8 05	19 15	26 13	0 47	2 41	2 23	17 59	21 54	16 33
16 F	9 41 58	26 47 40	19 01	16 55R	17 19	29 10	2 07	9 07	8 13	19 16	26 15	0 49	3 02	2 38	17 46	21 57	16 35
17 Sa	9 45 54	27 48 15	2♊24	16 55	19 00	0≈24	2 53	9 16	8 20	19 17	26 17	0 51	3 23	2 53	17 32	22 01	16 38
18 Su	9 49 51	28 48 49	15 27	16 54	20 42	1 39	3 39	9 25	8 27	19 18	26 19	0 53	3 44	3 08	17 18	22 05	16 40
19 M	9 53 48	29 49 22	28 12	16 50	22 25	2 53	4 25	9 33	8 34	19 19	26 21	0 55	4 04	3 23	17 04	22 09	16 43
20 T	9 57 44	0♓49 52	10♋44	16 45	24 09	4 07	5 11	9 42	8 42	19 20	26 23	0 56	4 25	3 37	16 50	22 14	16 46
21 W	10 1 41	1 50 21	23 03	16 37	25 54	5 21	5 58	9 51	8 49	19 21	26 25	0 58	4 45	3 51	16 36	22 19	16 48
22 Th	10 5 37	2 50 48	5♌13	16 29	27 40	6 36	6 44	10 01	8 56	19 23	26 27	1 00	5 05	4 05	16 21	22 24	16 51
23 F	10 9 34	3 51 13	17 15	16 20	29 27	7 50	7 30	10 10	9 04	19 24	26 29	1 01	5 25	4 18	16 06	22 30	16 54
24 Sa	10 13 30	4 51 36	29 12	16 12	1♓14	9 04	8 17	10 20	9 11	19 25	26 31	1 03	5 45	4 32	15 52	22 36	16 57
25 Su	10 17 27	5 51 58	11♍03	16 06	3 03	10 18	9 03	10 29	9 18	19 27	26 34	1 05	6 05	4 44	15 37	22 43	16 59
26 M	10 21 23	6 52 18	22 52	16 01	4 52	11 33	9 49	10 39	9 25	19 28	26 36	1 07	6 25	4 57	15 22	22 50	17 02
27 T	10 25 20	7 52 36	4♎41	15 59D	6 43	12 47	10 36	10 49	9 33	19 30	26 38	1 08	6 44	5 09	15 07	22 57	17 05
28 W	10 29 16	8 52 53	16 31	15 58	8 34	14 01	11 22	10 59	9 40	19 31	26 40	1 10	7 04	5 22	14 51	23 05	17 08
29 Th	10 33 13	9 53 09	28 26	15 59	10 26	15 15	12 09	11 09	9 47	19 33	26 42	1 11	7 23	5 33	14 36	23 13	17 11

March 2024

DATE	SID.TIME	SUN	MOON	NODE	MERCURY	VENUS	MARS	JUPITER	SATURN	URANUS	NEPTUNE	PLUTO	CERES	PALLAS	JUNO	VESTA	CHIRON
1 F	10 37 10	10 H 53 22	10 ♏ 29	16 ♈ 00	12 H 19	16 ≈ 30	12 ≈ 55	11 ♉ 19	9 H 55	19 ♉ 35	26 H 44	1 ≈ 13	7 ♉ 42	5 ♐ 45	14 ♍ 21 R	23 ♊ 21 R	17 ♈ 14
2 Sa	10 41 6	11 53 35	22 45	16 02	14 13	17 44	13 42	11 29	10 02	19 36	26 47	1 15	8 01	5 56	14 06	23 30	17 17
3 Su	10 45 3	12 53 45	5 ♐ 18	16 03R	16 08	18 58	14 28	11 40	10 09	19 38	26 49	1 16	8 20	6 07	13 50	23 39	17 20
4 M	10 48 59	13 53 55	18 13	16 03	18 03	20 12	15 15	11 50	10 17	19 40	26 51	1 18	8 39	6 17	13 35	23 49	17 23
5 T	10 52 56	14 54 02	1 ♑ 33	16 00	19 59	21 27	16 01	12 01	10 24	19 42	26 53	1 19	8 57	6 27	13 20	23 58	17 26
6 W	10 56 52	15 54 09	15 21	15 56	21 55	22 41	16 48	12 11	10 31	19 44	26 56	1 21	9 16	6 37	13 05	24 09	17 29
7 Th	11 0 49	16 54 13	29 37	15 52	23 52	23 55	17 34	12 22	10 39	19 46	26 58	1 22	9 34	6 46	12 50	24 19	17 32
8 F	11 4 45	17 54 17	14 ≈ 18	15 48	25 48	25 10	18 21	12 33	10 46	19 48	27 00	1 24	9 52	6 56	12 35	24 30	17 36
9 Sa	11 8 42	18 54 18	29 20	15 48	27 45	26 24	19 07	12 44	10 53	19 50	27 02	1 25	10 10	7 04	12 20	24 41	17 39
10 Su	11 12 39	19 54 17	14 H 33	15 45	29 41	27 38	19 54	12 55	11 01	19 52	27 05	1 26	10 28	7 13	12 05	24 52	17 42
11 M	11 16 35	20 54 15	29 48	15 43	1 ♈ 36	28 52	20 41	13 07	11 08	19 54	27 07	1 28	10 46	7 21	11 51	25 04	17 45
12 T	11 20 32	21 54 10	14 ♈ 54	15 42D	3 30	0 H 07	21 27	13 18	11 15	19 56	27 09	1 29	11 03	7 28	11 37	25 16	17 48
13 W	11 24 28	22 54 04	29 43	15 43	5 23	1 21	22 14	13 29	11 22	19 58	27 11	1 31	11 20	7 36	11 22	25 28	17 52
14 Th	11 28 25	23 53 55	14 ♉ 09	15 44	7 13	2 35	23 00	13 41	11 30	20 01	27 14	1 32	11 37	7 42	11 08	25 40	17 55
15 F	11 32 21	24 53 44	28 08	15 45	9 02	3 49	23 47	13 52	11 37	20 03	27 16	1 33	11 54	7 49	10 55	25 53	17 58
16 Sa	11 36 18	25 53 31	11 ♊ 41	15 46	10 48	5 04	24 34	14 04	11 44	20 05	27 18	1 35	12 11	7 55	10 41	26 06	18 02
17 Su	11 40 14	26 53 16	24 49	15 47R	12 31	6 18	25 20	14 16	11 51	20 08	27 20	1 36	12 28	8 01	10 28	26 20	18 05
18 M	11 44 11	27 52 59	7 ♋ 35	15 47	14 10	7 32	26 07	14 28	11 58	20 10	27 23	1 37	12 44	8 06	10 15	26 33	18 08
19 T	11 48 8	28 52 39	20 02	15 46	15 45	8 46	26 54	14 40	12 05	20 12	27 25	1 38	13 00	8 11	10 02	26 47	18 12
20 W	11 52 4	29 52 17	2 ♌ 15	15 44	17 15	10 01	27 40	14 52	12 13	20 15	27 27	1 39	13 16	8 15	9 50	27 01	18 15
21 Th	11 56 1	0 ♈ 51 53	14 17	15 42	18 40	11 15	28 27	15 04	12 20	20 17	27 30	1 41	13 32	8 19	9 37	27 16	18 19
22 F	11 59 57	1 51 26	26 12	15 39	20 00	12 29	29 14	15 16	12 27	20 20	27 32	1 42	13 48	8 23	9 26	27 30	18 22
23 Sa	12 3 54	2 50 58	8 ♍ 02	15 37	21 14	13 43	0 H 00	15 28	12 34	20 23	27 34	1 43	14 03	8 26	9 14	27 45	18 25
24 Su	12 7 50	3 50 27	19 51	15 36	22 22	14 58	0 47	15 40	12 41	20 25	27 36	1 44	14 18	8 29	9 03	28 00	18 29
25 M	12 11 47	4 49 54	1 ♎ 40	15 35	23 23	16 12	1 34	15 53	12 48	20 28	27 39	1 45	14 33	8 31	8 52	28 16	18 32
26 T	12 15 43	5 49 19	13 32	15 34D	24 17	17 26	2 20	16 05	12 55	20 30	27 41	1 46	14 48	8 33	8 41	28 31	18 36
27 W	12 19 40	6 48 42	25 28	15 34	25 04	18 40	3 07	16 18	13 02	20 33	27 43	1 47	15 03	8 34	8 31	28 47	18 39
28 Th	12 23 37	7 48 03	7 ♏ 32	15 35	25 44	19 54	3 54	16 30	13 09	20 36	27 45	1 48	15 17	8 35	8 21	29 03	18 43
29 F	12 27 33	8 47 22	19 45	15 36	26 17	21 08	4 41	16 43	13 16	20 39	27 48	1 49	15 31	8 36R	8 11	29 19	18 46
30 Sa	12 31 30	9 46 39	2 ♐ 09	15 36	26 42	22 23	5 27	16 56	13 22	20 41	27 50	1 50	15 45	8 36	8 02	29 36	18 50
31 Su	12 35 26	10 45 55	14 49	15 37	27 00	23 37	6 14	17 08	13 29	20 44	27 52	1 51	15 59	8 35	7 53	29 52	18 53

Tables are calculated for midnight Greenwich Mean Time

April 2024

DATE	SID.TIME	SUN	MOON	NODE	MERCURY	VENUS	MARS	JUPITER	SATURN	URANUS	NEPTUNE	PLUTO	CERES	PALLAS	JUNO	VESTA	CHIRON
1 M	12 39 23	11♈09	27♐46	15♈37	27♈10R	24♈51	7♓01	17♉21	13♓36	20♉47	27♓54	1≈52	16♑13	8♐34R	7♏45R	0♋09	18♈57
2 T	12 43 19	12 44 21	11♑03	15 37R	27 13	26 05	7 47	7 47	17 34	13 43	20 50	27 57	1 53	16 26	8 33	7 37	0 26	19 00
3 W	12 47 16	13 43 31	24 42	15 37	27 09	27 19	8 34	18 00	13 49	20 53	27 59	1 54	16 39	8 31	7 29	0 44	19 04
4 Th	12 51 12	14 42 40	8≈45	15 37D	26 58	28 33	9 21	18 00	13 56	20 56	28 01	1 55	16 52	8 29	7 22	1 01	19 07
5 F	12 55 9	15 41 47	23 09	15 37	26 41	29 48	10 07	18 13	14 03	20 59	28 03	1 55	17 04	8 26	7 15	1 19	19 11
6 Sa	12 59 6	16 40 52	7♓53	15 37	26 18	1♈02	10 54	18 26	14 09	21 02	28 05	1 56	17 17	8 23	7 08	1 37	19 15
7 Su	13 3 2	17 39 55	22 51	15 37	25 49	2 16	11 41	18 39	14 16	21 05	28 08	1 57	17 29	8 19	7 02	1 55	19 18
8 M	13 6 59	18 38 56	7♈54	15 38R	25 16	3 30	12 27	18 53	14 22	21 08	28 10	1 58	17 41	8 14	6 57	2 13	19 22
9 T	13 10 55	19 37 55	22 56	15 37	24 39	4 44	13 14	19 06	14 29	21 11	28 12	1 58	17 52	8 10	6 51	2 31	19 25
10 W	13 14 52	20 36 52	7♉46	15 37	23 58	5 58	14 01	19 19	14 35	21 14	28 14	1 59	18 04	8 04	6 46	2 50	19 29
11 Th	13 18 48	21 35 48	22 18	15 37	23 15	7 12	14 47	19 33	14 42	21 17	28 16	2 00	18 15	7 59	6 42	3 09	19 32
12 F	13 22 45	22 34 41	6♊27	15 36	22 31	8 26	15 34	19 46	14 48	21 20	28 18	2 00	18 25	7 52	6 38	3 28	19 36
13 Sa	13 26 41	23 33 32	20 09	15 35	21 45	9 41	16 21	19 59	14 54	21 24	28 20	2 01	18 36	7 45	6 34	3 47	19 39
14 Su	13 30 38	24 32 20	3♋25	15 34	21 00	10 55	17 07	20 13	15 01	21 27	28 23	2 01	18 46	7 38	6 31	4 06	19 43
15 M	13 34 35	25 31 07	16 16	15 34D	20 16	12 09	17 54	20 26	15 07	21 30	28 25	2 02	18 56	7 31	6 28	4 26	19 46
16 T	13 38 31	26 29 51	28 46	15 34	19 34	13 23	18 40	20 40	15 13	21 33	28 27	2 02	19 06	7 22	6 25	4 45	19 50
17 W	13 42 28	27 28 33	10♌59	15 34	18 54	14 37	19 27	20 54	15 19	21 36	28 29	2 03	19 15	7 14	6 23	5 05	19 53
18 Th	13 46 24	28 27 12	22 59	15 35	18 24	15 51	20 13	21 07	15 25	21 40	28 31	2 03	19 25	7 04	6 21	5 25	19 57
19 F	13 50 21	29 25 50	4♍51	15 36	17 44	17 05	21 00	21 21	15 31	21 43	28 33	2 04	19 33	6 55	6 20	5 45	20 01
20 Sa	13 54 17	0♉24 25	16 39	15 37	17 15	18 19	21 46	21 35	15 37	21 46	28 35	2 04	19 42	6 45	6 19	6 05	20 04
21 Su	13 58 14	1 22 58	28 27	15 39	16 50	19 33	22 33	21 48	15 43	21 49	28 37	2 04	19 50	6 34	6 18	6 26	20 08
22 M	14 2 10	2 21 29	10♎19	15 39R	16 30	20 47	23 19	22 02	15 49	21 53	28 39	2 05	19 58	6 23	6 18D	6 46	20 11
23 T	14 6 7	3 19 58	22 17	15 39	16 15	22 01	24 06	22 16	15 54	21 56	28 41	2 05	20 06	6 12	6 18	7 07	20 14
24 W	14 10 3	4 18 26	4♏24	15 38	16 05	23 15	24 52	22 30	16 00	21 59	28 43	2 05	20 13	6 00	6 19	7 27	20 18
25 Th	14 14 0	5 16 51	16 41	15 36	16 00D	24 29	25 38	22 44	16 06	22 03	28 45	2 05	20 21	5 48	6 19	7 48	20 21
26 F	14 17 57	6 15 15	29 09	15 34	15 59	25 43	26 25	22 58	16 11	22 06	28 47	2 06	20 27	5 35	6 21	8 09	20 25
27 Sa	14 21 53	7 13 36	11♐50	15 30	16 04	26 57	27 11	23 11	16 17	22 10	28 48	2 06	20 34	5 22	6 22	8 31	20 28
28 Su	14 25 50	8 11 57	24 45	15 27	16 14	28 11	27 57	23 25	16 22	22 13	28 50	2 06	20 40	5 08	6 24	8 52	20 32
29 M	14 29 46	9 10 15	7♑54	15 24	16 28	29 25	28 44	23 39	16 28	22 16	28 52	2 06	20 46	4 54	6 27	9 13	20 35
30 T	14 33 43	10 08 33	21 18	15 22	16 47	0♉38	29 30	23 53	16 33	22 20	28 54	2 06	20 51	4 40	6 29	9 35	20 39

225

May 2024

DATE	SID.TIME	SUN	MOON	NODE	MERCURY	VENUS	MARS	JUPITER	SATURN	URANUS	NEPTUNE	PLUTO	CERES	PALLAS	JUNO	VESTA	CHIRON
1 W	14 37 39	11♉06 48	4≈58	15♈21D	17♈11	18♉52	0♈16	24♉07	16♓38	22♉23	28♓56	2≈06	20♉56	4♐25R	6♍32	9♋57	20♈42
2 Th	14 41 36	12 05 02	18 53	15 21	17 39	3 06	1 03	24 21	16 43	22 27	28 58	2 06R	21 01	4 10	6 36	10 18	20 45
3 F	14 45 33	13 03 15	3♓03	15 22	18 11	4 20	1 49	24 35	16 49	22 30	28 59	2 06	21 06	3 55	6 39	10 40	20 49
4 Sa	14 49 29	14 01 26	17 27	15 23	18 47	5 34	2 35	24 49	16 54	22 34	29 01	2 06	21 10	3 39	6 43	11 02	20 52
5 Su	14 53 26	14 59 36	2♈02	15 24R	19 26	6 48	3 21	25 04	16 59	22 37	29 03	2 06	21 14	3 23	6 48	11 25	20 55
6 M	14 57 22	15 57 44	16 43	15 25	20 10	8 02	4 07	25 18	17 04	22 41	29 04	2 06	21 17	3 07	6 52	11 47	20 59
7 T	15 1 19	16 55 51	1♉24	15 24	20 57	9 16	4 53	25 32	17 09	22 44	29 06	2 06	21 20	2 51	6 57	12 09	21 02
8 W	15 5 15	17 53 56	16 00	15 21	21 48	10 30	5 39	25 46	17 13	22 47	29 08	2 06	21 23	2 34	7 03	12 32	21 05
9 Th	15 9 12	18 52 00	0♊23	15 17	22 42	11 44	6 25	26 00	17 18	22 51	29 09	2 06	21 26	2 17	7 08	12 54	21 08
10 F	15 13 8	19 50 02	14 29	15 12	23 39	12 57	7 11	26 14	17 23	22 54	29 11	2 06	21 28	2 00	7 14	13 17	21 12
11 Sa	15 17 5	20 48 02	28 12	15 07	24 39	14 11	7 57	26 28	17 27	22 58	29 13	2 05	21 29	1 42	7 21	13 40	21 15
12 Su	15 21 2	21 46 00	11♋30	15 01	25 42	15 25	8 43	26 42	17 32	23 01	29 14	2 05	21 31	1 25	7 27	14 03	21 18
13 M	15 24 58	22 43 57	24 25	14 57	26 48	16 39	9 29	26 57	17 36	23 05	29 16	2 05	21 32	1 07	7 34	14 26	21 21
14 T	15 28 55	23 41 52	6♌58	14 54	27 56	17 53	10 15	27 11	17 41	23 08	29 17	2 04	21 32	0 49	7 41	14 49	21 24
15 W	15 32 51	24 39 45	19 12	14 53D	29 08	19 07	11 01	27 25	17 45	23 12	29 19	2 04	21 33R	0 31	7 49	15 12	21 27
16 Th	15 36 48	25 37 37	1♍13	14 53	0♊22	20 20	11 46	27 39	17 49	23 15	29 20	2 04	21 32	0 13	7 56	15 36	21 30
17 F	15 40 44	26 35 26	13 05	14 54	1 38	21 34	12 32	27 53	17 53	23 19	29 22	2 03	21 32	29♍55	8 04	15 59	21 33
18 Sa	15 44 41	27 33 14	24 54	14 55	2 57	22 48	13 18	28 07	17 57	23 22	29 23	2 03	21 31	29 37	8 13	16 23	21 36
19 Su	15 48 37	28 31 01	6♎43	14 56R	4 19	24 02	14 03	28 21	18 01	23 26	29 24	2 03	21 30	29 19	8 21	16 46	21 39
20 M	15 52 34	29 28 45	18 39	14 57	5 43	25 16	14 49	28 36	18 05	23 29	29 26	2 02	21 28	29 00	8 30	17 10	21 42
21 T	15 56 31	0♊26 28	0♏44	14 55	7 09	26 29	15 35	28 50	18 09	23 33	29 27	2 02	21 27	28 42	8 39	17 34	21 45
22 W	16 0 27	1 24 10	13 01	14 52	8 38	27 43	16 20	29 04	18 12	23 36	29 28	2 01	21 24	28 24	8 48	17 58	21 48
23 Th	16 4 24	2 21 50	25 33	14 46	10 09	28 57	17 06	29 18	18 16	23 40	29 30	2 01	21 22	28 06	8 58	18 22	21 51
24 F	16 8 20	3 19 30	8♐21	14 39	11 42	0♊11	17 51	29 32	18 20	23 43	29 31	2 00	21 19	27 48	9 08	18 46	21 54
25 Sa	16 12 17	4 17 07	21 23	14 31	13 18	1 25	18 36	29 46	18 23	23 47	29 32	1 59	21 15	27 30	9 18	19 10	21 57
26 Su	16 16 13	5 14 44	4♑41	14 23	14 56	2 38	19 22	0♊00	18 26	23 50	29 33	1 59	21 11	27 13	9 28	19 34	22 00
27 M	16 20 10	6 12 20	18 11	14 15	16 36	3 52	20 07	0 15	18 30	23 53	29 35	1 58	21 07	26 55	9 39	19 58	22 02
28 T	16 24 6	7 09 55	1≈52	14 08	18 19	5 06	20 52	0 29	18 33	23 57	29 36	1 58	21 03	26 38	9 49	20 22	22 05
29 W	16 28 3	8 07 28	15 43	14 04	20 04	6 20	21 37	0 43	18 36	24 00	29 37	1 57	20 58	26 23	10 00	20 47	22 08
30 Th	16 32 0	9 05 01	29 41	14 02D	21 51	7 33	22 23	0 57	18 39	24 04	29 38	1 56	20 53	26 03	10 11	21 11	22 11
31 F	16 35 56	10 02 33	13♓46	14 02	23 41	8 47	23 08	1 11	18 42	24 07	29 39	1 55	20 47	25 46	10 23	21 36	22 13

Tables are calculated for midnight Greenwich Mean Time

June 2024

DATE	SID.TIME	SUN	MOON	NODE	MERCURY	VENUS	MARS	JUPITER	SATURN	URANUS	NEPTUNE	PLUTO	CERES	PALLAS	JUNO	VESTA	CHIRON
1 Sa	16 39 53	11Ⅱ00 04	27✶57	14♈02	25♉32	10Ⅱ01	23♈53	1Ⅱ25	18✶45	24♉10	29✶40	1≈55R	20♍31R	25♏30R	10♍34	22♋01	22♈16
2 Su	16 43 49	11 57 35	12♈11	14 03R	27 26	11 15	24 38	1 39	18 48	24 14	29 41	1 54	20 35	25 13	10 46	22 25	22 18
3 M	16 47 46	12 55 05	26 29	14 02	29 23	12 28	25 23	1 53	18 50	24 17	29 42	1 53	20 28	24 57	10 58	22 50	22 21
4 T	16 51 42	13 52 34	10♉45	14 00	1Ⅱ21	13 42	26 08	2 07	18 53	24 20	29 43	1 52	20 22	24 41	11 11	23 15	22 23
5 W	16 55 39	14 50 02	24 57	13 55	3 22	14 56	26 53	2 21	18 55	24 24	29 44	1 51	20 14	24 26	11 23	23 40	22 26
6 Th	16 59 35	15 47 29	8Ⅱ59	13 47	5 24	16 10	27 37	2 35	18 58	24 27	29 45	1 51	20 07	24 11	11 36	24 05	22 28
7 F	17 3 32	16 44 56	22 49	13 37	7 28	17 23	28 22	2 49	19 00	24 30	29 45	1 50	19 59	23 56	11 49	24 30	22 31
8 Sa	17 7 29	17 42 22	6♋21	13 27	9 34	18 37	29 07	3 03	19 02	24 34	29 46	1 49	19 50	23 42	12 02	24 55	22 33
9 Su	17 11 25	18 39 47	19 32	13 17	11 42	19 51	29 51	3 17	19 04	24 37	29 47	1 48	19 42	23 27	12 15	25 21	22 35
10 M	17 15 22	19 37 10	2♌24	13 07	13 51	21 04	0♉36	3 30	19 06	24 40	29 48	1 47	19 33	23 14	12 28	25 46	22 37
11 T	17 19 18	20 34 33	14 55	13 00	16 01	22 18	1 21	3 44	19 08	24 43	29 48	1 46	19 24	23 00	12 42	26 11	22 40
12 W	17 23 15	21 31 55	27 09	12 55	18 12	23 32	2 05	3 58	19 10	24 47	29 49	1 45	19 14	22 47	12 56	26 37	22 42
13 Th	17 27 11	22 29 16	9♍10	12 52	20 23	24 46	2 49	4 12	19 12	24 50	29 50	1 44	19 04	22 35	13 09	27 02	22 44
14 F	17 31 8	23 26 35	21 02	12 51D	22 35	25 59	3 34	4 25	19 13	24 53	29 50	1 43	18 54	22 23	13 24	27 28	22 46
15 Sa	17 35 4	24 23 54	2♎51	12 52R	24 47	27 13	4 18	4 39	19 15	24 56	29 51	1 42	18 44	22 11	13 38	27 53	22 48
16 Su	17 39 1	25 21 12	14 42	12 52	26 59	28 27	5 02	4 53	19 16	24 59	29 52	1 41	18 34	22 00	13 52	28 19	22 50
17 M	17 42 58	26 18 29	26 40	12 51	29 10	29 41	5 46	5 06	19 18	25 02	29 52	1 40	18 23	21 49	14 07	28 45	22 52
18 T	17 46 54	27 15 46	8♏50	12 48	1♋21	0♋54	6 30	5 20	19 19	25 05	29 53	1 39	18 12	21 38	14 22	29 10	22 54
19 W	17 50 51	28 13 01	21 16	12 43	3 31	2 08	7 14	5 34	19 20	25 08	29 53	1 37	18 00	21 29	14 37	29 36	22 56
20 Th	17 54 47	29 10 16	4♐00	12 36	5 39	3 22	7 58	5 47	19 21	25 12	29 53	1 36	17 49	21 19	14 52	0♌02	22 58
21 F	17 58 44	0♋07 31	17 05	12 26	7 46	4 35	8 42	6 01	19 22	25 15	29 54	1 35	17 37	21 10	15 07	0 28	23 00
22 Sa	18 2 40	1 04 45	0♑29	12 14	9 52	5 49	9 26	6 14	19 23	25 18	29 54	1 34	17 25	21 01	15 22	0 54	23 01
23 Su	18 6 37	2 01 58	14 11	12 03	11 56	7 03	10 10	6 27	19 23	25 20	29 54	1 33	17 13	20 53	15 38	1 20	23 03
24 M	18 10 34	2 59 12	28 06	11 52	13 58	8 17	10 54	6 41	19 24	25 23	29 55	1 32	17 01	20 46	15 53	1 46	23 05
25 T	18 14 30	3 56 25	12≈12	11 43	15 59	9 30	11 37	6 54	19 25	25 26	29 55	1 30	16 49	20 38	16 09	2 12	23 06
26 W	18 18 27	4 53 37	26 22	11 36	17 57	10 44	12 21	7 07	19 25	25 29	29 55	1 29	16 36	20 32	16 25	2 38	23 08
27 Th	18 22 23	5 50 50	10✶35	11 32	19 53	11 58	13 04	7 21	19 26	25 32	29 55	1 28	16 24	20 26	16 41	3 05	23 09
28 F	18 26 20	6 48 03	24 46	11 31D	21 48	13 11	13 48	7 34	19 26R	25 35	29 56	1 27	16 11	20 20	16 57	3 31	23 11
29 Sa	18 30 16	7 45 15	8♈55	11 31R	23 40	14 25	14 31	7 47	19 26	25 38	29 56	1 25	15 58	20 14	17 13	3 57	23 12
30 Su	18 34 13	8 42 28	22 59	11 30	25 30	15 39	15 14	8 00	19 26	25 40	29 56	1 24	15 45	20 10	17 30	4 24	23 14

DATE	SID.TIME	SUN	MOON	NODE	MERCURY	VENUS	MARS	JUPITER	SATURN	URANUS	NEPTUNE	PLUTO	CERES	PALLAS	JUNO	VESTA	CHIRON
1 M	18 38 9	9♋39 41	6♊59	11♈29R	27♋18	16♋53	15♉58	8♊13	19♓26R	25♉43	29♓56	1♒23R	15♑32R	20♏05R	17♍46	4♌50	23♈15
2 T	18 42 6	10 36 55	20 53	11 25	29 04	18 06	16 41	8 26	19 25	25 46	29 56R	1 22	15 19	20 01	18 03	5 16	23 16
3 W	18 46 3	11 34 08	4♋41	11 19	0♌48	19 20	17 24	8 39	19 25	25 49	29 56	1 20	15 06	19 58	18 20	5 43	23 18
4 Th	18 49 59	12 31 22	18 18	11 10	2 30	20 34	18 07	8 52	19 25	25 51	29 56	1 19	14 52	19 55	18 37	6 10	23 19
5 F	18 53 56	13 28 35	1♌45	10 59	4 09	21 47	18 50	9 05	19 24	25 54	29 56	1 18	14 39	19 52	18 54	6 36	23 20
6 Sa	18 57 52	14 25 49	14 57	10 46	5 47	23 01	19 33	9 17	19 24	25 56	29 56	1 16	14 26	19 50	19 11	7 03	23 21
7 Su	19 1 49	15 23 03	27 54	10 34	7 22	24 15	20 16	9 30	19 23	25 59	29 56	1 15	14 13	19 49	19 28	7 30	23 22
8 M	19 5 45	16 20 17	10♍35	10 22	8 55	25 29	20 58	9 43	19 22	26 02	29 55	1 14	13 59	19 47	19 45	7 56	23 23
9 T	19 9 42	17 17 30	22 59	10 13	10 26	26 42	21 41	9 55	19 22	26 04	29 55	1 12	13 46	19 47	20 03	8 23	23 24
10 W	19 13 38	18 14 44	5♍09	10 06	11 55	27 56	22 23	10 08	19 21	26 06	29 55	1 11	13 33	19 46D	20 20	8 50	23 25
11 Th	19 17 35	19 11 58	17 07	10 02	13 22	29 10	23 06	10 20	19 19	26 09	29 55	1 09	13 20	19 47	20 38	9 17	23 26
12 F	19 21 32	20 09 11	28 58	10 00D	14 46	0♌24	23 48	10 33	19 18	26 11	29 54	1 08	13 07	19 47	20 56	9 44	23 26
13 Sa	19 25 28	21 06 24	10♎46	10 00R	16 08	1 37	24 30	10 45	19 17	26 14	29 54	1 07	12 54	19 48	21 14	10 11	23 27
14 Su	19 29 25	22 03 38	22 36	10 00	17 28	2 51	25 13	10 57	19 16	26 16	29 54	1 05	12 41	19 50	21 32	10 38	23 28
15 M	19 33 21	23 00 51	4♏34	10 00	18 45	4 05	25 55	11 09	19 14	26 18	29 53	1 04	12 29	19 52	21 50	11 05	23 29
16 T	19 37 18	23 58 05	16 46	9 58	20 00	5 19	26 37	11 21	19 13	26 20	29 53	1 02	12 16	19 54	22 08	11 32	23 29
17 W	19 41 14	24 55 19	29 15	9 53	21 13	6 32	27 19	11 33	19 11	26 23	29 52	1 01	12 04	19 57	22 26	11 59	23 30
18 Th	19 45 11	25 52 33	12♐07	9 47	22 23	7 46	28 01	11 45	19 09	26 25	29 52	1 00	11 52	20 00	22 44	12 26	23 30
19 F	19 49 7	26 49 47	25 22	9 38	23 31	9 00	28 42	11 57	19 08	26 27	29 51	0 58	11 40	20 03	23 03	12 53	23 31
20 Sa	19 53 4	27 47 02	9♑01	9 27	24 36	10 13	29 24	12 09	19 06	26 29	29 51	0 57	11 28	20 07	23 21	13 21	23 31
21 Su	19 57 1	28 44 17	23 03	9 17	25 38	11 27	0♊06	12 21	19 04	26 31	29 50	0 55	11 16	20 11	23 40	13 48	23 31
22 M	20 0 57	29 41 32	7♒21	9 07	26 37	12 41	0 47	12 32	19 02	26 33	29 50	0 54	11 04	20 16	23 58	14 15	23 32
23 T	20 4 54	0♌38 48	21 52	8 58	27 33	13 55	1 29	12 44	18 59	26 35	29 49	0 53	10 53	20 21	24 17	14 42	23 32
24 W	20 8 50	1 36 04	6♓27	8 52	28 26	15 08	2 10	12 55	18 57	26 37	29 48	0 51	10 42	20 27	24 36	15 10	23 32
25 Th	20 12 47	2 33 22	21 01	8 49	29 16	16 22	2 51	13 07	18 55	26 39	29 48	0 50	10 31	20 32	24 55	15 37	23 32
26 F	20 16 43	3 30 40	5♈29	8 48D	0♍02	17 36	3 32	13 18	18 52	26 40	29 47	0 48	10 21	20 39	25 14	16 05	23 32R
27 Sa	20 20 40	4 27 59	19 46	8 48	0 45	18 49	4 13	13 29	18 50	26 42	29 46	0 47	10 10	20 45	25 33	16 32	23 32
28 Su	20 24 36	5 25 19	3♉52	8 48R	1 25	20 03	4 54	13 40	18 47	26 44	29 46	0 45	10 00	20 52	25 52	17 00	23 32
29 M	20 28 33	6 22 40	17 45	8 48	2 00	21 17	5 35	13 51	18 44	26 46	29 45	0 44	9 51	20 59	26 11	17 27	23 32
30 T	20 32 30	7 20 03	1♊26	8 46	2 32	22 30	6 16	14 02	18 42	26 47	29 44	0 43	9 41	21 07	26 30	17 55	23 32
31 W	20 36 26	8 17 26	14 55	8 41	2 59	23 44	6 57	14 13	18 39	26 49	29 43	0 41	9 32	21 15	26 50	18 22	23 32

Tables are calculated for midnight Greenwich Mean Time

DATE	SID.TIME	SUN	MOON	NODE	MERCURY	VENUS	MARS	JUPITER	SATURN	URANUS	NEPTUNE	PLUTO	CERES	PALLAS	JUNO	VESTA	CHIRON
1 Th	20 40 23	9♌14 51	28♊11	8♈34R	3♍22	24♌58	7♊37	14♊24	18♓36R	26♉51	29♓42R	0♒40R	9♋23R	21♍23	27♍09	18♌50	23♈31R
2 F	20 44 19	10 12 16	11♋15	8 25	3 40	26 12	8 18	14 35	18 33	26 52	29 41	0 38	9 14	21 31	27 28	19 18	23 31
3 Sa	20 48 16	11 09 43	24 06	8 15	3 54	27 25	8 58	14 45	18 30	26 54	29 40	0 37	9 06	21 40	27 48	19 45	23 31
4 Su	20 52 12	12 07 10	6♌44	8 05	4 03	28 39	9 39	14 56	18 27	26 55	29 39	0 36	8 58	21 49	28 07	20 13	23 30
5 M	20 56 9	13 04 38	19 09	7 56	4 06R	29 53	10 19	15 06	18 23	26 56	29 38	0 34	8 50	21 59	28 27	20 41	23 30
6 T	21 0 6	14 02 08	1♍23	7 48	4 05	1♍06	10 59	15 16	18 20	26 58	29 37	0 33	8 43	22 09	28 47	21 08	23 29
7 W	21 4 2	14 59 38	13 25	7 43	3 58	2 20	11 39	15 27	18 17	26 59	29 36	0 32	8 36	22 19	29 07	21 36	23 29
8 Th	21 7 59	15 57 09	25 19	7 40	3 46	3 34	12 19	15 37	18 13	27 00	29 35	0 30	8 29	22 29	29 26	22 04	23 28
9 F	21 11 55	16 54 41	7♎07	7 39D	3 28	4 47	12 58	15 47	18 10	27 01	29 34	0 29	8 23	22 40	29 46	22 32	23 27
10 Sa	21 15 52	17 52 14	18 53	7 40	3 05	6 01	13 38	15 56	18 06	27 03	29 33	0 27	8 17	22 51	0♎06	23 00	23 27
11 Su	21 19 48	18 49 47	0♏43	7 41	2 37	7 15	14 18	16 06	18 02	27 04	29 32	0 26	8 11	23 02	0 26	23 28	23 26
12 M	21 23 45	19 47 22	12 40	7 42R	2 05	8 28	14 57	16 16	17 59	27 05	29 31	0 25	8 06	23 14	0 46	23 56	23 25
13 T	21 27 41	20 44 58	24 50	7 42	1 27	9 42	15 36	16 25	17 55	27 06	29 29	0 23	8 01	23 26	1 06	24 23	23 24
14 W	21 31 38	21 42 34	7♐19	7 41	0 46	10 56	16 15	16 35	17 51	27 07	29 28	0 22	7 56	23 38	1 26	24 51	23 23
15 Th	21 35 35	22 40 12	20 10	7 38	0 01	12 09	16 55	16 44	17 47	27 08	29 27	0 21	7 52	23 50	1 47	25 19	23 22
16 F	21 39 31	23 37 50	3♑27	7 33	29♌13	13 23	17 33	16 53	17 43	27 08	29 26	0 20	7 48	24 03	2 07	25 47	23 21
17 Sa	21 43 28	24 35 30	17 11	7 27	28 23	14 37	18 12	17 02	17 39	27 09	29 25	0 18	7 45	24 15	2 27	26 15	23 20
18 Su	21 47 24	25 33 10	1≈21	7 20	27 31	15 50	18 51	17 11	17 35	27 10	29 23	0 17	7 42	24 28	2 47	26 44	23 19
19 M	21 51 21	26 30 52	15 54	7 14	26 40	17 04	19 30	17 20	17 31	27 11	29 22	0 16	7 39	24 42	3 08	27 12	23 18
20 T	21 55 17	27 28 35	0♓43	7 09	25 49	18 17	20 08	17 28	17 27	27 11	29 21	0 15	7 36	24 55	3 28	27 40	23 17
21 W	21 59 14	28 26 19	15 40	7 06	25 00	19 31	20 47	17 37	17 23	27 12	29 19	0 13	7 34	25 09	3 49	28 08	23 15
22 Th	22 3 10	29 24 05	0♈36	7 04D	24 14	20 44	21 25	17 45	17 19	27 13	29 18	0 12	7 33	25 23	4 09	28 36	23 14
23 F	22 7 7	0♍21 52	15 25	7 04	23 32	21 58	22 03	17 53	17 14	27 13	29 16	0 11	7 31	25 37	4 30	29 04	23 13
24 Sa	22 11 3	1 19 42	0♉00	7 05	22 54	23 11	22 41	18 02	17 10	27 14	29 15	0 10	7 30	25 52	4 50	29 32	23 11
25 Su	22 15 0	2 17 32	14 17	7 07	22 23	24 25	23 19	18 10	17 06	27 14	29 14	0 09	7 30	26 06	5 11	0♍00	23 10
26 M	22 18 57	3 15 25	28 14	7 08R	21 57	25 39	23 56	18 17	17 01	27 14	29 12	0 08	7 29D	26 21	5 31	0 29	23 08
27 T	22 22 53	4 13 20	11♊52	7 08	21 39	26 52	24 34	18 25	16 57	27 15	29 11	0 06	7 29	26 36	5 52	0 57	23 07
28 W	22 26 50	5 11 16	25 12	7 06	21 28D	28 06	25 12	18 33	16 53	27 15	29 09	0 05	7 30	26 52	6 13	1 25	23 05
29 Th	22 30 46	6 09 14	8♋14	7 03	21 25	29 19	25 49	18 40	16 48	27 15	29 08	0 04	7 31	27 07	6 34	1 53	23 04
30 F	22 34 43	7 07 14	21 00	6 59	21 30	0♎33	26 26	18 47	16 44	27 15	29 06	0 03	7 32	27 23	6 54	2 22	23 02
31 Sa	22 38 39	8 05 16	3♌33	6 54	21 43	1 46	27 03	18 54	16 39	27 15	29 05	0 02	7 33	27 39	7 15	2 50	23 00

September 2024

DATE	SID. TIME	SUN	MOON	NODE	MERCURY	VENUS	MARS	JUPITER	SATURN	URANUS	NEPTUNE	PLUTO	CERES	PALLAS	JUNO	VESTA	CHIRON
1 Su	22 42 36	9♍03 20	15♌54	6♈50R	22♌05	2♎59	27♊40	19♊01	16♓35R	27♉15R	29♓03R	0≈01R	7♑35	27♏55	7♎36	3♍18	22♈58R
2 M	22 46 33	10 01 25	28 05	6 45	22 35	4 13	28 17	19 08	16 30	27 15	29 02	0 00	7 37	28 11	7 57	3 47	22 57
3 T	22 50 29	10 59 32	10♍07	6 42	23 13	5 26	28 54	19 15	16 25	27 15	29 00	29♑59	7 40	28 28	8 18	4 15	22 55
4 W	22 54 26	11 57 40	22 01	6 40	23 59	6 40	29 30	19 21	16 21	27 15	28 59	29 58	7 43	28 44	8 39	4 43	22 53
5 Th	22 58 22	12 55 51	3♎50	6 39D	24 53	7 53	0♋06	19 28	16 16	27 15	28 57	29 57	7 46	29 01	9 00	5 12	22 51
6 F	23 2 19	13 54 02	15 37	6 39	25 54	9 07	0 43	19 34	16 12	27 15	28 55	29 56	7 49	29 18	9 21	5 40	22 49
7 Sa	23 6 15	14 52 16	27 23	6 40	27 02	10 20	1 19	19 40	16 07	27 15	28 54	29 55	7 53	29 35	9 42	6 09	22 47
8 Su	23 10 12	15 50 31	9♏14	6 42	28 16	11 33	1 54	19 46	16 03	27 14	28 52	29 54	7 57	29 52	10 03	6 37	22 45
9 M	23 14 8	16 48 47	21 12	6 43	29 36	12 47	2 30	19 52	15 58	27 14	28 51	29 53	8 02	0♐10	10 24	7 05	22 43
10 T	23 18 5	17 47 06	3♐21	6 45	1♍02	14 00	3 06	19 57	15 53	27 14	28 49	29 53	8 07	0 28	10 45	7 34	22 41
11 W	23 22 1	18 45 25	15 48	6 45R	2 32	15 13	3 41	20 03	15 49	27 13	28 47	29 52	8 12	0 45	11 06	8 02	22 39
12 Th	23 25 58	19 43 47	28 35	6 45	4 07	16 27	4 16	20 08	15 44	27 13	28 46	29 51	8 17	1 03	11 27	8 31	22 37
13 F	23 29 55	20 42 10	11♑46	6 44	5 45	17 40	4 51	20 13	15 40	27 12	28 44	29 50	8 23	1 21	11 48	8 59	22 34
14 Sa	23 33 51	21 40 34	25 25	6 43	7 27	18 53	5 26	20 18	15 35	27 12	28 43	29 49	8 29	1 40	12 09	9 28	22 32
15 Su	23 37 48	22 39 00	9≈31	6 41	9 11	20 07	6 01	20 23	15 30	27 11	28 41	29 49	8 36	1 58	12 31	9 56	22 30
16 M	23 41 44	23 37 28	24 03	6 39	10 57	21 20	6 35	20 27	15 26	27 10	28 39	29 48	8 42	2 17	12 52	10 25	22 28
17 T	23 45 41	24 35 57	8♓56	6 38	12 45	22 33	7 10	20 32	15 21	27 09	28 38	29 47	8 49	2 35	13 13	10 53	22 25
18 W	23 49 37	25 34 28	24 03	6 37D	14 35	23 46	7 44	20 36	15 17	27 09	28 36	29 47	8 57	2 54	13 34	11 22	22 23
19 Th	23 53 34	26 33 01	9♈15	6 37	16 25	25 00	8 18	20 40	15 12	27 08	28 34	29 46	9 04	3 13	13 55	11 50	22 20
20 F	23 57 30	27 31 36	24 21	6 37	18 16	26 13	8 52	20 44	15 08	27 07	28 33	29 45	9 12	3 32	14 17	12 19	22 18
21 Sa	0 1 27	28 30 13	9♉15	6 38	20 07	27 26	9 26	20 47	15 04	27 06	28 31	29 45	9 20	3 51	14 38	12 47	22 16
22 Su	0 5 24	29 28 53	23 49	6 38	21 59	28 39	9 59	20 51	14 59	27 05	28 29	29 44	9 29	4 10	14 59	13 16	22 13
23 M	0 9 20	0♎27 34	7♊58	6 39	23 50	29 52	10 32	20 54	14 55	27 04	28 28	29 44	9 37	4 30	15 21	13 44	22 11
24 T	0 13 17	1 26 18	21 43	6 39R	25 42	1♍05	11 05	20 57	14 51	27 03	28 26	29 43	9 46	4 50	15 42	14 13	22 08
25 W	0 17 13	2 25 05	5♋03	6 39	27 32	2 18	11 38	21 00	14 46	27 02	28 24	29 43	9 56	5 09	16 03	14 41	22 06
26 Th	0 21 10	3 23 53	18 00	6 39	29 23	3 31	12 11	21 03	14 42	27 01	28 23	29 42	10 05	5 29	16 24	15 10	22 03
27 F	0 25 6	4 22 44	0♌38	6 39	1♎12	4 44	12 43	21 05	14 38	27 00	28 21	29 42	10 15	5 49	16 46	15 38	22 00
28 Sa	0 29 3	5 21 37	13 00	6 39	3 01	5 57	13 16	21 08	14 34	26 58	28 19	29 41	10 25	6 09	17 07	16 07	21 58
29 Su	0 32 59	6 20 32	25 08	6 39D	4 50	7 10	13 48	21 10	14 30	26 57	28 18	29 41	10 35	6 29	17 29	16 35	21 55
30 M	0 36 56	7 19 29	7♍08	6 39	6 37	8 23	14 19	21 12	14 26	26 56	28 16	29 41	10 46	6 49	17 50	17 04	21 53

Tables are calculated for midnight Greenwich Mean Time

October 2024

DATE	SID.TIME	SUN	MOON	NODE	MERCURY	VENUS	MARS	JUPITER	SATURN	URANUS	NEPTUNE	PLUTO	CERES	PALLAS	JUNO	VESTA	CHIRON
1 T	0 40 53	8≏18 28	19♍01	6♈39	8≏24	9♎36	14♋51	21Ⅱ13	14♓22R	26♉54R	28♓14R	29♑40R	10♍57	7♐10	18≏11	17♍33	21♈50R
2 W	0 44 49	9 17 30	0≏49	6♈39R	10 10	10 49	15 22	21 15	14 18	26 53	28 13	29 40	11 08	7 30	18 33	18 01	21 47
3 Th	0 48 46	10 16 33	12 36	6 39	11 55	12 02	15 53	21 16	14 14	26 51	28 11	29 39	11 19	7 51	18 54	18 30	21 45
4 F	0 52 42	11 15 39	24 24	6 39	13 39	13 15	16 24	21 17	14 10	26 50	28 10	29 39	11 31	8 11	19 15	18 58	21 42
5 Sa	0 56 39	12 14 46	6♏14	6 38	15 23	14 28	16 55	21 18	14 06	26 48	28 08	29 39	11 42	8 32	19 37	19 27	21 39
6 Su	1 0 35	13 13 56	18 10	6 37	17 06	15 41	17 25	21 19	14 02	26 47	28 06	29 39	11 54	8 53	19 58	19 55	21 37
7 M	1 4 32	14 13 07	0♐13	6 36	18 47	16 54	17 56	21 20	13 59	26 45	28 05	29 39	12 07	9 14	20 19	20 24	21 34
8 T	1 8 28	15 12 21	12 27	6 35	20 28	18 07	18 25	21 20	13 55	26 43	28 03	29 39	12 19	9 35	20 41	20 52	21 31
9 W	1 12 25	16 11 36	24 55	6 34	22 09	19 20	18 55	21 20R	13 52	26 42	28 02	29 39	12 32	9 56	21 02	21 21	21 28
10 Th	1 16 22	17 10 53	7♑40	6 34D	23 48	20 32	19 24	21 20	13 48	26 40	28 00	29 39	12 45	10 17	21 24	21 49	21 26
11 F	1 20 18	18 10 12	20 46	6 34	25 27	21 45	19 53	21 20	13 45	26 38	27 59	29 39	12 58	10 39	21 45	22 18	21 23
12 Sa	1 24 15	19 09 32	4≈15	6 34	27 05	22 58	20 22	21 20	13 41	26 36	27 57	29 39D	13 11	11 00	22 06	22 46	21 20
13 Su	1 28 11	20 08 54	18 09	6 35	28 42	24 11	20 51	21 19	13 38	26 35	27 56	29 39	13 25	11 22	22 28	23 15	21 17
14 M	1 32 8	21 08 18	2♓28	6 36	0♏18	25 23	21 19	21 18	13 35	26 33	27 54	29 39	13 38	11 43	22 49	23 43	21 15
15 T	1 36 4	22 07 44	17 10	6 37	1 54	26 36	21 47	21 17	13 32	26 31	27 53	29 39	13 52	12 05	23 10	24 12	21 12
16 W	1 40 1	23 07 11	2♈09	6 38R	3 29	27 49	22 15	21 16	13 29	26 29	27 51	29 39	14 07	12 26	23 32	24 40	21 09
17 Th	1 43 57	24 06 41	17 20	6 37	5 04	29 01	22 42	21 14	13 26	26 27	27 50	29 39	14 21	12 48	23 53	25 09	21 06
18 F	1 47 54	25 06 12	2♉32	6 36	6 38	0♏14	23 09	21 13	13 23	26 25	27 48	29 39	14 35	13 10	24 14	25 37	21 04
19 Sa	1 51 51	26 05 46	17 35	6 34	8 11	1 26	23 36	21 11	13 20	26 23	27 47	29 39	14 50	13 32	24 35	26 05	21 01
20 Su	1 55 47	27 05 21	2Ⅱ22	5 32	9 44	2 39	24 02	21 09	13 18	26 21	27 45	29 39	15 05	13 54	24 57	26 34	20 58
21 M	1 59 44	28 04 59	16 45	5 29	11 16	3 51	24 29	21 07	13 15	26 19	27 44	29 40	15 20	14 16	25 18	27 02	20 56
22 T	2 3 40	29 04 40	0♋40	5 26	12 47	5 04	24 54	21 04	13 13	26 17	27 43	29 40	15 35	14 38	25 39	27 31	20 53
23 W	2 7 37	0♏04 22	14 07	5 24	14 18	6 16	25 20	21 01	13 10	26 14	27 41	29 40	15 51	15 00	26 00	27 59	20 50
24 Th	2 11 33	1 04 07	27 08	5 23D	15 48	7 28	25 45	20 59	13 08	26 12	27 40	29 41	16 06	15 22	26 21	28 27	20 47
25 F	2 15 30	2 03 54	9♌45	5 23	17 18	8 41	26 10	20 56	13 06	26 10	27 39	29 41	16 22	15 45	26 43	28 56	20 45
26 Sa	2 19 26	3 03 43	22 03	5 24	18 47	9 53	26 34	20 52	13 04	26 08	27 37	29 41	16 38	16 07	27 04	29 24	20 42
27 Su	2 23 23	4 03 34	4♍06	5 26	20 15	11 05	26 58	20 49	13 01	26 06	27 36	29 42	16 54	16 30	27 25	29 52	20 39
28 M	2 27 20	5 03 28	16 00	5 28	21 43	12 18	27 22	20 45	13 00	26 03	27 35	29 42	17 11	16 52	27 46	0≏21	20 37
29 T	2 31 16	6 03 23	27 48	5 29R	23 10	13 30	27 45	20 42	12 58	26 01	27 34	29 43	17 27	17 15	28 07	0 49	20 34
30 W	2 35 13	7 03 21	9≏34	5 30	24 37	14 42	28 08	20 38	12 56	25 59	27 32	29 43	17 44	17 37	28 28	1 17	20 31
31 Th	2 39 9	8 03 20	21 22	5 28	26 03	15 54	28 31	20 33	12 54	25 56	27 31	29 44	18 01	18 00	28 49	1 45	20 29

November 2024

DATE	SID.TIME	SUN	MOON	NODE	MERCURY	VENUS	MARS	JUPITER	SATURN	URANUS	NEPTUNE	PLUTO	CERES	PALLAS	JUNO	VESTA	CHIRON
1 F	2 43 6	9♏03 22	3♏14	6♈26R	27♏28	17♐06	28♋53	20♊29R	12♓53R	25♉54R	27♓30R	29♑44R	18♑18	18♐23	29♎10	2♎13	20♈26R
2 Sa	2 47 2	10 03 26	15 12	6 21	28 53	18 18	29 14	20 24	12 51	25 52	27 29	29 45	18 35	18 45	29 32	2 41	20 24
3 Su	2 50 59	11 03 31	27 18	6 15	0♐16	19 30	29 36	20 20	12 50	25 49	27 28	29 45	18 52	19 08	29 53	3 10	20 21
4 M	2 54 55	12 03 39	9♐33	6 09	1 39	20 42	29 56	20 15	12 49	25 47	27 27	29 46	19 09	19 31	0♏13	3 38	20 19
5 T	2 58 52	13 03 48	21 59	6 02	3 01	21 54	0♌17	20 10	12 47	25 44	27 26	29 47	19 27	19 54	0 34	4 06	20 16
6 W	3 2 49	14 03 58	4♑37	5 56	4 22	23 06	0 37	20 05	12 46	25 42	27 25	29 47	19 45	20 17	0 55	4 34	20 14
7 Th	3 6 45	15 04 11	17 28	5 51	5 42	24 18	0 56	19 59	12 45	25 40	27 24	29 48	20 02	20 40	1 16	5 02	20 11
8 F	3 10 42	16 04 25	0♒34	5 48	7 01	25 30	1 15	19 54	12 45	25 37	27 23	29 49	20 20	21 03	1 37	5 30	20 09
9 Sa	3 14 38	17 04 40	13 58	5 47D	8 19	26 42	1 34	19 48	12 44	25 35	27 22	29 50	20 38	21 26	1 58	5 58	20 07
10 Su	3 18 35	18 04 57	27 41	5 47	9 35	27 53	1 51	19 42	12 43	25 32	27 21	29 51	20 57	21 49	2 19	6 26	20 04
11 M	3 22 31	19 05 15	11♓44	5 48	10 50	29 05	2 09	19 36	12 43	25 30	27 20	29 51	21 15	22 12	2 39	6 53	20 02
12 T	3 26 28	20 05 34	26 06	5 50R	12 02	0♑17	2 26	19 30	12 42	25 27	27 19	29 52	21 34	22 35	3 00	7 21	20 00
13 W	3 30 24	21 05 55	10♈46	5 50	13 13	1 28	2 42	19 24	12 42	25 25	27 18	29 53	21 52	22 59	3 21	7 49	19 57
14 Th	3 34 21	22 06 17	25 39	5 48	14 22	2 40	2 58	19 17	12 42D	25 22	27 18	29 54	22 11	23 22	3 41	8 17	19 55
15 F	3 38 18	23 06 41	10♉38	5 44	15 28	3 51	3 14	19 11	12 42	25 20	27 17	29 55	22 30	23 45	4 02	8 44	19 53
16 Sa	3 42 14	24 07 07	25 35	5 38	16 31	5 02	3 28	19 04	12 42	25 17	27 16	29 56	22 49	24 09	4 22	9 12	19 51
17 Su	3 46 11	25 07 34	10♊21	5 31	17 31	6 14	3 43	18 57	12 42	25 15	27 15	29 57	23 08	24 32	4 43	9 40	19 49
18 M	3 50 7	26 08 03	24 47	5 22	18 28	7 25	3 56	18 50	12 42	25 12	27 15	29 58	23 27	24 55	5 03	10 07	19 46
19 T	3 54 4	27 08 33	8♋49	5 14	19 20	8 36	4 10	18 43	12 42	25 10	27 14	29 59	23 46	25 19	5 24	10 35	19 44
20 W	3 58 0	28 09 05	22 23	5 07	20 08	9 47	4 22	18 36	12 43	25 07	27 13	0♒00	24 06	25 42	5 44	11 02	19 42
21 Th	4 1 57	29 09 39	5♌29	5 02	20 50	10 58	4 34	18 29	12 43	25 05	27 13	0 01	24 25	26 06	6 04	11 30	19 40
22 F	4 5 53	0♐10 15	18 10	4 59	21 27	12 09	4 45	18 21	12 44	25 02	27 12	0 02	24 45	26 29	6 25	11 57	19 38
23 Sa	4 9 50	1 10 52	0♍30	4 59D	21 57	13 20	4 56	18 14	12 44	25 00	27 12	0 04	25 05	26 53	6 45	12 24	19 37
24 Su	4 13 47	2 11 31	12 33	4 59	22 20	14 30	5 06	18 06	12 45	24 57	27 11	0 05	25 25	27 16	7 05	12 52	19 35
25 M	4 17 43	3 12 12	24 26	5 00R	22 34	15 41	5 15	17 59	12 46	24 55	27 11	0 06	25 45	27 40	7 25	13 19	19 33
26 T	4 21 40	4 12 54	6♎13	5 00	22 40R	16 52	5 24	17 51	12 47	24 52	27 10	0 07	26 05	28 03	7 45	13 46	19 31
27 W	4 25 36	5 13 38	17 59	4 59	22 36	18 02	5 32	17 43	12 48	24 50	27 10	0 08	26 25	28 27	8 05	14 13	19 29
28 Th	4 29 33	6 14 23	29 50	4 56	22 22	19 13	5 39	17 35	12 50	24 47	27 10	0 10	26 45	28 50	8 25	14 40	19 28
29 F	4 33 29	7 15 10	11♏48	4 50	21 57	20 23	5 45	17 27	12 51	24 45	27 09	0 11	27 06	29 14	8 45	15 07	19 26
30 Sa	4 37 26	8 15 58	23 55	4 42	21 21	21 33	5 51	17 19	12 53	24 43	27 09	0 12	27 26	29 38	9 05	15 34	19 24

Tables are calculated for midnight Greenwich Mean Time

December 2024

DATE	SID.TIME	SUN	MOON	NODE	MERCURY	VENUS	MARS	JUPITER	SATURN	URANUS	NEPTUNE	PLUTO	CERES	PALLAS	JUNO	VESTA	CHIRON
1 Su	4 41 22	9✗16 48	6✗15	♎31R	20✗35R	22♑43	5♌56	17♊11R	12♓54	24♉40R	27♓09R	0♒14	27♑47	0♒01	9♏25	16≏01	19♈23R
2 M	4 45 19	10 17 39	18 47	18	19 37	23 53	6 00	17 03	12 56	24 38	27 08	0 15	28 28	0 25	9 44	16 28	19 21
3 T	4 49 16	11 18 31	1♈31	06	18 31	25 03	6 04	16 55	12 58	24 35	27 08	0 16	28 28	0 49	10 04	16 55	19 20
4 W	4 53 12	12 19 24	14 28	54	17 17	26 13	6 07	16 47	12 59	24 33	27 08	0 18	28 49	1 12	10 24	17 21	19 18
5 Th	4 57 9	13 20 18	27 36	44	15 57	27 23	6 09	16 39	13 01	24 31	27 08	0 19	29 10	1 36	10 43	17 48	19 17
6 F	5 1 5	14 21 12	10≈55	37	14 35	28 33	6 10R	16 31	13 04	24 28	27 08	0 21	29 31	2 00	11 03	18 15	19 16
7 Sa	5 5 2	15 22 08	24 25	33	13 12	29 42	6 10	16 23	13 06	24 26	27 08D	0 22	29 52	2 24	11 22	18 41	19 15
8 Su	5 8 58	16 23 04	8♓07	♍31D	11 52	0≈51	6 10	16 14	13 08	24 24	27 08	0 23	0≈13	2 47	11 41	19 07	19 13
9 M	5 12 55	17 24 01	22 01	♍31R	10 37	2 01	6 09	16 06	13 10	24 22	27 08	0 25	0 34	3 11	12 01	19 34	19 12
10 T	5 16 51	18 24 58	6♈07	31	9 30	3 10	6 07	15 58	13 13	24 19	27 08	0 26	0 56	3 35	12 20	20 00	19 11
11 W	5 20 48	19 25 56	20 25	30	8 32	4 19	6 04	15 50	13 15	24 17	27 08	0 28	1 17	3 59	12 39	20 26	19 10
12 Th	5 24 45	20 26 54	4♉53	27	7 44	5 27	6 00	15 42	13 18	24 15	27 08	0 30	1 38	4 22	12 58	20 52	19 09
13 F	5 28 41	21 27 54	19 27	21	7 08	6 36	5 56	15 34	13 21	24 13	27 08	0 31	2 00	4 46	13 17	21 18	19 08
14 Sa	5 32 38	22 28 54	4♊01	12	6 42	7 44	5 50	15 26	13 24	24 11	27 08	0 33	2 21	5 10	13 36	21 44	19 07
15 Su	5 36 34	23 29 54	18 29	♍01	6 28D	8 53	5 44	15 18	13 27	24 09	27 09	0 34	2 43	5 34	13 54	22 10	19 06
16 M	5 40 31	24 30 56	2♋44	49	6 24	10 01	5 37	15 10	13 30	24 07	27 09	0 36	3 05	5 57	14 13	22 36	19 05
17 T	5 44 27	25 31 58	16 39	36	6 30	11 09	5 29	15 02	13 33	24 05	27 09	0 38	3 27	6 21	14 32	23 01	19 05
18 W	5 48 24	26 33 00	0♌12	25	6 45	12 16	5 20	14 54	13 36	24 03	27 10	0 39	3 49	6 45	14 50	23 27	19 04
19 Th	5 52 21	27 34 04	13 19	16	7 09	13 24	5 11	14 46	13 40	24 01	27 10	0 41	4 10	7 09	15 09	23 52	19 03
20 F	5 56 17	28 35 08	26 02	10	7 40	14 31	5 01	14 38	13 43	23 59	27 10	0 43	4 32	7 32	15 27	24 18	19 03
21 Sa	6 0 14	29 36 13	8♍25	♍07	8 18	15 39	4 49	14 31	13 47	23 57	27 11	0 44	4 55	7 56	15 45	24 43	19 02
22 Su	6 4 10	0♑37 19	20 30	♍06	9 02	16 46	4 37	14 23	13 50	23 55	27 11	0 46	5 17	8 20	16 03	25 08	19 02
23 M	6 8 7	1 38 25	2≏24	06	9 51	17 52	4 25	14 15	13 54	23 53	27 12	0 48	5 39	8 43	16 21	25 33	19 01
24 T	6 12 3	2 39 33	14 12	05	10 45	18 59	4 11	14 08	13 58	23 51	27 12	0 50	6 01	9 07	16 39	25 58	19 01
25 W	6 16 0	3 40 40	26 00	04	11 43	20 05	3 57	14 01	14 02	23 49	27 13	0 51	6 23	9 31	16 57	26 23	19 01
26 Th	6 19 56	4 41 49	7♏53	00	12 45	21 11	3 41	13 54	14 06	23 48	27 14	0 53	6 46	9 54	17 15	26 47	19 00
27 F	6 23 53	5 42 58	19 55	♍54	13 50	22 17	3 25	13 47	14 10	23 46	27 14	0 55	7 08	10 18	17 33	27 12	19 00
28 Sa	6 27 50	6 44 07	2✗11	45	14 58	23 23	3 09	13 40	14 14	23 44	27 15	0 57	7 30	10 42	17 50	27 37	19 00
29 Su	6 31 46	7 45 17	14 42	33	16 09	24 28	2 51	13 33	14 18	23 43	27 16	0 58	7 53	11 05	18 08	28 01	19 00D
30 M	6 35 43	8 46 28	27 30	19	17 21	25 33	2 33	13 26	14 23	23 41	27 16	1 00	8 16	11 29	18 25	28 25	19 00
31 T	6 39 39	9 47 38	10♑35	♍06	18 36	26 38	2 14	13 19	14 27	23 40	27 17	1 02	8 38	11 53	18 42	28 49	19 00

The Planetary Hours

The selection of an auspicious time for starting any activity is an important matter. Its existence tends to take on a nature corresponding to the conditions under which it was begun. Each hour is ruled by a planet, and the nature of any hour corresponds to the nature of the planet ruling it. The nature of the planetary hours is the same as the description of each of the planets. Uranus, Neptune, and Pluto are considered here as higher octaves of Mercury, Venus, and Mars.

Sunrise Hour	Sun	Mon	Tue	Wed	Thu	Fri	Sat
1	☉	☽	♂	☿	♃	♀	♄
2	♀	♄	☉	☽	♂	☿	♃
3	☿	♃	♀	♄	☉	☽	♂
4	☽	♂	☿	♃	♀	♄	☉
5	♄	☉	☽	♂	☿	♃	♀
6	♃	♀	♄	☉	☽	♂	☿
7	♂	☿	♃	♀	♄	☉	☽
8	☉	☽	♂	☿	♃	♀	♄
9	♀	♄	☉	☽	♂	☿	♃
10	☿	♃	♀	♄	☉	☽	♂
11	☽	♂	☿	♃	♀	♄	☉
12	♄	☉	☽	♂	☿	♃	♀

Sunset Hour	Sun	Mon	Tue	Wed	Thu	Fri	Sat
1	♃	♀	♄	☉	☽	♂	☿
2	♂	☿	♃	♀	♄	☉	☽
3	☉	☽	♂	☿	♃	♀	♄
4	♀	♄	☉	☽	♂	☿	♃
5	☿	♃	♀	♄	☉	☽	♂
6	☽	♂	☿	♃	♀	♄	☉
7	♄	☉	☽	♂	☿	♃	♀
8	♃	♀	♄	☉	☽	♂	☿
9	♂	☿	♃	♀	♄	☉	☽
10	☉	☽	♂	☿	♃	♀	♄
11	♀	♄	☉	☽	♂	☿	♃
12	☿	♃	♀	♄	☉	☽	♂

Table of Rising and Setting Signs

To find your approximate Ascendant, locate your Sun sign in the left column and determine the approximate time of your birth. Line up your Sun sign with birth time to find Ascendant. Note: This table will give you the approximate Ascendant only. To obtain your exact Ascendant you must consult your natal chart.

Sun Sign	6–8 a.m.	8–10 a.m.	10 a.m.–12 p.m.	12–2 p.m.	2–4 p.m.	4–6 p.m.
Aries	Taurus	Gemini	Cancer	Leo	Virgo	Libra
Taurus	Gemini	Cancer	Leo	Virgo	Libra	Scorpio
Gemini	Cancer	Leo	Virgo	Libra	Scorpio	Sagittarius
Cancer	Leo	Virgo	Libra	Scorpio	Sagittarius	Capricorn
Leo	Virgo	Libra	Scorpio	Sagittarius	Capricorn	Aquarius
Virgo	Libra	Scorpio	Sagittarius	Capricorn	Aquarius	Pisces
Libra	Scorpio	Sagittarius	Capricorn	Aquarius	Pisces	Aries
Scorpio	Sagittarius	Capricorn	Aquarius	Pisces	Aries	Taurus
Sagittarius	Capricorn	Aquarius	Pisces	Aries	Taurus	Gemini
Capricorn	Aquarius	Pisces	Aries	Taurus	Gemini	Cancer
Aquarius	Pisces	Aries	Taurus	Gemini	Cancer	Leo
Pisces	Aries	Taurus	Gemini	Cancer	Leo	Virgo

Sun Sign	6–8 p.m.	8–10 p.m.	10 p.m.–12 a.m.	12–2 a.m.	2–4 a.m.	4–6 a.m.
Aries	Scorpio	Sagittarius	Capricorn	Aquarius	Pisces	Aries
Taurus	Sagittarius	Capricorn	Aquarius	Pisces	Aries	Taurus
Gemini	Capricorn	Aquarius	Pisces	Aries	Taurus	Gemini
Cancer	Aquarius	Pisces	Aries	Taurus	Gemini	Cancer
Leo	Pisces	Aries	Taurus	Gemini	Cancer	Leo
Virgo	Aries	Taurus	Gemini	Cancer	Leo	Virgo
Libra	Taurus	Gemini	Cancer	Leo	Virgo	Libra
Scorpio	Gemini	Cancer	Leo	Virgo	Libra	Scorpio
Sagittarius	Cancer	Leo	Virgo	Libra	Scorpio	Sagittarius
Capricorn	Leo	Virgo	Libra	Scorpio	Sagittarius	Capricorn
Aquarius	Virgo	Libra	Scorpio	Sagittarius	Capricorn	Aquarius
Pisces	Libra	Scorpio	Sagittarius	Capricorn	Aquarius	Pisces

Blank Horoscope Chart

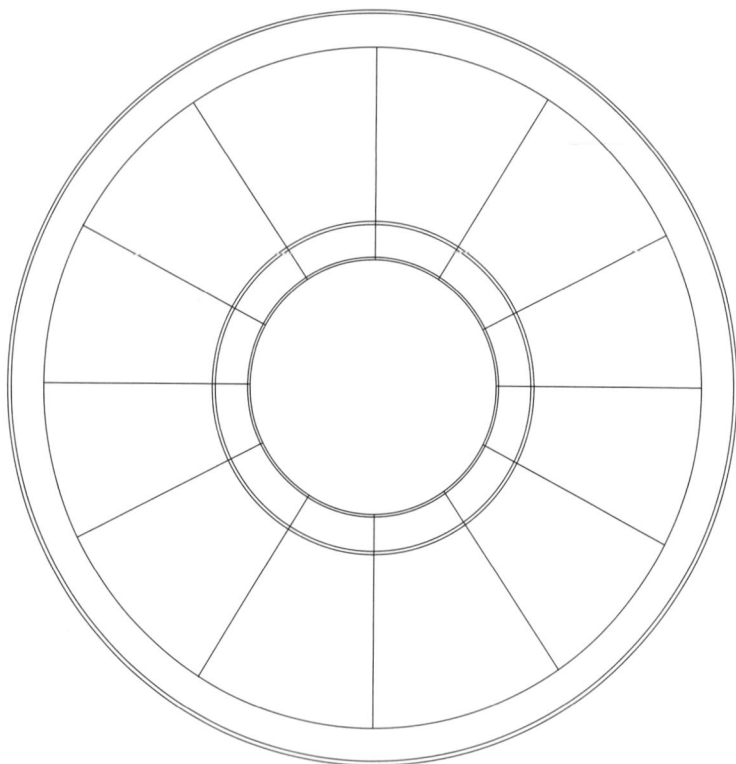

Notes

Notes

Notes

2023

SEPTEMBER
S	M	T	W	T	F	S
					1	2
3	4	5	6	7	8	9
10	11	12	13	14	15	16
17	18	19	20	21	22	23
24	25	26	27	28	29	30

OCTOBER
S	M	T	W	T	F	S
1	2	3	4	5	6	7
8	9	10	11	12	13	14
15	16	17	18	19	20	21
22	23	24	25	26	27	28
29	30	31				

NOVEMBER
S	M	T	W	T	F	S
			1	2	3	4
5	6	7	8	9	10	11
12	13	14	15	16	17	18
19	20	21	22	23	24	25
26	27	28	29	30		

DECEMBER
S	M	T	W	T	F	S
					1	2
3	4	5	6	7	8	9
10	11	12	13	14	15	16
17	18	19	20	21	22	23
24	25	26	27	28	29	30
31						

2024

JANUARY
S	M	T	W	T	F	S
	1	2	3	4	5	6
7	8	9	10	11	12	13
14	15	16	17	18	19	20
21	22	23	24	25	26	27
28	29	30	31			

FEBRUARY
S	M	T	W	T	F	S
				1	2	3
4	5	6	7	8	9	10
11	12	13	14	15	16	17
18	19	20	21	22	23	24
25	26	27	28	29		

MARCH
S	M	T	W	T	F	S
					1	2
3	4	5	6	7	8	9
10	11	12	13	14	15	16
17	18	19	20	21	22	23
24	25	26	27	28	29	30
31						

APRIL
S	M	T	W	T	F	S
	1	2	3	4	5	6
7	8	9	10	11	12	13
14	15	16	17	18	19	20
21	22	23	24	25	26	27
28	29	30				

MAY
S	M	T	W	T	F	S
			1	2	3	4
5	6	7	8	9	10	11
12	13	14	15	16	17	18
19	20	21	22	23	24	25
26	27	28	29	30	31	

JUNE
S	M	T	W	T	F	S
						1
2	3	4	5	6	7	8
9	10	11	12	13	14	15
16	17	18	19	20	21	22
23	24	25	26	27	28	29
30						

JULY
S	M	T	W	T	F	S
	1	2	3	4	5	6
7	8	9	10	11	12	13
14	15	16	17	18	19	20
21	22	23	24	25	26	27
28	29	30	31			

AUGUST
S	M	T	W	T	F	S
				1	2	3
4	5	6	7	8	9	10
11	12	13	14	15	16	17
18	19	20	21	22	23	24
25	26	27	28	29	30	31

SEPTEMBER
S	M	T	W	T	F	S
1	2	3	4	5	6	7
8	9	10	11	12	13	14
15	16	17	18	19	20	21
22	23	24	25	26	27	28
29	30					

OCTOBER
S	M	T	W	T	F	S
		1	2	3	4	5
6	7	8	9	10	11	12
13	14	15	16	17	18	19
20	21	22	23	24	25	26
27	28	29	30	31		

NOVEMBER
S	M	T	W	T	F	S
					1	2
3	4	5	6	7	8	9
10	11	12	13	14	15	16
17	18	19	20	21	22	23
24	25	26	27	28	29	30

DECEMBER
S	M	T	W	T	F	S
1	2	3	4	5	6	7
8	9	10	11	12	13	14
15	16	17	18	19	20	21
22	23	24	25	26	27	28
29	30	31				

2025

JANUARY
S	M	T	W	T	F	S
			1	2	3	4
5	6	7	8	9	10	11
12	13	14	15	16	17	18
19	20	21	22	23	24	25
26	27	28	29	30	31	

FEBRUARY
S	M	T	W	T	F	S
						1
2	3	4	5	6	7	8
9	10	11	12	13	14	15
16	17	18	19	20	21	22
23	24	25	26	27	28	

MARCH
S	M	T	W	T	F	S
						1
2	3	4	5	6	7	8
9	10	11	12	13	14	15
16	17	18	19	20	21	22
23	24	25	26	27	28	29
30	31					

APRIL
S	M	T	W	T	F	S
		1	2	3	4	5
6	7	8	9	10	11	12
13	14	15	16	17	18	19
20	21	22	23	24	25	26
27	28	29	30			

MAY
S	M	T	W	T	F	S
				1	2	3
4	5	6	7	8	9	10
11	12	13	14	15	16	17
18	19	20	21	22	23	24
25	26	27	28	29	30	31

JUNE
S	M	T	W	T	F	S
1	2	3	4	5	6	7
8	9	10	11	12	13	14
15	16	17	18	19	20	21
22	23	24	25	26	27	28
29	30					

JULY
S	M	T	W	T	F	S
		1	2	3	4	5
6	7	8	9	10	11	12
13	14	15	16	17	18	19
20	21	22	23	24	25	26
27	28	29	30	31		

AUGUST
S	M	T	W	T	F	S
					1	2
3	4	5	6	7	8	9
10	11	12	13	14	15	16
17	18	19	20	21	22	23
24	25	26	27	28	29	30
31						